C.E. WYMAN.

THE WATERBURY RECORD

By R. L. Duffus

WILLIAMSTOWN BRANCH
Impersonal Memories of a Vermont Boyhood

THE WATERBURY RECORD
More Vermont Memories

THE WATERBURY RECORD

More Vermont Memories

BY

R. L. DUFFUS

W · W · NORTON & COMPANY · INC ·
NEW YORK

Contents

———————

As I Was Saying

———◆◆◆►———

*I*N A BOOK called *Williamstown Branch* I tried to picture a small town in Vermont as seen through the eyes of a boy of ten. In the present volume I have taken a look at a somewhat larger Vermont town, as it is now remembered by a young man who was then seventeen or eighteen years old. The young man was quiet and law-abiding, almost to a fault, but he was observant. In the office of a weekly newspaper, *The Waterbury Record and Stowe Journal,* he had a good spot from which to do his observing.

I have followed the policy of the earlier book in using real names or fictitious names as seemed best to me in each case. I haven't wished to hurt the feelings of any living person and I hope I haven't done so. There are some foolish people in these pages, my younger self included, but nobody who was thoroughly sinful. I have invented one or more characters where I judged this would be true to the spirit of the town if not to its actual list of inhabitants in the years 1905–1906.

My younger sister and older brother will not read this book until it is in print, and are therefore not responsible for anything I have said about anything or anybody. I hope they will like it, for I have tried to tell the truth to quite a large extent, and I have fond memories of them in their younger days and fond thoughts of them now that they have grown up.

THE WATERBURY RECORD

CHAPTER ONE

———◄••••►———

... And Members of the Graduating Class

1

*I*N 1905, when I graduated, the Waterbury (Vt.) High
School had forty-five students and the senior class had
five members. The tininess of this group of half-baked
young Vermonters made it possible for each of us to have
some kind of honor. It fell to my lot to be the valedictorian,
though I was not really saying good bye to the two boys and
two girls who completed the class, nor, for another year, to
Waterbury.

However, it was thought suitable to make a ceremony of
it, and each of us had to make, or read, some kind of speech.
The girls were lucky, for they carried their manuscripts with
them and could refer to them if they wished. We boys had to
memorize our eloquence, and there wasn't any hole deep
enough in or near Waterbury to hide our disgrace if we forgot.

Nearly every adult in town turned out, as well as most of
the nongraduating adolescents. Parents and friends were
there for what I take to be good motives. Others, as I even
then suspected, came to see the graduates squirm. Indeed,
one of the great pleasures of life in every generation is surely
to sit in a comfortable chair in an auditorium and watch some-

one who does not like to make speeches make a speech. Some do like to, unhappily.

I was not an exhibitionist of that particular variety, but when prodded I reacted like a frightened rabbit and struck out at destiny. The ordeal of appearing in public threw me into a coma, and in this condition I went through the motions expected of me with an outward calm that surprised my relatives and well-wishers.

Shortly before graduation day, if I may illustrate this point, some of us staged a high-school play in which I had one of the main roles. All the roles were main, I should add. I was the baffled lover pretending to be something else, I forget what—either not a lover, or another person or not baffled—and the play was called *The Cool Collegians*. We had picked this drama out of a catalogue, with the aid of Professor Hosmer, the principal. To us it seemed sophisticated, which we longed to be. To him, I imagine, it seemed something we couldn't do any harm with, or get lost in. (He wouldn't like that sentence—in those days high-school students who ended sentences with prepositions got into trouble.)

Fussing around with the scenery and trying to make the curtain work took our minds off the coming ordeal, but in time, like all well-trained ordeals, it arrived. I remember all too well my sensations as I waited for my cue to enter— I was supposed to come on whistling, as a sign of a gay, free, unworried spirit. I had hoped that the black moustache that Mr. Hosmer had pasted onto my face would make me feel like somebody else, but it did not. I could not whistle, my mouth was too dry.

I knew then, as I faced the drama-loving population of Waterbury, that whatever career I subsequently chose, whatever I became famous for (and we all expected to become famous for something), it would not be acting. Not if I could help it.

However, it was impossible to run. I was like one of those unhappy soldiers who are afraid of the enemy but much more afraid of the military police.

The consequence was that I walked right out on the stage and kissed a girl who was supposed, in the play, to be my aunt or my friend's aunt. A burst of applause greeted this feat. I suppose now is as good a time as any to admit that I was an excessively shy boy and not given to kissing girls, least of all in public.

A certain amount of derision was mingled, in this applause, with a much larger amount of good will. That is about all that an adolescent, in any generation, in any community, has a right to expect.

In fact, and I might as well state this at the beginning of this exploration into the adventures and observations of an adolescent of some years back, I do not believe adolescents have any rights at all, except those guaranteed to all by the Federal Constitution.

Adolescence is something a person gets over. I learned this by hard experience, and I hereby pass it along to those who come after me. I think I knew this in that strange June of 1905, when I also knew quite a lot about Virgil (I could turn Virgil into something almost like English verse), plain and solid geometry (I could sometimes prove theorems in ways the books hadn't figured out), French to a certain point but not to the point the soldiers thought up a dozen years and more later, a quantity of history, some English and American literature, and the names of the customers on my paper route and which paper each one wanted.

I knew about adolescence, because I knew that if I did not get over it I would die, either by a slow decline which no doctor, not even Dr. Henry Janes, could recognize and prescribe for, or by my own hand. The trouble with dying by

my own hand was that I could never think of any really
pleasant way of accomplishing it; and for this and other reasons I finally gave up the whole idea.

When I had kissed the girl who was supposed to be my
aunt, or my friend's aunt, in the play called *The Cool Collegians,* I suddenly realized that I could, under pressure, do
things that were ordinarily beyond me. I would not have
dreamed of intercepting that girl on Main Street or Stowe
Street and kissing her, even on the left cheek, even a glanc-
ing kiss.

I was as surprised as the rest of the population, including
the girl who was supposed to be my friend's aunt or my own
aunt—especially because I had never ventured to come within
two and a half inches of her during rehearsals.

I had also surprised a female high-school teacher, a rosy-
cheeked, blue-eyed creature of great self-assurance, who had
told a friend of mine that I couldn't possibly act in a play—
I was too bashful. For a year or so afterwards I always hoped
that this teacher would have chilblains or be disappointed
in love or get poison ivy—nothing fatal or permanently dis-
abling, but just enough to remind her she shouldn't make
rash judgments on insufficient evidence.

The reason I know I did well in the play called *The Cool
Collegians* was that Harry Whitehill, the editor of *The Waterbury Record* and *Stowe Journal,* and my employer of two
years' standing during most of my out-of-school waking hours,
said so.

Harry said I could write a criticism of the play, leaving
out any mention of my own performance. I knew what he
meant by criticism; he meant some well-chosen words that
wouldn't lose the *Record* any readers or advertisers. So I
wrote a paragraph or two about how well everybody else
had done, and Harry Whitehill inserted in my piece the
gratifying comment:

Rob Duffus's performance in the role of the young man who had trouble convincing his aunt that he was somebody else showed that even the quietest of our young men can do well on the stage.

I don't know quite what this meant. But after a fairly rugged four years, during which I had been busy out of school as well as in school, Mr. Whitehill's words did me good. I never asked myself, of course, what he would have said if he had decided I was a bad actor, even for a high-school play. I think, however, he would have said I was a good actor, for he had a naturally kindly heart, and, besides, I was a good investment; I was going to work for him full time for a year at a bargain rate.

2

It was with this slight glow of success that I entered the month of June, 1905, and realized that before long I would have to make a speech and become a graduate of the Water-bury High School. I knew I could make such a speech, but I did not really care to.

In the early morning, in those idyllic days, it was my duty and habit to sweep out Mr. Whitehill's store and news-paper office. I have never felt cheerful in the early morning; I did not then and I do not now. I have little use for persons who feel cheerful in the early morning, unless they have other and more endearing qualities.

Thus there comes back to me, bleak and somber, the dawn of the day which was destined to end with the graduating exercises of the class of 1905 of the Waterbury High School.

It did not seem to me, as I slunk about the shop in my dingy working-clothes, with the dust and ink of my trade on my hands and face, and nobody to talk to—not even the lady hereinafter called Lilith, who was imaginary but real—that I

could possibly stand up on the stage in the high-school
auditorium and deliver that valedictory oration. I had re-
hearsed it till I knew it by heart, I had been taught gestures
to go with each phrase—the right hand up and forward,
palm up, pause, proceed, wait for laugh—but all this belonged to some other prospective high-school graduate, in
a kindlier clime and time.

My success as a Cool Collegian did me no good, as I
thought of it. Tonight I couldn't be a Cool Collegian. I had
to be myself. And what was the thing called Myself? Why
should anybody listen to It talk?

I sweated with more than work as I thought this situation
over. I wished I could enlist in the army and get sent to the
Philippines.

Wishing did me no good—it never has, before or since.
Suddenly there I was, like a prisoner who has had his walk
in the sun and finds the firing squad impatient to get back
to its morning beer.

The salutatorian had done his best, and it was good. The
two girls had read their essays. One of the other boys had
produced the class prophecy—peering into the dim shadows
of the next ten years, when we would all be married, rich
and happy. He had been instructed to pause for his laughs,
and did so; he got them because the audience soon perceived that this was the only way to get on with the program.

My name was mentioned as my grinning fellow student
sat complacently down. I rose. I had to rise, though I did
not then want to. I would have felt no stronger urge if somebody had built a fire under me.

For some occult reason I recall the precise words of the
opening phrase: "In the beginning there was no such thing
as education."

My general theme was that once upon a time, in man's
early history, there was nothing to know, because nothing

had been discovered, and therefore there didn't have to be institutions such as the Waterbury High School.

I went on to say that it was, in my opinion, a good thing that we now had such institutions as the Waterbury High School. I heard my voice going on and on, as though somebody else were talking, and a certain portion of my mind detached itself from the immediate topic and went back over the four years I had spent in high school.

A drowning man is believed to see in a flash all his past life; I have not yet drowned myself and do not know, but I did live again some meaningful years of my existence while I delivered the words I had so well memorized, with the gestures that had been hammered into me.

The machine had been wound up and would run. I could let it run and, in a way, think of something else. I wasn't even scared any more. A sort of sadness seized me. I'd never be a high-school student again. I couldn't go back over it and do it better and maybe have a better time.

And so, members of the faculty, fellow classmates, friends, I seemed to be saying—and so what?

3

There was the first principal, a peppery little man not long out of college. Our high-school principals were usually passing time while waiting to find something better, and I suppose this was the case with Mr. Roscoe.

He was a well-meaning young man, with wit rather than humor and with some gifts for teaching. Why do I remember his inconsequential moments? One morning he told his history class, who had been, as it were, studying the Crusades, that the Crusaders had brought back pink sugar to Western Europe and that this was probably what we would remember, forgetting the political and economic meaning of this excursion of Europeans into the Near East. He did not talk down to us, not Mr. Roscoe.

So I still remember that the Crusaders brought back pink sugar, just as Mr. Roscoe said I would. I also remember that Mr. Roscoe made a blistering comment on a theme I turned in for the English composition class because, like a medieval monk (and in some respects I did then resemble one) I had illumined the initial letter of the first paragraph. I got more or less even with Mr. Roscoe when we were reading Macbeth aloud in class one day and he took a small part in order to get on with it. I was reading the lines that required me to call Mr. Roscoe a "lily-liver'd boy," and suddenly I found myself throwing much more vehemence into the part and making much more noise than anybody, myself included, had expected.

Mr. Roscoe, I imagine, didn't sympathize with my particular brand of adolescence. All I can now say is, he should have waited a few years and experimented to find out if he liked the various brands of lost generations and beat generations any better. My generation was lost and beat, as a matter of course; the difference was, we forgot to mention it.

As for Mr. Roscoe, he went out riding in a sleigh with a lady in the month of January, 1907, after I had left Waterbury, the horse ran away, the sleigh upset, and Mr. Roscoe was married the very next spring. At the time I thought this served him right, when I heard of it in California. My position then was that being married took too much of a young man's spare time; I changed this position later.

The second principal, and the last in my Waterbury period, was Mr. Hosmer, a long, lean, scholarly man who may have been teaching merely to save money for further study but who really did seem to like adolescent boys and girls. He was kindly, firm and wholesome. I think of him still with gratitude, just as I do of the late Mrs. Frankum (how I wish she wasn't "late," but still with us and teaching fortunate young generations) of the Williamstown Graded School.

Mr. Hosmer being present at the graduation exercises, I could think about him while I delivered my oration without getting too far from the stage. Mr. Hosmer, a graduate of Williams College, thought some of us—not me, so much, for I was getting exercise enough working for Mr. Whitehill—ought to get outdoors more. He worked out plans for cross-country running, with competitions, prizes and perhaps meets with other high schools.

Some of the boys did run a little, but the enterprise fizzled out. My contemporaries in Waterbury were not especially athletic. It seemed foolish to them to go in for exercise merely for the sake of exercise; they were perhaps a little too near the farm to think highly of that. They would skate, because skating was customarily social, and there would be girls around. They would play basketball, because the game was highly competitive and the good players received favorable attention. They would fish, ride bicycles, or walk in the woods.

But run through the woods? No, Mr. Hosmer.

Mr. Hosmer, moderately disappointed, encouraged basketball and there was a little haphazard high-school baseball. I didn't get into either, for I was believed to have a heart lesion. However, this did not keep me from wading through blizzards and cloud-bursts to deliver papers and otherwise serve Harry Whitehill. I did not mind this irony too much then, I do not mind it at all now, for Harry Whitehill unwittingly taught me more than I could ever have learned playing basketball or baseball.

Having failed to get us running through the woods, Mr. Hosmer fell back on educating us, and this, indeed, he partially succeeded in doing. I don't remember his methods. Maybe he had none. Mainly he educated us by taking an interest in us as persons and persuading us that learning was worth while. It was just at this time that it began to seem natural for a Waterbury High School graduate to go to college. We were stepping up our educational level, and Mr. Hosmer, a good man and a good teacher, was doing his part.

So, as I went on with my valedictory oration I thought about Mrs. Frankum in Williamstown and wished she could be present, and about Mr. Hosmer in Waterbury, and how good it was that he was present; a youngster couldn't fail when Mr. Hosmer was calmly sure he would do all right . . .

I thought back over the four long years, out of school as well as in school, which hadn't seemed too long to me as I ploughed through them: the sense of failure and futility which I often had, and thought was peculiar to myself, and didn't know was a common phase of growing up; the cold winter mornings, sometimes with a blizzard blowing in from the northwest, when I went up to fix the fires for Mr. Whitehill's store and printing shop; the tender winds of late March and early April, so caressingly charged with emotions I wanted to write poetry about, and sometimes could and sometimes couldn't, only it wasn't poetry, it wasn't as good as William Cullen Bryant and Shakespeare and poets like that; and spring coming, and now this latest spring.

In the beginning there was no such thing as education. I was elaborating this point as much as it could be elaborated in a fifteen-minute speech. And I was thinking of many other things that didn't need to be elaborated.

Now I was a graduate of the Waterbury High School, or would be if I could get out a few more words before that old heart lesion carried me off. I was, in a way, educated.

The high-school auditorium was a vast room, as I saw it then, not so large in recent years. We used to have what were called promenades in it, because it was still considered slightly wicked, even in sophisticated Waterbury, to do round dances. A promenade was square dancing, but if a girl was going to be squeezed on a certain evening she got squeezed on the evening of a square dance just as she would have been on the evening of a round dance. Not by me, for I was diffident, but I did notice things.

The auditorium wouldn't have seemed more crowded if it had been filled with thousands of people. I couldn't see faces clearly except for those down front: Mr. Hosmer, Miss Collins (the teacher who thought I wouldn't be able to perform in The Cool Collegians and who, unhappily, did not get poison ivy as a consequence), my mother, aunt, and sister (my grandmother couldn't come, but I had recited the whole oration to her before I left the house); even the faces I could see were blurred from time to time; but my voice went on and on, rather smoothly as I thought, listening to it as I did in a detached sort of way, and I didn't have to be prompted.

In the beginning there was no such thing as education. And now, members of the faculty, fellow classmates, friends . . . I was doing all right, I believed.

I caught a smile on one or two faces among my contemporaries, a smile mingled with some surprise, for I seemed to be getting along better as an orator than I did when I had to go up front with my class and recite.

We were still following this system when I was a student in the Waterbury High School, just as we had followed it in the Williamstown Graded School. It doubtless encouraged concentration. When a class went forward to recite, a boy working on a geometry problem at a desk four seats from the back row was expected to go right on working in spite of the fact that the girl he most admired—or one of them, for in those days a boy could admire half a dozen girls at once—was up front describing the life and times of Julius Caesar, or over at one side writing French sentences on the blackboard.

The fact that I had thus learned to divide my mind and

attention into two or more parts may help to account for the peculiar experience I was having as I delivered my gradua-tion speech. I could reflect on my past life while I also went on explaining why in the beginning there was no such thing as education, and why this happy state had long since passed . . .

So sweet they were, I thought, some of those lost mornings and dawns before mornings, in those dear old days now three or even four years back, so full of ecstasy the winds and fragrance that came off the meadows and the wooded hills, so sweet and aching they were . . . and what had it all been about? And what would come next, now that I was committed to spend another year in thrall to Harry Whitehill instead of going away immediately to college?

Meanwhile, youth would be slipping away. I was sixteen years old as I stood there declaiming, but in a few weeks I would be seventeen, in a year after that I would be eighteen, and what had I to show for all this time of living? The paths of glory, as I well knew, led but to the grave, but I hadn't even found where they started.

As I was saying, in the beginning there was no such thing as education, but now I was somewhat educated, and the result was I could ask more questions than before and answer fewer than before.

Now I was finished with my oration, and the applause was just about the same that my predecessors had stirred up. I may not have swayed my audience to any great extent but at any rate I hadn't unswayed it. I also picked up a small extra clatter of approval because I was the last of the lot and people felt relieved because there weren't going to be more speakers.

Mr. Hosmer took up the diplomas and handed them out. As I took mine from him he smiled in his pleasant, one-sided way and said: "Well done, Rob." Later he added: "It

wasn't as bad as you thought it would be, was it? It lived up
to that class motto."

I had found the class motto somewhere in the back of a
Latin dictionary. Unless I am mistaken it read: "Velle est
posse" or, for the benefit of those who specialized in Greek,
"If you think you can wangle it you probably can."

My relatives assured me, with one accord, that Daniel
Webster couldn't have done it better, not at my age, anyhow. I received some other congratulations from well-wishers who had been certain my tongue would cleave to the
roof of my mouth or that I would fall down and have to be
carried off the stage as soon as I tried to start speaking.

Next morning Harry Whitehill asked me to write a few
paragraphs for the *Record* and *Stowe Journal* about the
graduation exercises. He gazed at me with unusual approval.

"You can leave out your own speech," he said. "I'll take
care of that."

So what the *Record* carried in its next issue was substantially the following:

Rob Duffus, the valedictorian, pointed out the necessity for
education in a well-written and excellently delivered speech,
and appealed to the classes still to come to carry on the tradition established by the Class of 1905. Following this, etc.

Following this, etc., to fill in what Harry Whitehill didn't
write, I became for a year a full-time employee of *The Waterbury Record* and *Stowe Journal*—and when I say full-time
I mean full-time. This was my graduate year, though it
yielded no degree. I did not realize that though my education had formally come to a halt it was in fact continuing.

It was an education in the nature of the town of Waterbury, Vermont, a larger and more complicated town than
Williamstown, Vermont, with all the dramas, dreams, and
tragedies that Williamstown ever had, and some that were

peculiar to itself.

A town on the main line of a railroad in those days could be different in kind as well as in size from a town on a branch line. You couldn't have anything resembling a slum in Williamstown, but there were a few houses on the wrong side of the tracks in Waterbury that didn't smell as sweet as they might have done; you couldn't have serious corruption in Williamstown but it could occur in Waterbury, along with other symptoms of an advanced civilization; you had a more positive and self-conscious culture in Waterbury than in Williamstown, but you also had a sharper and in some ways more painful division between the cultured and the uncultured.

In short, you had more in Waterbury, and you paid for it.

Such was the course in higher education to which I more or less wittingly committed myself when I decided, or was persuaded, to wait over a year after graduation and grow up a little more before proceeding to college.

And grow up I did, though I am not sure anybody noticed it—not even myself.

CHAPTER TWO

---◄•••►---

That Makes Us Square

1

*M*Y *EMPLOYER,* H. C. Whitehill, editor and publisher of the *Waterbury Record* (weekly circulation, 1,000) and *Stowe Journal* (circulation, 200) paused as I came in from my paper route a week or so after my graduation from the Waterbury (Vt.) High School, in that, for me, historic year 1905. He stood in the aisle between the stationery and the chinaware as I headed back through the front store toward the printing office in back. He waved an admonitory finger. I was taller than he but he was fatter than I, and older, and I paused with the feeling that I must have done something wrong.

I was a hard-working young man, accustomed to getting up at half-past five on winter mornings, regulating stoves or a steam-heating boiler during the colder months, sweeping out both store and shop, carrying the morning paper that came from Burlington and the papers that later came up from Boston on the 4.20 afternoon train, setting type, running job presses and the big flat-bed newspaper press; I was also a bright boy, though I am not sure now that I showed any brightness when I worked for Mr. Whitehill for two dollars a week during my last two high-school years and for six dollars a week after graduation.

This must have been Tuesday, the day we went to press.

I was not at the moment, in Mr. Whitehill's eyes, the promising young man who had so recently instructed and edified a graduation audience by declaring that in the beginning there was no such thing as education. Mr. Whitehill was annoyed because I had lingered too long for breakfast, which my beloved grandmother, aunt, and mother had provided for me. I had eaten too much or too slowly, with an appetite increased by the hour and a half or so I had spent doing Mr. Whitehill's chores.

"Rob," he began, looking at his watch with a slow, plump gesture. "You are late this morning. I counted on you to help us out a little more."

I looked sidewise at the now empty coal stove, an old-fashioned bulbous affair, with a scuttle at its side, that Mr. Whitehill did not abandon even after he got the steam heat. Ancient parties from the hills used to come to town and sit around that stove, summer or winter, aiming to hit the scuttle when they spat out their tobacco juice but, as even then I had noticed could happen in the best-regulated human affairs, not always succeeding.

Mr. Whitehill, I knew, had not got out of bed at half-past five. He didn't have to. Still, he was my employer and by Waterbury lights a highly successful man, well-filled-out, lively, usually jovial.

I did not tell Mr. Whitehill to go jump in the Winooski River, though he could easily have done so after a brisk ten-minute walk. I did not tell him to go dredge up somebody else who could do as much work and as good work as I did for less pay and longer hours. I rather liked Mr. Whitehill. I was even grateful to him, for he had given me my first smell of printer's ink—a perfume for which in half a century I was never to lose my taste.

"Well—" I began.

Mr. Whitehill's severity relaxed. He could never be severe

very long. He could be stingy and sparing much longer, but that was different. He could misunderstand a boy about as thoroughly as did his father-in-law and partner, Justin Moody, who was approximately two and a half times his age, but he could not continue to scold me for lingering at home long enough to eat two more griddle cakes. He himself had once been young. I knew this because he had on the wall of his private office a photograph of the Goddard Seminary basketball team of some years earlier, with himself sitting in front in the role of business manager. I think the title is correct. It should be. Managing anything, even a Sunday school class, would have been a business for Harry White-hill.

"Rob," said Mr. Whitehill, "you're a bright boy. How'd you like to go to Norwich University? I could maybe get you a scholarship and a chance to earn board and room by writing for the Burlington and Barre newspapers. And the *Record*, too, of course."

Norwich was, and is, a military school, located at North-field, Vermont. In bygone times it had been at Norwich, Vermont, and its militant undergraduates, so legend had it, used to cross the Connecticut River and damage the under-graduates of Dartmouth College, who had not been taught how to deploy, skirmish, and come in on the flank. The move to Northfield had been a logical one, since there was no nearby college or university whose students would be in danger from the extracurricular activities of the Norwich boys.

Several boys from Waterbury had gone to Norwich dur-ing my time. The education was good, if you wanted to be an engineer or go into the army. It was not so good for boys with literary tastes, which was what bothered me. But when a boy came home from Norwich University, clad in a fancy military uniform, it didn't matter whether or not he had been learning anything. The girls followed that boy around and wouldn't look at anybody else.

So I said to Mr. Whitehill, "I'd certainly like to."

"I might also," said Mr. Whitehill grandly, "get you a scholarship at Brown University, in Providence, Rhode Island. And you could write for the newspapers from there, too. How would you like that?"

I knew I'd like it better than Norwich, even though there would be no fancy dress. Underneath the ingenuous surface of my illusions about the world I knew even then what the United States Army found out many years later, that I was not cut out to be a soldier; a war with me in it would be from the start more likely to be a lost war for the side I was on; I would forget orders, retreat when ordered to advance, refuse to salute my officers unless they merited that token of respect—that sort of thing.

"I'd like it fine," I said.

Mr. Whitehill smiled approvingly. "Is there anything you wouldn't like fine?" he inquired. "Well, I'm glad you want to get ahead." He paused, as his thinking processes caught up with him. "What is worth having," he went on, "is worth asking for."

He took a chance in saying this, because I might have turned suddenly into a young man who believed that people believed what they said. But I was still gullible. I was pleased to notice that Mr. Whitehill was now in a good mood, in spite of his mild irritation at my being late. He didn't even seem to be in a hurry, even though he would still have to see to it that the *Record* and *Journal* were slapped together, run off on the flat-bed presses, folded and mailed.

"To show you what I mean," Mr. Whitehill continued, "I have just pulled off a transaction with two men from Boston who thought we were what you might call hayseeds up this way. You know the old Watkins place?" I did, and he resumed. "When old man Watkins died and his widow moved away to live with her son in Brattleboro the house and wood lot came on the market. You remember that?" I did. It had been in the *Record* and also in the *Stowe Journal,* because the Watkins place lay up Stowe way, anyhow.

"Well," Mr. Whitehill proceeded, looking like a chubby angel, "I bought that wood lot, though I didn't have any use for the house. Know what I did? I sold the house to Elijah Henry for one hundred dollars more than I paid for it. Elijah needed it that much, with that invalid wife of his." He paused for my approval, which I signified. I wasn't inclined, at that time, to question the moral codes of individuals who lived in Waterbury and who were older and richer than I was. And for some reason I wanted to go on working for Mr. Whitehill and not tell him precisely what I thought of some of the things he did.

"Then," said Mr. Whitehill, who evidently had not read my thoughts, and indeed never would, "I ran into these two men from Boston—smart men, too, with their shoes shined so you could shave with them and white collars up to their ears."

Mr. Whitehill looked at me again, as though he expected me to admire him. So I did. I perceived that while he enjoyed making money without doing any real work for it (I sort of enjoyed that idea, too, and wished I could do it), he enjoyed even more being looked up to as a man who could outsmart two city slickers from Boston with white collars that came up to their ears.

"I sold that land to these men from Boston," declaimed Mr. Whitehill, "for three thousand dollars more than I paid for it. What do you think of that, Rob?"

"Why, that's fine," I said, wishing I had the three thousand dollars and could go away to college at once, and live like a king and sleep late in the morning.

I did a little inside figuring. The three thousand dollars Mr. Whitehill had just picked up would have paid my former school-term salary of two dollars a week for almost thirty years. Mr. Whitehill could have raised me to three dollars a week for thirty years and still have had a clear profit, on the one-dollar raise, of $1,440. Or he could have hired me, at six dollars a week, for almost ten years. Not counting interest, of course, and I imagine Mr. Whitehill would have counted the interest.

"What is worth having," Mr. Whitehill had said, "is worth asking for."

But I didn't ask him. A Barre, Vt., daily newspaper asked Mr. Whitehill if he knew of a young man who could fill its needs for an inexpensive general reporter. I don't know what Mr. Whitehill told them, though he could have told them that I was, at least in theory, the brightest member of a class of five, and the only one who would rather write for a newspaper than work. The Barre newspaper offered eight dollars a week. Mr. Whitehill told me that was fine, but the way he figured it, he said, was that if I went to Barre I couldn't live with my grandmother, mother, and aunt, and would probably have to pay at least two dollars a week for room and board. And probably more, said Mr. Whitehill, with a rueful smile at the grasping nature of the Barre people. I was, in theory, paying my grandmother a dollar a week —that was the way we did things in Vermont—but she gave the dollar back, and more, too, by beautifully subtle devices, which was also the way we did things in Vermont.

So I stayed in Waterbury, working full time for Mr. Whitehill, during the year and more between my graduation from the Waterbury High School in June, 1905, and my departure for Stanford University in August, 1906.

Mr. Whitehill's semi-sleeping partner, his father-in-law, Justin Moody, was one of my monitors and philosophical guides during this period. Mr. Moody had side-whiskers much like those of the late President Chester A. Arthur, to whose photographs I hereby refer the curious. He had other characteristics, too, some of them baffling to me but none of them vicious or needlessly cruel. He was amiable when nothing disturbed his amiability. He was also careful.

To give an idea of the relationship between Mr. Whitehill, Mr. Moody, and their hired help, long before unions arrived in Vermont in the small-town newspaper industry and made things difficult for small-town publishers, I might mention the time when I went down-cellar in the *Record* office, stepped on the loose board of a packing case, and whanged a long nail into my left leg. I know this happened because the scar is still there.

I had to run across the street to Dr. Minard, though he was not my regular physician. Dr. Minard opened the wound up and put liquid fire into it—or maybe corrosive sublimate. This was supposed to stop infection, and it, or something else, did. It was not supposed to quite kill the patient, and in this case it did not.

I thereupon retired to my grandmother's house for approximately a week, and was thus of no use to Mr. Whitehill and Mr. Moody. I remember sitting in an easy chair, with my injured leg on another chair, and reading *Midsummer Night's Dream*, but this didn't help get out the *Record*.

What strikes me as interesting, after all these years, is what Mr. Whitehill said to me when I reported for work, limping a little but free from the danger of blood poisoning.

"I'm glad to see you back, Rob," Mr. Whitehill briskly remarked. He was, indeed, glad, for he had had to hire a boy who was nowhere near as brisk and eager as I was, and to pay him what he had paid me. Or possibly a little less. I imagine he may have got Fred Allerton for five dollars instead of six.

Mr. Moody, from the side of the counter nearest the street, where he could see pretty women going by in case any such did go by (and I am not blaming him for this amiable weakness), chimed in. "You'll remember, Rob," he remarked, "I warned you against running around in the cellar with all those—er—boards down there."

He hadn't warned me. I knew he hadn't. He knew he hadn't. He knew I knew he knew he hadn't. But I knew his conscience would trouble him if he couldn't persuade himself he had, and that I knew he had. So I kept still. I had a patience with the hypocritical elderly that is sadly lacking today.

Mr. Whitehill, smiling blandly, was doing some figuring on a piece of wrapping paper. "Let me see," he mused. "You hurt yourself at about eleven o'clock Tuesday morning. I spoke to you about the cellar, too, as you will recall." He waited for me to recall, but for once I didn't. I kept stubbornly silent. "Let's say twelve o'clock," he finally resumed. "Let's say half a day." He beamed at his own generosity. "That makes a day and a half you worked last week. That's four and a half days off, not counting Sunday, but it was so warm we didn't need any fires and didn't need you." He held out his hand, with the gesture of the senior John D. Rockefeller bestowing a dime on a deserving young man. "So here's a dollar and a half, and I guess that makes us square, doesn't it?"

I took the dollar and a half. Did it make us square? Maybe Dr. Minard wouldn't charge more than that for his services. He wasn't my regular doctor. That was Dr. Henry Janes, a surgeon who had come young out of the Civil War with an amazing record of service and an equally amazing willingness to devote himself and all his knowledge and experience to the people of one small Vermont town. Dr. Minard would go easy on me, because he would feel that he was out of his jurisdiction in saving my life—as he may have been. Maybe he shouldn't have saved my life, maybe he should have let me die for the glory of what used to be called medical ethics. However, he did save my life, and I am glad he did.

"But this week you'll get six dollars as usual," Mr. White-hill was saying. "If," he added, "you keep well and don't get careless and get hurt again."

I wondered if Mr. Whitehill knew how I used to turn on the water power that ran the presses, and later the electric power, to see if they would respond to my desires, to find out if I were that powerful. I was.

But Mr. Whitehill seldom reproached me for anything, and when he did reproach me it was for things of which I wasn't ashamed, such as taking time over a hearty breakfast, and not over my sins, such as turning on the power when it wasn't needed.

2

I don't suppose anybody ever had a broader beginning experience in journalism than I had when I worked for Mr. Whitehill. I learned how to set type by hand, and I still think I could do about four sticks—or fifty-two eight-point, thirteen-em lines—an hour after brushing up a bit. In this adventure I also learned something of no subsequent use to me but of continued interest: the letter "e" is the letter most used in the English alphabet (even by the most egocentric writers) and is therefore, in the old-style printers' case, nearest to the hand and in the biggest compartment.

I also learned to run the job press, which required me to insert a blank sheet of paper with my right hand and take the printed sheet out with my left hand at a rapid pace, and still have a hand or two left at the end of the day. At a pinch I could step on a foot pedal and save a hand from being obliterated, but good printers did not believe in getting into this predicament. Even at my present age I sometimes take one of my hands out of my pocket and look at it, and marvel that it is still there.

If it hadn't been there, at the end of some working day in 1906, Mr. Whitehill and Mr. Moody would have been honestly sorry. They might also have been fair enough to pay my wages to the very end of the day on which the accident happened. Am I being unfair to Mr. Whitehill and Mr. Moody? I don't think so. I am, rather, mentioning one of the folkways of the period—and this especially for the benefit of those who are convinced that as the years pass matters get worse and worse.

However, the press I liked best was the flat-bed, not because it was safer than the job-press but because it was more dramatic. This sort of press, which was then common on small newspapers and common on big ones until two or three generations earlier still—something like that, and let us not worry about details—consisted essentially of a big roller, under which the "flat-bed" carried the page or pages of type. If the pages were not securely locked up they "pied"—and if the gentle reader doesn't know what that means I am not going to torture myself by explaining.

The operator of this press stood on a sort of running-board (as we would have called it later, but not now, because at this writing there aren't any running-boards, just fins), and fed large sheets of paper into the revolving cylinder as it came round. Since the paper was full of static electricity we sprinkled it with water first, and since it was still full of electricity after this ritual, we gave each sheet a twist and flop as we fed it into the grippers. This was an art. I learned to do it well, as I will demonstrate if somebody will produce a flat-bed press. There are some skills one cannot forget.

Sometimes the big sheet went in crooked, in spite of all I could do, and came out crooked. In that case it wrapped itself tenderly and completely around the ink rollers, tore itself into tatters, and had to be removed by hand, with the waste of much time, benzine and ink. I did not much care for this. What I cared for was to be standing there running off the paper and have a beautiful girl come in, as one did once (but this was a long time ago, and I can't now prove she was beautiful, or even existed, and I am not sure which one she was), and admire my control of the thundering old machine. And how it did thunder, girls or no girls! I have never since got so much fun out of any machine, not even out of the first automobile my family owned, back in 1931.

Another thing I did for Mr. Whitehill, without any complaint from him, and I now suspect with his covert encouragement, was to sneak into the office on Sundays to attend to the fires when fires were in season, or to look the place over at other seasons, and then practice on the Smith-Premier typewriter he may have bought for just such an emergency. He never asked me to learn how to typewrite, but when I had learned, without much damage to the typewriter (you had to take a sledgehammer to hurt a typewriter in those halcyon days), he exploited my skill. I think Mr. Whitehill was one of the most ingenious men I ever met.

I did not learn much from my daily, year-in-year-out chore of sweeping out the shop and store. Nobody expected me to learn anything from this. All they hoped for was that it would improve my character, which I am now sure it did—something must have.

Why it did not also kill me I am not now sure. The store and printing office at the end of a day were littered with paper—especially the printing office at the rear. I fed this paper, in winter, into the red-hot stoves. In summer I burned it in the same stoves. When the stoves gave way to the central steam plant I used it in the same way.

Then I cleaned the dirt and rust off the stoves or the steam firebox with benzine—a chemical related to kerosene on its mother's side and to gasoline on its father's side, and a sort of cousin of the devil—in a saturated rag. I have often wondered why I did not set the shop on fire and why I did not blow myself up. It is an idle speculation, no doubt. I was reserved for a different fate, if not a higher one. The *Record* Office never did burn down, even after I left it.

Another part of my duties was, as I have said, to "carry" the *Burlington Free Press* in the morning and the Boston newspapers at night. This meant going to the railway station and then careering around for three-quarters of an hour or more in the summer on a bicycle (I could then ride no hands, and maybe still could if anybody wants to bet), and in winter on foot.

Blizzards delayed me sometimes but they never stopped me. To this day, I believe, I could repeat both the morning and the afternoon routes, leaving the right papers with the right people—except that most of the former customers would not be taking newspapers any more; they would now know all the past, all the present and all the future, in their heavens or their hells, as the cases might be, and not have to strain their eyes.

However, Brown's Livery Stable, which is no longer in business, did take the *Boston Journal;* Randall Blodgett, just as surely, did take the *Boston Globe;* Mrs. Shepley, widow of a good business man, combined the coal and wood trade with the *Boston Herald;* and there was a dissolute stone cutter in the Waterbury Inn, no credit to a noble vocation, who took both the *Journal* and *Globe,* and never, to my knowledge, was completely paid up for either. This grieved Mr. Whitehill, who thought that if I were a little firmer everybody on my paper route would pay his bills promptly and this would be a better world.

Mr. Whitehill also thought that if I expected to become a

newspaperman I should do some reporting. This involved, to take small things first, picking up what Harry Whitehill called "items." An "item" was somebody going to Montpelier for a day, or somebody coming to Waterbury for a day from Montpelier, or a marriage, or somebody starting a new house (which didn't often happen), or somebody getting sick or getting better after being sick. Deaths we procured with no trouble from Will Boyce the undertaker, who needed and, because he was a good and kindly man, deserved, the advertising. Arrivals and departures we could copy from the registration book at the Waterbury Inn.

I didn't do so well with items. The trouble with me was I was too polite to ask people about their private affairs. I didn't then understand how eager most people were to get their private affairs—that is, when they weren't in jail or being sued—into print. So the items I brought in disappointed Mr. Whitehill. It seems to me we needed two or three hundred a week, and my half dozen weren't much of a contribution.

What I was good in was assignments to stories which nobody could possibly want to conceal, and where about all I had to do was to notice what was going on. In this field I was sometimes useful and even profitable to Mr. Whitehill.

Mr. Whitehill was, among other things, the Waterbury correspondent of the *Burlington Free Press.* Usually this responsibility called for "items," which could be extracted from the *Record* and rewritten—by me. Once I went on a week's vacation—the only one I ever had while I worked for Mr. Whitehill—and at his suggestion fixed up six sets of "items" for the *Free Press* in advance. These bits of news must have had mildew on them when they reached the *Free Press,* for after my return from Highgate Springs (but that is another story) Mr. Whitehill showed me a reproachful letter from the Burlington editor.

The moral was, as near as I could figure it out, that I had better not take any more vacations so long as I worked for Mr. Whitehill. Or that I should set up as a prophet and write items about things that hadn't happened but were going to —and in fact this practice is now a recognized journalistic technique.

But sometimes I ran into a real story while operating for the *Free Press* on Mr. Whitehill's behalf. One such story, the pattern of many with which I was to become familiar in later years, was an investigation of what was then called the Waterbury State Asylum for the Insane. This was an impressive group of brick buildings, somewhat resembling the campus of a college or university—and maybe, in the light of what we now know about the human mind and emotions, the institution contained as much creative fervor as other institutions of (as Veblen loved to put it) the higher learning.

It appeared, however, that the attendants had not been kind to the patients, that the food had not been good, and, in short, that the bad Republicans (the Democrats didn't have any say in such matters then, in Vermont) who had been handing out the patronage were not as honest or as efficient as the good Republicans who hadn't got their hands on it.

I already knew that the Waterbury Asylum was not precisely a happy place. Sometimes we saw—and also heard— the inmates when they went out buggy-riding with the attendants. This was supposed to be good for them, but some of them screamed. Once I heard a woman's voice through a barred window at the Asylum. "I want my money," she was shouting. "I want them to bring back my money."

Money and sex were the two things that upset people, it seemed, and when both were involved in a single case the results were dismaying.

Once I saw Mildred Brewster walking quietly with a group of women inmates. Mildred had been the central figure in a famous murder case in Barre. She had shot her lover, presumably for not loving her enough. Now she walked, quiet and drab, under the elms of Waterbury, with a guard watching her just as he watched the others. She walked with a crooked mouth that could never smile or look beautiful again, for she had shot herself there in preference to her poor, broken heart.

I didn't know that this was the high romance; I don't know yet. What I suspect is that Mildred came to the Asylum because the State of Vermont could not bring itself to hang her—as it did, and wickedly, hang two other unfortunate women, one of them from Waterbury.

Being of the Puritan tradition, we were fond of justice. Being kindly disposed toward most of our neighbors, as a community can be when there is plenty of room and each is dependent on the other in time of dire need, and being especially tender toward women, we—and I don't mean high-school boys working for newspapers but also grown Vermonters, with whiskers—we tempered justice with mercy.

Was it mercy in Mildred Brewster's case? Again, I don't know. I do know that there was no horror when I saw her. There she walked, quiet, sad, not beautiful any more, if ever she was, and I could not think she took any joy, as I did, as normal people did, in spring and fall and the glory of first snow.

But there was this investigation, from which my mind and memories wander. Maybe Mildred Brewster figured in it, what she ate and how she was treated. Male patients figured in it, too. One of them, troubled with a remorse the Freudians much later carefully explained to me (but it bothered me somewhat, then), went into a toilet and emasculated himself. Why, asked the investigator, was this sort of thing allowed to happen? Happily for me, it was not my duty to answer. All I had to do was to record the question and see that the *Burlington Free Press* got it. And any answer to it— but not my answer.

Other patients, not driven to emasculate themselves, yet somehow difficult to deal with, were beaten or tied up or deprived of proper food. The investigator asked, why?

I didn't and don't know what the trouble was. The patients were victims. Every person is entitled to be physically and mentally normal, and these, in spite of the Declaration of Independence, the Constitution and the Gettysburg Address, were not normal.

The attendants were victims, too—of poor pay, of poor education (they had no Mrs. Frankum, no Professor Hosmer to help them and stir their ambition), of a half-medical, half-punitive system that tried at one and the same time to cure people of insanity and punish them for being insane.

But I put none of these thoughts into the stories I wrote about the investigation. The thoughts came later. All I had at the time was a sort of indigestion, part physical, part emotional. Day by day I wrote down the testimony, as I could reconstruct it from my amateurish notes. One of the great thrills of my life was when the *Burlington Free Press* picked up what Mr. Whitehill had telegraphed them from my stories, changed the first paragraphs little or not at all, put headlines on them and ran them on page one. I had no by-line. I did not become famous. I just had an inner glow that began below my chin and ran down as far as my belt.

Mr. Whitehill complimented me. He said that if I could only get up a little more gumption I would have the makings of a first-class newspaperman. He also collected space rates from the *Free Press,* and kept the money, as he had a legal right to do.

3

Justin Moody, Mr. Whitehill's father-in-law, regarded me, and perhaps the world in general, with a great deal of humorous toleration. I believe—and, indeed, I believed then, but didn't have enough words lying around to express it—that he had been quite a lady's man in his day. He dressed neatly still, and smelled faintly of cologne. Most male Vermonters didn't smell of cologne.

What he did in the office, in the way of work, was never evident, but I imagine he kept an eye on the cash drawer to make sure his son-in-law did not do anything rash with Mr. Moody's part of the investment. Mr. Moody and Mr. Whitehill, I am sure, did not suspect each other of wrongdoing. Neither one could possibly have done wrong, in the legal sense; they had been too well brought up. But they watched each other, in a pleasant sort of way, and I never heard a cross word between them.

Mr. Moody liked to repeat a couplet he had heard in his youth, running as follows, in what Mr. Moody took to be the Irish dialect:

> *"The rich people ride in chaises,*
> *The poor have to walk, by Jaises."*

But Mr. Moody didn't plan to be poor, if he could help it. If there were any chaises he would do his best to ride in them. I had the impression that if Mr. Whitehill had proposed to raise me to three dollars a week during my part-time and apprentice years, or to seven dollars a week during my full-time year, Mr. Moody would have been shocked. What could a boy of seventeen going on eighteen be wanting with seven dollars a week? The foreman of the printing plant got only twelve. The young journeyman who worked

under him—and over me, except that we were good friends
—got eight. Mr. Moody thought the more you didn't pay out
the more you had left.

Yet Mr. Moody wasn't mean. He was always genial, always
leisurely, never outwardly hurried or worried. He could be
relaxed, for he had no work to do except to wait on an occasional customer. He could be more relaxed than Mr. Whitehill, who was ambitious in an unimaginative way, and wanted
to be rich or politically powerful, or both, and popular with
everybody.

I lived in this atmosphere for four years—three while I was
going to high school and one after I graduated. I started in
with the faith that if I worked hard enough and long enough
I would get ahead in the world. I did not learn until much
later that this is not the only way—perhaps not even the sur-
est way—to do it. Mr. Whitehill and Mr. Moody profited, to
a certain extent, by this superstition of mine.

Yet in a way I loved the circumstances of my semi-servi-
tude. I loved Mr. Whitehill's printing office. I loved the smell
of ink and wet newsprint. I was proud of ink stains on my
shirt, not to mention on my hands and behind my ears. As
the foreman, Walter Robinson, said, these were the badges
of my trade, and I should not be ashamed of them. I loved
the rattle and bang of the presses. I asked no ethical questions. I didn't see the iniquity when Mr. Whitehill bought
syndicated "boiler plate"—stereotyped metal strips—and used
the material twice. I was fond of boiler plate, partly because
I liked to read the proofs that came with it and partly because you didn't have to distribute it into the type cases when
you were through with it.

I loved so many things about that old *Record* shop. I even
loved the smell of decaying oranges and other fruits and
vegetables that came up from Charlie Haines's nearby grocery store on hot summer days, and was wafted, along with

multitudinous flies, into our windows.

I thrilled with honest pride the day Mr. Whitehill went off, leaving me to make up the front page (well, perhaps the foreman helped a little), and I wrote, set and published my first editorial. It read: "Twenty below zero this morning. Some winter." Fortunately, it did not occur to me to come out for the Democratic candidate for the State Legislature.

Mr. Whitehill and Mr. Moody exploited me. I know that now. I think I sensed it then. But in a way, after my fashion, without their knowledge, I exploited Mr. Whitehill and Mr. Moody.

Mr. Whitehill paid me an intangible salary, of which he was not even aware. Or was he so aware? For he seemed to know that I did not wish to be a clerk in Bert Lyford's dry-goods store, though Bert offered me a dollar more than Mr. Whitehill did; or in Jim Morton's drugstore, though Jim said I could turn the freezer that made the ice cream—and this meant, though not so stated, that I could lick the dasher. Mr. Whitehill was like Keats' Belle Dame sans Merci, whom he did not otherwise resemble; Mr. Whitehill, or rather the trade he permitted me to learn, in part, had me in thrall.

But this was not the whole of the intangible salary Mr. Whitehill paid me. Indeed, for that intangible salary—and I am sorry for him and glad for myself that he did not know this damaging fact—he could have had my services while I was in high school for about a dollar and a half and all my time and some of my loyalty after my graduation, for a whole year and more, for as little as five dollars a week. Mr. Whitehill and I cannot do each other any good or any harm now, but I wish I could tell him this and study his expression. I would not worry too much about the results. Men who publish newspapers, even small newspapers, even newspapers that exist only in memory, as do themselves, have ink in their veins. Mr. Whitehill could have lived comfortably by dealing in real estate or in some other legal but not dramatic occupation. He chose to publish a newspaper. He chose to run a printing office. For these choices, I still salute him.

For Harry Whitehill was not a bad or feeble man. His character would have passed an x-ray test without revealing anything more than the customary shadows that result from being alive at all. What I mean is, I could have been had cheaper, because of the immaterial rewards that came to me —rewards on which I have earned invisible dividends for many long and not altogether disenchanting years.

And I would say this about Justin Moody—and to him if he were around. It is safe to say this, now, in 1959. Neither Mr. Whitehill nor Justin Moody can cut my pay, not any more. The adolescent youth who worked so hard for them is no longer an asset to either of them—he no longer exists. Nor do they.

But what uncounted wealth Mr. Whitehill and his father-in-law did shower on me! They enabled me to learn a little about one of the noblest of trades. They inoculated me with a disease which neither of them caught, yet which, happily, I have never shaken off. As I write these words I think of the composing room of a great newspaper, into which room I am privileged on occasion to enter (though not to touch the type), and I know that I was privileged, also, in my bewildered beginnings, to come into the borderland of a great tradition—and this through the gullibility of Mr. Whitehill and Mr. Moody.

The ink is in my soul as well as on my collar, and if Anybody in any hereafter looks at my soul in a critical or inquiring way, I shall be proud to testify I was in my small way a printer once.

Of course this was not all that Mr. Whitehill and Mr. Moody paid me. In summer they did not pay me so handsomely, for in warm weather I did not have to keep the fires going, and it might be almost daylight when I got up and went to the *Record* office—a quiet office, deep in silence as in waste paper.

In winter, however, they paid me beyond the dreams of avarice, in a gold neither of them had ever known, or, knowing, had put by and lost. In winter they made it possible for me to get up in the darkness and cold and go up to the office, through drifted snow or North Pole breezes; they made it possible for me to do the miracle that brought a little warmth out of the chill that had enveloped the store and shop; they made it possible for me to see something they could seldom have seen in their later years, the flush of dawn, glowing tenderly on that noble little range of mountains we stubbornly called the Hogbacks; and later in the season they paid me, without knowing it and without drawing down their bank accounts, in the first warm, lascivious breezes of spring, that then came early into town to bless all those who loved them and waited for them.

I like to lie abed in the morning now. Yet I would not now surrender those visions of beauty and of dawn, of love divine and human, that Mr. Moody and Mr. Whitehill all unconsciously paid me. Perhaps even now they would not begrudge this wage. Where could they have cashed it if they had held it back?

The dust of sweeping lingered in my nostrils, but the glory of morning came in upon me like a song.

Mr. Whitehill and Mr. Moody paid me, also, without intending to, in the hearty blizzards that came upon our town in the depth of winter, when I picked up the Burlington or Boston newspapers, before school and after school, and struggled through the snow with them. I was not quite sure of my manliness in those adolescent days, but when I took the buffets of the storms I felt a little more secure. I loved this challenge and encounter, I love the memory of it today, and I thank Mr. Moody and Mr. Whitehill for exposing me to it.

These matters were part of an unintended treasure. I feel somewhat guilty about having kept them so long to myself. Perhaps I cheated Mr. Whitehill and Mr. Moody.

4

Let me picture a January day during that last postgraduate year, when I learned so much. My Aunt Alice would wake me up at half-past five by pounding on the stovepipe that passed through my upstairs room, and, in a mild way, warmed it, but not by half-past five in the mornings. My Aunt Alice would then go downstairs to the cellar and fix our own furnace—she did this every cold morning during the five years I lived in that house, and never once trusted me to do it, though I was explicitly trusted, and perhaps over-trusted, to keep the *Record* fires burning brightly but not brightly enough to burn the place down.

This meant, of course, that my aunt got up before I did, but I took it for granted that aunts and mothers did that sort of thing and didn't mind; and the gratitude I feel now is overdue and useless.

The only way I could manage to get out of bed at all on a very cold morning was to start rolling at the very first tap on the stovepipe. If I had hesitated even for a moment I might have withdrawn under the bedclothes—and maybe be there yet, or at least until the following spring.

I then dressed, sliding into my cold underwear with shuddering haste, put on my overcoat, overshoes, muffler, mittens and "took," as we called the knitted headgear we wore on cold mornings, and waded through the snow, if there was any, to the office, a distance of perhaps a quarter of a mile. I had no coffee and no breakfast at that hour. I didn't expect to have them and wouldn't have considered it right to have them; I knew that in this world of stern duty one earned one's breakfast before one ate it.

The reward came later. When I had finished my work at the office I went home and had a breakfast that would astound me today, a breakfast, sometimes, with griddle cakes, fried sausages, eggs in various styles, popovers (though these were mainly for Sunday mornings), vast quantities of butter, and coffee. Dr. Janes said a growing boy at that time in the morning could handle coffee without hurting himself and referred to the coffee substitutes that were then coming into the market as slop.

After this I went to the depot and picked up the *Burlington Free Press*, distributed it along a paper route, left the surplus copies at the front office, and was then ready to begin my day's work. This was what I expected, this was a routine suited to the place and time.

I was learning something during that postgraduate year. I wasn't learning what my relatives thought I was learning. I wasn't even learning what I myself thought I was learning, for I never afterwards got any real use out of being able to run a job press or feed a flat-bed. I was learning something, a very little but something, about human nature. I was learning, for example, that the words people spoke didn't always mean what they seemed to.

Mr. Whitehill, for instance, used many words expressive of good will toward the ingenuous adolescent who did so much work for him for so little monetary pay. Mr. Whitehill really did have the good will that was in the words. He really wanted me to go to college and get educated and be a successful man, and reflect credit on Mr. Moody and himself and the *Waterbury Record*. However, he did not plan to have this happen at any extra cost or inconvenience to himself.

Moreover, like every successful man—and in his field, place, and time he was successful—he had a degree of contempt for those who were not yet successful and perhaps never would be. He was confident and at times swaggering, which I wasn't. I was also young, which he no longer was. The result was that he patronized me.

Mr. Whitehill was not a doggy man. He was not an outdoor man at all. Once, however, he did have a dog—a collie, I believe, which was ordinarily kept at home but sometimes found her way to the office. I liked dogs well enough, though our family had never had one, and I struck up a casual acquaintance with the collie. After all, we both belonged to Mr. Whitehill—the collie permanently, since Abraham Lincoln had not abolished the private ownership of dogs, myself temporarily. We both worked for Mr. Whitehill. The collie's pay was bigger than mine, perhaps, for it covered board and lodging, which mine really didn't.

So one day I heard Mr. Whitehill speak to the collie, in a certain recognizable tone of voice, and for a flashing instant thought he was speaking to me.

Anger flamed in me like the active end of a Fourth-of-July rocket. I didn't know why, and I didn't say anything. I merely remembered—and still remember. The incident gave me a measure of a man who might have been one of my youthful heroes if he had cared to take the trouble to understand what went on in the minds of other persons, even in the minds of quite young persons.

But he didn't understand; in spite of his natural amiability he didn't try to.

So, therefore, but with a diminishing respect for Harry Whitehill, I completed my day's rounds. At about four-twenty it was time to go to the depot and pick up the Boston papers —the *Globe,* the *Herald,* and the *Journal.* Weather or no weather, this was what I did.

Then I went home and had supper with my always solicitous grandmother, mother, and aunt and, during the last months, with my quiet-voiced sister, who was congenial at all times and comfortable to talk to. My father and brother had gone to California—the former threatened with tuberculosis. We were a small family in that last year in Waterbury —and sometimes a sad one.

After supper, in winter, I went back to the *Record* office and bedded down the stoves or the steam boiler for the night. It was quiet there, the store was closed to customers, and I felt secure and almost successful. Not successful like Mr. Whitehill, or even Mr. Moody, who had mainly succeeded in becoming a father-in-law, but successful in knowing just how to bed down a fire and adjust dampers and steam valves.

When I had fixed the fires and maybe experimented with the power apparatus I would go home and spend an hour or so in getting cultured. During my high-school days I had tried to turn Virgil into English verse. Maybe I succeeded. I wouldn't know now, for I lost my manuscript and haven't read Virgil since. In fact, so far as translations go (and I am like Shakespeare, or even more so, in knowing little Latin and no Greek beyond the alphabet), I prefer Homer.

After I had got as cultured as I could stand after an active day, which would be at about nine o'clock, I went to bed. There wasn't much chance to get into mischief when a boy was working for H. C. Whitehill. He couldn't become a juvenile delinquent—he didn't have time.

5

My Aunt Alice asked me one day if I knew Mr. Whitehill's story. At first the question confused me, for Mr. Whitehill was full of stories—almost as full as Justin Moody was. Some of Mr. Whitehill's stories I heard when he didn't know I was around, but I heard them.

"About when he first came to Waterbury," said my aunt.

I didn't know that part of Mr. Whitehill's biography. There was no especial reason why he should tell it to me. I took it for granted he had been in Waterbury for many years. I knew he had once been in Barre, and had studied, if that is the word for it, at what was then Goddard Seminary. I wondered if Mr. Whitehill had ever been as young as I felt. I supposed not. I supposed he had been born running things, and making money, even as a baby. Maybe he had bought rattles at one cent each and sold them at twenty-five cents a dozen. That was the way I felt about Mr. Whitehill.

"Well," went on my aunt. She paused, trying to find words that would interest her and still not shock her refined young nephew, and continued.

It seemed that when Mr. Whitehill had first come to Waterbury to buy and operate the *Waterbury Record* and *Stowe Journal* he had fallen into the clutches of a Bad Woman. A Bad Woman was one who got her means of support from a number of men instead of just one man. Obviously this woman had come from somewhere else. There was a story during my time in the town of a sinful female from somewhere else who had set up light housekeeping on the edge of town, and before the sheriff had had time to sit on the complaints and make out a warrant and arrest her there was a line of men reaching all the way from near the top of Blush Hill (which was its real name, even before this episode) to the lumber mill at Colbyville. It was a dark and rather foggy night, of course.

Mr. Whitehill's Bad Woman had not only caused him to err but had done it in such a way as to create a scandal and leave him with an ailment we never mentioned by name. My aunt, who was a direct and forceful woman, made this clear to me. She was also an honest-minded and loving woman. She didn't want me to fall into the same trap as Harry Whitehill when I grew up. But in all fairness to Mr. Whitehill she wanted to make one more point.

"Most men in his position," she said, "would have left

town. Mr. Whitehill didn't. He said the story would go anywhere he might go in Vermont, and he might as well face it out here, where people knew some of his good points as well as his bad points."

"That was mighty brave of him," I commented.

"It was mighty sensible of him," my aunt said. "And in spite of his faults, and that one mistake, he does have many good points."

I took a good look at Harry Whitehill the next day. He certainly didn't look like a hero. But I knew, even then, in all my callowness and calfishness, they don't always.

I still like to think of H. C. Whitehill facing it out, as he did, marrying into a good old family, becoming a respected member of the Methodist Church, and helping me to learn something about printing and journalism. I used to speculate about the woman who had caused his mishap. What did she look like? Was it her passionate beauty that carried Mr. Whitehill off his feet? Was there a strain of romance in him that I had not detected? Did he want, as a young man, the things that I, as a young man, desired?

At any rate, I could bear with Mr. Whitehill's frailties, even with his good-natured and only half-conscious contempt for my own awkward and bungling ways, after I learned of his adventure and his valiant recovery.

I didn't even mind his strut so much as I once had. Maybe he was scared inside, just the same as I, an eighteen-year-old boy, was. Maybe this woman, this Lilith, as I had come to call her, had seemed to give him courage when he needed it.

Did I really think these things? I know I felt them. As for Lilith, a name I had run across in my reading, and with which name I christened the lady who had crossed Mr. Whitehill's path so inopportunely—I wished I could lay eyes on her; sometimes, at night, I wished I could be ruined by her.

But Harry Whitehill wasn't ruined. He rose in his little

world in spite of his misadventure—perhaps partly because of it, for though the women of the community condemned him the men had an admiration for the especial kind of sin of which Harry was believed to be guilty.

Years later he established a radio station on top of Blush Hill. He had been long dead when, on a slippery winter afternoon, I drove up Blush Hill to look at the station. But there was a trace of his personality still about the place. It swaggered a little.

CHAPTER THREE

———◆•••◆———

A Patient of Dr. Janes

1

*T*HOSE WERE quiet times, before anybody felt it necessary to trespass upon his neighbor's silences. The radio was far in the future, and television still further, though I had read, in some story that came into the *Record* office in the ready-set "boiler plate" that Mr. White-hill bought, of an imaginary future kingdom in which the ruler spoke and appeared to his people by some miraculous electrical gadget. I didn't believe this possible. I still don't.

So what I heard at night, as I half-slept, half-waked, in my bedroom in my grandmother's house in Waterbury, were the sounds of the weather (the same then as now), the rumble of trains going by enchanted on the Central Vermont Railroad, sometimes the murmured conversation downstairs of my grandmother, mother and aunt, and once in a while the deep accents of Dr. Janes' organ. These were sometimes mournful, sometimes seeming to accept, in quiet philosophy, all the sorrows of mankind, but rarely gay.

I would not be hearing all the notes, of course. The doctor's left hand would speak a little louder than his right. He seemed to like to go down into the bass and rumble around there.

People said Dr. Janes built his own organ. I imagine that he installed it himself, with his strong and delicate surgeon's hands, in the front room of the house, used after his death as a part of the public library. How he learned to play I don't know. He had had enough else to do. Perhaps this music was the medicine he prescribed for himself as a cure for what he had gone through as a surgeon in the Civil War and what he went through daily, in his undramatic fashion, as a general practitioner in and around Waterbury.

It would be remembered of him all his life that he had served his time manfully, first with troops in action, later as a director of hospitals for the Army of the Potomac. He was said to have had under his supervision at one time twenty thousand sick and wounded soldiers. No doubt he could have gone on after the war to some larger community and made a name for himself. But he came back to his own town and his own people.

An old, sad story about Henry Janes ran in the legends of our village. He had been, so the old-timers said, a young man of extraordinary attraction for women, and this with no particular effort on his part. He went off to the war, so far as was announced, without making promises to anybody. His first assignments carried him into danger with a fighting Vermont regiment. One day, advancing under artillery fire, Dr. Janes was seen to fall and word came back from another Waterbury soldier that he was dead.

The news saddened everybody in Waterbury, including one young woman who at once put on mourning (and mourning was tragically easy to find in the stores in those days) and said that she and the doctor had been secretly engaged to be married. They had known each other, of course, but seemingly not well. Yet nobody could prove the young lady was wrong; nobody but the dead, that is; nobody but the doctor himself, who presently sent word that though he had stumbled into a shell hole while advancing with his regiment he was not only not dead and not hurt beyond a few bruises, but was coming home soon on furlough.

The girl did what her poor, frightened, humiliated heart urged her to do. She spoke to nobody about her trouble, but she did go down to the Winooski River, which was then running in a high spring flood, and drown herself.

"Poor girl!" said my grandmother. "Poor, poor girl! Such a sweet, gentle child she was, as I remember her."

"What did the doctor do?" I asked.

"He didn't do anything," replied my grandmother. "It hurt him terribly. You could see that. But it was all over before he got home, and nobody blamed him."

When the war was over and all his military duty done Dr. Janes came home for good, and soon after was married to a young lady who had said nothing at all about his supposed death and therefore had nothing to unsay. She must have been a lovely young person, for Mrs. Henry Janes, when I used to see her forty years later, was still a beautiful woman.

2

Dr. Janes, when I knew him best, must have been at least in his middle sixties, which at that time was very old. He was, however, extremely rugged, as an old-fashioned general practitioner had to be to stay alive, and as a veteran of the battles, camps and hospitals of the Army of the Potomac naturally was. Even now I cannot associate him with debility.

He resembled Dr. Watson of Williamstown, whom I had dumbly and trustingly revered, only in his selfless devotion to the art and science of medicine and in the wisdom with which he approached all human problems. Dr. Freud could have learned much from each of them; each understood, within the limits of the evidence, the strange connection between the body and the emotions.

Dr. Watson was profoundly religious. Dr. Janes was not

religious, not in the sense of going to church, or wanting to go. He had a kind of tough kindness. He could be grumpy if, in his opinion, grumpiness was indicated. I first went to him, or was taken to him, as a child. I saw him last when I was a troubled adolescent. Between these two periods he remained, so far as I could tell, the same.

Perhaps Henry Janes had learned in the Army of the Potomac, an army of bewildered boys thrust into history with great ideals and many confusions, how to deal with adolescents. He was, as I now understand, all the specialists that were later to blossom; he was acquainted with surgical and medical skills that did not then concern me, but he also knew why a high-school boy was uncertain, and at times scared, and yet driven by hopes and dreams.

Once he glared at me, almost fiercely, and demanded: "Are you ambidextrous?"

I felt a guilty flush rise in my ears and cheeks. What did ambidextrous mean? Was I, without meaning to be, ambidextrous?

Dr. Janes smiled and explained. The truth was, I was left-handed in most respects where being left-handed was inconvenient and unprofitable, but right-handed in fields where an eccentricity might have done me some good: for example, I threw a baseball right-handed and so could never be a left-handed pitcher, or any kind of pitcher worth mentioning; I batted right-handed and so could never puzzle the man who was trying to get three strikes on me. These accidents depressed me somewhat, but to Dr. Janes they were matters of a detached but kindly interest.

He studied me as an entomologist studies a pinned insect, but he studied me, also, with a fatherly good will. My deviations from the expected normal symptoms, physiological and psychological, interested him profoundly, but what he tried to do was to make me function better and feel better.

3

Dr. Janes had inherited a farm on the edge of town, a few minutes' walk from all the business section there seemed likely ever to be in Waterbury. It ran down to the rivers, to Little River where it came under the old bridge across Main Street, and to the Winooski. This was good land, except when now and then part of it was overflowed in the spring freshets; and of course these overflowings during countless years gone by had helped to make it good land.

The doctor didn't want to let the farm go, or lie fallow, or be cultivated by persons who didn't understand it and love it. He continued to maintain his meadows, and a herd of milk cattle to graze on them, and be largely supplied by what could be grown on them. He also had to have a horse, probably two horses, to get him on his rounds. He hadn't taken on an automobile at the time I left Waterbury.

The milk his cows produced Dr. Janes sold, to those who were willing and able to come for it or send for it. I now assume that all the sanitary precautions and observances known in that day were taken in the handling of his milk. The times were changing. In Williamstown, where I had observed the practices of the Sibley farm, the milkmen washed their hands before milking, and also used strainers to keep large impurities from getting into the pails. In Waterbury I had watched an early pasteurization process at the creamery; you let the milk get hot enough to kill the microbes, as we called anything smaller than an ant, but you didn't let it boil, because that would also have killed the flavor. The milk from Dr. Janes' cows was not pasteurized in my time, but it was clean, it tasted good, and I knew quite a few persons who drank it and lived to die of other ailments, such as old age, and not of the diseases ascribed to milk.

What I now remember is that milk and cream never looked

so good as they did in the pantry—or buttery—where they were kept for Dr. Janes' customers and patients. The cream lay thick on the shallow pans set out for it to rise, it was yellow and delicious, just to look at, a growing adolescent craved it. The milk was warm from the milking, and was poured into the cans the customers brought.

Mrs. Janes came in sometimes to make sure all was going well, a gracious lady of the manor. Mostly, though, it was Morris and Ellen who presided. These were among the friendliest and most unassuming persons I ever knew. They were a long-continuing and necessary part of the Janes household. Without Morris and Ellen it would never have been the same; it seemed to me, even though I knew better, that they had been in the Janes household always, and always would be.

They had at least been there a long time. Neither was married, or ever had been. Morris hid his natural mildness behind a formidable moustache, but this never fooled anybody. Ellen had brown hair, parted in the middle, and brown eyes.

Each, I soon understood, had found a refuge in the doctor's house. Neither really wanted out of life more than could be found there: friendship, safety, the little that each felt to be the necessities of existence. I suppose I saw them both on the street, I suppose both went to church when their work permitted, but I have no memory picture of them outside of the Janes house. That was where they belonged, like images in a painting in a frame. Take away the frame, let the outside world flow in, and they might disappear.

My Aunt Alice said that Morris used to come to Ellen's room in the evening, after all the chores and dish-washing and pan-scalding were finished with, and talk. The door would be wide open, of course, for no one would suspect that Morris or Ellen would break the least of our social and moral rules. No one really supposed, either, that they would do anything wrong if the door were closed and locked on the inside.

They were not that sort of persons. They were by nature good and proper. They also lacked, each of them, I suspect, the passionate necessity to do Wrong—or whatever the word is for putting Nature ahead of Mother Grundy. What they wanted was security, not ecstasy, and in the Janes household it was security they found.

My Aunt Alice wondered, out loud, why Morris and Ellen didn't get married. My grandmother said, maybe because they didn't want the responsibility of supporting each other. My mother suggested, perhaps they were fond of each other in a different, more restrained way.

I think everybody was right. Marriage would have meant another establishment, another house, an adventure that neither of them really desired. They liked each other—loved each other, like brother and sister—but they knew a little of the town's problems, the way Dr. Janes saw and experienced those problems; he didn't tell Morris and Ellen in so many words, but they knew. They were not impelled to go out into the chill of domesticity and take its risks, including children. And by the time I gave much thought to them I supposed Ellen was past the age for having children.

So their lives were placid, and without ambition. I don't even now know whether to be sorry for them or not. When Morris went among the cows at milking time, in the barn that smelled of fodder as of milk, in the warmth of the mild pastoral creatures that found relief in his coming; when he rose before sunrise, as he surely did a good part of the year; when he bedded his charges down for the night and knew that he had done his duty as well and faithfully as he could, did he not have his reward?

And Ellen, doing much of the cooking, priding herself on her shining pans, looking after the cream and butter, receiving a kindly smile from the doctor now and then (well, maybe that was what she lived for) and an affectionate word from Mrs. Janes (who did not know that Ellen unconsciously loved the doctor) on holidays: was that the worst lot that ever befell a woman?

Ellen couldn't help loving the doctor, consciously or otherwise. Every woman loved the doctor, I do believe. Mrs. Janes, who possessed him, body and soul, might have been disappointed if she had ever thought they didn't.

Henry Janes died, though not during my time in Waterbury. At that sad moment Ellen and Morris realized the lonesomeness that was about to descend on them, knew that they could not endure a situation in which they could not have quiet, thoughtful and unchaperoned talks together, and were married. I wonder if they were able to break themselves of the habit of keeping the door open when they talked together in the evening.

So Tristan came to his Isolde at last, not passionately but not tragically, either. They may have had more satisfaction out of life, in the end, than the Tristan and Isolde of the legend and the opera.

4

When I think of the story I am about to tell I also think of Dr. Janes, though he wasn't in it at the beginning, and only professionally at the end. However, when there was bad trouble everybody thought of Dr. Janes and what he might be able to do about it.

Once upon a time there was a boarding house down Bolton way, but within the confines of our town. In the boarding house there resided a number of stalwart, sex-hungry young men, and one young woman, whom I shall call, for various reasons, Lilith.

The men were working on the dam at Bolton Falls that

later added to our supply of electricity, and it did seem that a lot of electricity was running around in that boarding house, only not the kind that would light the streets of Waterbury.

What Lilith did I don't know, but somehow I guess. Lilith waited on table in that boarding house. I half-remember seeing her there, once, before or after the episode I am thinking of; Lilith was the sort of woman an adolescent boy would half-remember, without much certainty as to where or how or when he saw her.

So I do have some recollection, from somewhere, of a young woman who reached for plates, or laid plates down, with a wreathed and sinuous arm, so that it must have been a torment as well as a pleasure for full-grown and full-blooded men to watch her. I suspect, at this later date, that she was flattered by the attention she received, loved herself more than she loved any one man, distributed her largess according to her daily whims, and in time came thriftily, in a logic hard for New Englanders to controvert, to sell the only commodity she had.

Such things should not have happened in a Vermont village at that time. What we have to bear in mind is that then as now things that should not happen do happen. Of this I shall speak later.

At any rate, Lilith lived fully and joyously, but she overlooked some complications in the plain human nature with which she was surrounded. One day word came up to Waterbury village that a man named Bill Higgins had shot and badly wounded a man named Jim O'Neill at Mrs. Maxwell's boarding house. Dr. Janes had been called; everybody felt better when they heard that; but Jim O'Neill was in a bad way.

Bill Higgins had shot Jim O'Neill, so the word ran, because Jim had been too successfully attentive to Lilith, whom Bill Higgins liked to think of as his own personal property. I knew, of course, what this success of Jim O'Neill's consisted in, but I couldn't understand what Bill expected to gain by shooting Jim. Would it, for instance, make Lilith like Bill any better?

Such a tragedy was a real occasion in our town, for as a rule nobody in Waterbury got shot unless he shot himself while hunting, or unless some shortsighted neighbor mistook him for a deer. As for sexual passion, it was known to exist, but the general assumption was that if a girl didn't like a man that was her business, and there wasn't much he could do, or ought to do, about it. Except, of course, look for another girl, which I am told is advised by many psychiatrists even today.

The fate of Jim O'Neill consequently stirred the village up. It so happened that we had in our midst several men who had been out West during the days before law and order spoiled the fun. One of these was J. C. Randall, who had found money in California or somewhere, and then had returned and seemed wholly satisfied to settle down and be an old-fashioned, extremely dignified Vermonter. He was an admirable man with a beard, and a lovely daughter named Pearl, who married a doctor from the asylum and who died, to everybody's sorrow, during the great influenza epidemic of 1918–19.

Another former Westerner was of a different type. He didn't get rich in California or anywhere else, though he remained an industrious and seemingly a reasonably well-to-do citizen after he got home. And he retained, as Mr. Randall apparently hadn't, a kind of homesickness for the old free days in the West.

It was this man, therefore, who turned up with a Winchester rifle and a coil of rope as Sheriff C. C. Graves arrived at the intersection of Main and Stowe Streets, with Bill Higgins beside him in the buggy, handcuffed and evidently wishing he was somewhere else.

Hobart Riley, which was scarcely his name, strode out into the intersection, followed at a decent interval by a sprinkling of curious or indignant citizens, nobody could tell which. The makings of a mob were present, in case anybody wanted one; it was only the inclination and leadership that were lacking. We weren't used to lynching people in our town; we didn't know how.

But Hobart Riley spoke out loudly and bravely. "We'll take that man, C. C.," he said.

Bill Higgins looked scared. C. C. Graves clucked to his horse, as though he were on a country road. He also produced his revolver and laid it on his lap. "Hobart," he replied, in a level voice, "you go home. You take that God-damned rifle and go home."

And this was what Hobart Riley did. He took his God-damned rifle and went home. He even took the coil of rope. He was a Vermonter, and no Vermonter, after all, not even a frustrated lyncher, was going to leave a dollar's worth of perfectly good rope lying around in the middle of the street. You could do a lot of useful things with a rope besides hanging people.

Somebody asked Dr. Janes if he didn't think Hobart Riley was right. Dr. Janes had seen and examined the wounded man and should have been indignant.

"Hobart acted like a damn fool," said Dr. Janes, and that was all he was ever known to say about that incident. But everybody knew what he meant. It wasn't justice he was thinking about, at least not justice in the narrow sense, it was keeping the human machine going and getting as much and as good work out of it as possible.

He did what he could for Jim O'Neill. I saw an article in the *Burlington Free Press* some weeks later; it said that Dr. Janes had testified at Bill Higgins' trial, and that Dr. Janes had made quite a reputation among the medical fraternity for keeping Jim alive as long as he did.

Bill Higgins got five years in jail, which I am sure he liked better than being lynched—especially by an amateur such as Hobart Riley. As for the lady I call Lilith, with some recall of a quickened pulse after all these postadolescent years, she stuck with Jim until she was sure Jim would never be a well man again, and then went off with another boarder. For a while, anyway.

5

Henry Janes was not merely a physician, he was, whether he so desired it or not, a power in the community. I don't suppose he ever ran for any public office. What office could there be that would carry more weight than merely being Henry Janes? If any running had to be done it would be the office running after Dr. Janes, and this, too, he managed to escape.

But he did attend town meetings and village meetings— the latter, of course, having to do with affairs that the farmers and outlying residents wouldn't naturally be concerned with.

I attended those meetings, too, in my journalistic capacity, and took voluminous notes, to be transcribed and sweated down for later use in the *Record*. I wish I had those notes now, for the *Record* could not contain them.

Everybody says nowadays that the old New England town meeting was the most democratic institution that ever existed. In a way it was and in a way it wasn't. The town or village meeting reflected the community. Anybody at all, paupers, women, criminals and the mentally indisposed excepted, could rise and try to make a speech. He could go on speaking until the moderator cut him off, or until there was a loud enough yell for him to sit down, or until some friend and admirer grabbed his coattails and yanked him down.

It was stated in Waterbury by the old-timers that there

was once a man from Waterbury Center (he lived on the lefthand side of the road as you went up, in a shingled house painted brown with a dormer window) who got up in a town meeting and proposed that the school tax be reduced from three-fifths of a mill on the dollar to three-fourths of a mill. I forget whether or not his motion carried. It might have, for there could have been a few others whose notions of arithmetic were similar to his, and there may have been some who thought that the schools really did need more money— as they did and still do.

Town and village meetings could be funny, there was no doubt about that. However, they did have an undertone of deep seriousness, because money and some other serious things were involved. At some time or other during each important debate people would begin to wonder what C. C. Warren and Dr. Janes, respectively our richest and our wisest citizen, would think about it.

C. C. Warren was a tanner who had a home with a curved-glass bay window off the front porch and a stone dog on the lawn. If he did not have a real dog it was not because he could not afford one. Some persons thought C. C. had as much as a hundred thousand dollars. He had enough, at any rate, to buy the first horseless carriage ever owned in Waterbury. The town and village meetings listened to him because it seemed right that a big taxpayer should have more to say than a small taxpayer or a man who didn't pay any taxes at all. The town bum, as long as he kept out of the poor house, had one vote, just like C. C. Warren and Dr. Janes, but people weren't eager to get his opinions.

C. C. Warren's character and personality were all right, too. If he had been a mean man, with a tendency to lord it over people he might as well have kept his mouth shut. We didn't take that sort of nonsense from anybody; we didn't have to; we were Vermonters.

Still, Mr. Warren's money did help him. On the other hand, I never heard anybody speculate as to how much money Dr. Janes had. He had his land, his cows and dairy, the proceeds of his practice, maybe some cash or securities handed down from his parents or his wife's parents. He lived comfortably— that is, he did so when he was not making himself uncomfortable looking after his patients. But he didn't have to be rich to command attention.

For an example of his influence, I might mention an issue that came up about providing a water-cart to lay the dust in summer on the village roads. We didn't have hard-surfaced streets then, though we did have a sort of tar sidewalk that got so soft in hot weather that when you walked on it you felt like a fly on sticky flypaper.

The argument against having a water-cart was that the cart, the horse, and the driver would cost money, and money was hard to come by. Opponents of the water-cart said it rained often enough in spring, summer, and fall to lay the dust, and what was wrong with dust, anyhow? Waterbury had managed to get along for more than a century with dust, and why shouldn't it continue to do so? This wasn't, these persons said, a big city, it wasn't Boston, or even Burlington, it was just a plain little village, and we loved it, and why spend so much money to make it different?

I took these arguments down for use in the *Record*, though of course I wrote them for the *Record* in much finer language than any I am able to think of today. I knew how to write in those days; if a word of three or four syllables was available I didn't cheat my dozens of readers by using words of one syllable, any more than I could help.

Then Dr. Janes appeared. No doubt he had been looking after some sick person down the river, or up in Colbyville, or maybe across the bridge, in Duxbury or Moretown.

You could feel Dr. Janes in a room, even before you saw or

heard him. He hardly had to call for the moderator's attention. Whoever had been speaking, or trying to speak, stopped speaking or trying and waited for what the doctor had to say.

"The streets in this village," that was what he had to say, "are a disgrace. I wouldn't dare drive around here after dark if I didn't have business that required it. Those streets are so full of holes and ruts you could drop a cow in and never find her."

He waited for this preamble to take effect. Then he continued: "Some of you seem to think that dust is something you can brush off your clothes and get rid of. A doctor knows, because that is his business, that dust can make you sick—and it does, too, every summer. If we can't have streets in this village that are a little flatter than a ploughed field we can at least do something to keep the dust down."

Dr. Janes snorted a good, manly, Army-of-the-Potomac snort. "It's the damnedest nonsense to make out you're spending money when you get rid of something that's doing you harm. You aren't spending it, you're investing it, you're putting it in the bank for future use. I'd say that if it was necessary for this village to slap a mortgage on the town hall to buy and operate a water-wagon it had better do it."

There wasn't a dissenting vote, not even from the town bum, who was generally against spending tax money, on the theory that the more you wasted on schools, hard roads, water-wagons and such things the less you had left to invest in liquor.

6

Other young doctors—and Henry Janes was certainly young enough when he came wearily home from the Civil War—had to exert themselves to get attention. I mention this matter by way of contrast. One such young man, so my Aunt Alice said, used to get out his horse and buggy and drive like mad down Main Street or out Stowe Street, in the hope that people would notice this and believe that Dr. Stimson, youthful though he might be, was in great demand.

Somebody came on Dr. Stimson once, on a dirt road (and dirt roads weren't hard to find then) a few miles out of town. He had tied his horse to a tree, and was sitting under the tree in the shade.

"Ain't you feeling well, Doc?" asked the intruder.

"I feel all right," replied the physician. "I'm just trying to get my breath. I've just finished with one case and I'm trying to figure out the next one."

The passer-by snickered as he slapped the reins on his own horse. "I'll be on hand at both funerals," he said, "if you or the relatives will let me know."

That was Dr. Stimson, who later got to be quite a physician, much respected and extremely dignified, with, I believe, some chin whiskers, and whose real name I have not used.

New doctors always interested a few restless people. If a person had something difficult or impossible to cure, he or his family would shop around from one physician to another. And there was occasionally a newcomer in the medical world who made quite a stir by a new idea, such as drinking three quarts of water every day or never eating anything made out of white flour. The same as today, in fact, except that few persons worried about their weight; if they were fat or thin to a noticeable degree they took that to be the Lord's intention and made the best of it.

But Dr. Janes went right along, with few hobbies. He had his office in his home, directly across the street from my grandmother's house. This office was a room lined with books, with windows on the south side, clean and light and at the same time, or maybe just in some seasons of the year, a little dark and, in a medicinal way, musty. Dr. Janes sat behind a large desk and it seems to me I sat facing him at the end of the desk, on his left.

I knew he watched me carefully but in spite of my adolescent shyness this scrutiny never embarrassed me. It never seemed to me I had anything to hide from Dr. Janes—or could hide anything, even if I wanted to. I have wished that some modern doctors, specialists in various ailments, could make me feel the same way, and a little less like a prisoner in the dock.

He rarely had to come to my grandmother's house to see me, though he did come regularly to see her and sometimes to visit my mother or aunt. Once, in that final year in Waterbury, I had pleurisy. He listened to my chest and to a strange whisper in my heart that puzzled doctors for many a year, before and afterwards, though it had no especial significance and, as I write, has not yet carried me off.

Then he shook his head indignantly. "Harry Whitehill has been making you lift things too heavy for you," he declared.

For some reason I stood up for Harry Whitehill, or perhaps for my own virility. I was tired of being considered a delicate young man. I must have had a fever at the time, but I remember what I said: "No, he hasn't. I'm pretty strong. I can lift anything around the shop that has to be lifted."

He laughed and gave me a sedative—perhaps what we called a Dover Powder—and I went to sleep.

He was interested in my future—even concerned about it. Once I went into his office on some trivial occasion and found him talking with some elderly male relative of his, a cousin, maybe, who had arrived for a visit. This man was from way out West—Ohio, let us say—and was in the railway business. He had been telling Dr. Janes, or maybe he brought up the subject because he wanted to impress the callow youngster from across the street, about the time Coxey's Army was seizing railway trains in order to march on Washington and get the depression of 1893 annulled or repealed.

The railway man, glowing with self-admiration, told how he had armed himself and his office staff and gone down to the yards. When Coxey, or one of his lieutenants, had come along, the rioters had found themselves looking into gun-muzzles.

"They didn't ride out on any of our trains," concluded the man from Ohio grimly. "They walked out."

Dr. Janes looked at me inquiringly, as though he, too, was waiting to judge from my response what manner of young man I really was.

But I wasn't sure what I wanted to say. I had been reading a book called *Poverty*, by Robert Hunter. I had shocked my Aunt Alice and startled my mother by saying I didn't believe anybody could honestly acquire a million dollars. My aunt was afraid I might grow up and not be a good Republican.

"What do you think of that?" Dr. Janes asked finally.

The man from Ohio had his eye on me, too. Maybe he was wondering if I would make a good railroad man and eventually keep some homespun, ragged Army of tramps from commandeering railway trains and going to Washington to overthrow the Government. I knew it wasn't right to steal trains. I suspected it wasn't right for men to be so poor that they were tempted to steal trains.

"I don't know," I replied.

The man from Ohio looked at me with distaste. If he had had some thought of offering me a job as a freight clerk in the Sandusky yards he gave it up, then and there.

But I thought Dr. Janes' face showed a slight trace of approval.

7

Dr. Janes moved across the highways of my life like a demigod, but I realize now that I have not made him dramatic. I don't believe he wished to be dramatic. I suspect that after the high tragedy of the Civil War he was weary of noise and strutting, tired of make-believe and empty sentiments.

He could be human, as he was when I went to Dr. Minard to have my injured leg fixed up in a hurry; he could be hurt because I didn't come to him for the rest of the cure. He could be human when he played the organ at night, trying in that mournful music to forget the unforgettable.

Perhaps he thought of his life as simple and uneventful, after that first explosion of war violence. Perhaps all the drama, later on, was inward.

I can't remember when I saw him for the last time, for that time was mixed up with all the other times, with the slightly musty but always antiseptic atmosphere of his books and his office in general, with the benevolent scowl with which he greeted and studied me whenever I came in, with the feeling I had that once in his office nothing could go badly wrong with me. I may have been confusing him with the Deity— though I doubt that he believed in a Deity.

There was some final visit, of course, when I was going away, never to return to Waterbury again for more than a few days, never to be his patient again, never to see him again, for I believe he died during the five years of my first absence.

Yet I was, and would always be, a patient of Dr. Janes.

CHAPTER FOUR

The Ascent of Mount Mansfield

1

I WAS out of doors a good part of every day when I worked for Harry Whitehill, but except for brief strolls on Sundays in summer, when I didn't have to keep any fires going at the *Record* Office, I never got deeply into raw nature. I loved the woods, I read about wildernesses in the mild pages of Henry Van Dyke and the more robust passages in Stewart Edward White, I went once in a while up Sunset Hill or to the Split Rock, where you could (and can) still see the marks of an ancient glacier, but it was only in imagination that I was a woodsman, a pioneer, a hunter.

Especially was I a young Vermonter of my own day and generation in my instinctive dislike for wild country with six or seven feet of snow on it. In that period of Vermont history a man who went up Mount Mansfield in the dead of winter, or tried to do so, would have been pursued, and if caught thrown forthwith into the Waterbury State Hospital for the Insane.

I skated a little, and badly, mostly on the shallow pond on the far side of the track, near the railway depot. Early in my social career in Waterbury I was skating on this pond with a female contemporary who had a nice figure but a hot temper, when I lost my balance—and hers, too. This young person never did forgive me, during the five years I spent in Waterbury, for making a ridiculous spectacle of her, and I never forgave her for never forgiving me. In my mellow advanced years I assume that everybody has forgiven everybody, and we might try it again tomorrow if we had skates and some ice, but this did not help at the time.

I sometimes wondered if it would not be fun to go snow-shoeing, the way our ancestors had to do, whether they liked it or not, but I had no snowshoes, and I could arouse no interest in the subject among my friends. One elderly person said to me—I suppose he was at least thirty-five at the time —that a man lost interest in that sort of thing after he was married and settled down and had children of his own.

Fun in Waterbury, except in a very restricted field, was understood to terminate with marriage. I am informed that conditions have changed since I moved away.

If I had mentioned skis I presume I would have been listened to with blank stares of amazement. But I couldn't mention skis, because I didn't know what they were. Nobody but the Scandinavians knew what skis were.

But even in the gentler months of the year not many people went out and really wallowed in nature. A few of the business and professional men built themselves what they called a shack on Lake Mansfield, an artificial pond at the foot of the mountain of the same name. I wouldn't even try to guess what they did there, as a rule, in addition to fishing. They couldn't have done any drinking, of course, because Vermont was then a prohibition state, and the only way a man could get liquor was to fall ill or order some sent to his address by express. But I do suppose that this was part of the infant country-club movement in that section.

Once these gentlemen invited the Rev. Kellogg for an overnight stay at the camp. I heard Mr. Whitehill telling, with some surprise, how human Mr. Kellogg turned out to be.

"He didn't pray all the time," said Mr. Whitehill. "He was

—well, almost—just like the rest of us. He even told stories."

"What kind of stories?" asked Justin Moody, whose rheumatism or something had kept him at home.

"Clean stories," replied Mr. Whitehill sharply. "What kind of stories did you expect him to tell?"

"There are some stories in the Bible," Mr. Moody mused, "that aren't exactly—"

"He didn't tell those, either." Mr. Whitehill laughed. "He took it we already knew them."

"Did he say grace?"

"Certainly. Why shouldn't he?"

"No reason at all why he shouldn't." Mr. Moody worked with his toothpick and gazed as usual at the passersby through the big front window. "Lots of perfectly normal people do. But it don't sound to me like life in the open country."

It wasn't. I could see that. I wouldn't have put it beyond Henry van Dyke to pray and say grace when he was camping out, because he was, after all, a minister and wouldn't want to get out of practice; but I was sure Stewart Edward White wouldn't, and Henry David Thoreau hadn't, and I was quietly resolved that I wouldn't, either, if I ever got into the real woods or way out on the plains or mountains of the West.

I wanted to be real tough and self-reliant, and not ask favors of the Almighty.

2

However, I did sleep out in the woods one night before I left Waterbury; in the summer of 1905, that memorable year, I made the ascent of Mount Mansfield with two companions. Since the way to Stowe, near the foot of the mountain, was almost all uphill, we put our bicycles on the interurban trolley car and went that far in luxury.

The trolley car waited at Waterbury depot for chance

passengers on the afternoon northbound train who might, for some mysterious reason, wish to go to Stowe. Some did, as a rule. So Earl, Joe and myself, attired and equipped for a rugged life, paraded around the depot platform for half an hour or so. I had on an old pair of pants with holes nearly through the knees, a bandana handkerchief and a hat that had been new when I was a freshman in high school. Tied to my belt in various places by string were a tin cup, a small tin kettle and possibly a Spanish-War canteen. We each carried a bundle of provisions—we must have, for we made use of them later—but I imagine these were in the wire baskets we had on the fronts of our bicycles.

Harry Whitehill put a little piece in the *Record* about us: "Rob Duffus, Joe Smith and Earl Boyce went camping on Mount Mansfield on their bicycles last week. The boys weren't armed to do any shooting but if no bears dropped dead on the mountain last week it must have been because they didn't catch sight of our young friends."

We detrained at Stowe, which was a quiet country town, and caused a small commotion as we pedaled slowly along the principal street past the stores. We didn't mind this much, because Stowe wasn't on the main line and we felt like city folks, and extremely sophisticated. Of course this was long before an Austrian mountaineer in full regalia could prance through Stowe, stopping to yodel now and then as he readjusted his skis, and never cause more than a weary yawn among the bored but acquisitive natives.

Mount Mansfield itself then boasted nothing more elaborate than an ancient and rickety hotel, balanced precariously between the winds, and approached by a corkscrew dirt road. It was plain to us that we could not ride our bicycles all the way up this dirt road. Soon we found ourselves pushing slowly up the steep grade, with darkness filtering in. It was evident that the time was near, and indeed had already arrived, when we would be in the dark and on our own resources in what one of my favorite books called the beast-haunted wilderness.

I had never, prior to this, slept outdoors. I do not know why the descendants of pioneers, as we all were, should be so skittish about open country after dark, but that was what we were.

We turned off the road with sinking hearts. At least, my own heart sank, and I thought I detected anxious looks on the faces of my two companions.

Earl Boyce's father, the undertaker, sometimes took his son along on his professional errands, and at more suitable times and under more cheerful circumstances Earl had often told me what his father had to do to make a corpse an attractive feature of a funeral. He went into the subject again that night, but I wished he hadn't.

There was, for instance, the impoverished French-Canadian who had taken too much cold tea or something and then gone for a stroll along the right-of-way of the Central Vermont Railroad, not far northwest of my grandmother's house. Earl said his father had succeeded in piecing the remains together so that the relatives had been pleased. It was, he said, a little like one of those cut-up picture puzzles.

There was also the farmer hauling wood down a steep slope on the Blush Hill Road, where Harry Whitehill later built the radio station. This farmer had stopped at what was called a thank-ye-ma'am—a sort of bump in the road left in for drainage purposes, and maybe also to make life more difficult—to put a stick under the wheels and rest the horses. In some strange, sad way he had managed to get his own foolish head under a wheel just as the whole wagon started to slide. Earl said he looked pretty well after his father had finished. "Except," said Earl, "his eyes—." I shudderingly closed my own eyes, and didn't listen to any more of Earl's anecdotes. A man like that might be walking around in the dark, on the side of a lonesome mountain, trying to find somebody to—well, poke his eyes back in for him.

I thought of these things as we scratched the stones and twigs away and started to settle down for the night.

Joe hadn't any information in any way comparable with Earl's. Joe's father, being a hardware merchant, saw the insides of many houses, because he often fixed up whatever plumbing there was, but as a rule his stories wouldn't keep a person awake nights. All Joe could think of that night was a lady we knew who had tuberculosis and was living in a tent on the lawn near her house, summer and winter. The lady thought this would cure her, but nobody else, not even Dr. Janes, agreed. All Dr. Janes would say was that if she felt happier living in a tent why shouldn't she?

Earl said that if this lady shut her eyes and kept still, at the stage she had got to now, she wouldn't look any better than most remains did.

I kept right on thinking of these things as we settled down, built a small fire, and huddled together to make coffee and eat our sandwiches and apples.

"I suppose this would have seemed second nature to old Ethan Allen," I said.

"You just got to get used to it," commented Joe Smith. "If we did it every night it would seem funny sleeping in a bed." He jumped slightly. "What was that?"

"A dead tree falling, maybe," said Earl Boyce. "A long way off."

"I wouldn't want to have one fall on me, dead or alive," I half whispered.

We ate in comparative silence. "Anyhow, no girls to bother us," Earl observed.

"A girl," Joe sneered, "would be scared out of her senses up here."

I had been reading about a legendary monster that haunted the Canadian North Woods. It traveled in big jumps, moaning and lamenting as it traveled. If it happened to light on a sleeping camper, it picked him up and swept off with him, because there wasn't anything it liked better than a really juicy camper.

"I wish you'd keep your damn mouth shut," said Earl.

"I wish I would, too," I promptly agreed.

Something else that I did not mention came into my mind and stayed there after we had eaten and lain down on the extremely hard ground beside the dying fire. What we didn't know about making ourselves comfortable in the woods would have been enough to equip a whole battalion of today's Eagle Scouts, and leave something over for the Campfire Girls.

It would have been hard for me to go to sleep with a quiet mind and an easy conscience, which I never did have during my adolescent years. However, what I found myself thinking about was something I had read in one of my favorite outdoor authors. In the North Woods there was not only the fun-loving monster I have mentioned, there was also an institution known as the Wild Huntsmen.

You never saw these creatures, at least not if you were lucky, but you heard their voices, now distinct, now far away—but never far enough away—sweeping through the woods in search of a prey one hardly dared try to picture.

I listened. I heard them. There were clear, high-pitched shouts, and the sound of magic horns.

I said nothing to my possibly slumbering companions. It was good when dawn began to come, after many long years. We rose with shouts of joy. We had slept out in the woods for the first time, and it was wonderful, it was something to tell stories about when we got back among our peers.

If a night in the woods could make a young man a woodsman, then that was what we were.

I brought some water from a spring that fed down a trough into a wooden cask by the side of the road. It was cold and enlivening. We made coffee and ate something—probably more sandwiches, for I, at least, didn't then know how to cook bacon. Then I walked a hundred feet westward through the trees and came on a rocky ledge, and an ocean of low clouds that rolled brightly in the rising sun for miles and miles, in every direction that wasn't cut off by the bulk of the mountain.

That was one of the sights on Mansfield, and in this world, that stayed with me. I can today shut my eyes and see it.

The other spectacle of that trip that I have remembered is the valley of the Winooski and the glitter of Lake Champlain, as we saw them when we reached the rocky saddle at the top of the road, beyond and above the hotel, toward the middle of the day. In the noon clearness and stillness we could see Camel's Hump, and the Burlington breakwater, and in the far distance the Adirondacks.

I thought, as I gazed at these new miracles, that I couldn't bear to leave Vermont if I could always be where I could see over it and beyond it in this fantastic fashion. Yet in all my eighteen years I had never had this opportunity. We lived shut in, even as boys and young men, down in the valleys, seldom coming up high into the hills; in one sense we knew our homeland, our beautiful Vermont, less well than had Ethan Allen and the other pioneers.

But the sight of the blue Adirondacks did not fully satisfy me. If the ridge of Mansfield made me love my native state, with pride and passion, the distance, cloud beyond cloud, plains beyond plains, mountains beyond mountains, all the way to the Pacific, also summoned me.

3

In the amiable foolishness of our time of life and deficit of experience we decided to camp a few feet west of the hotel, in a sort of swamp where melting snow enabled moss and stunted cedars to grow in a thin layer of soil above the eternal rocks.

We felt safer, though none of us said so, near the hotel. We also discovered, first, that the hotel people would rather we didn't build a fire right there—if they wanted to burn the hotel down they could do it themselves; second, that this seemed to be Old Home Week for half the mosquitoes in Vermont and adjoining states.

Almost with one impulse, with hardly a word among us, we left that lordly place, which I was not to visit again for more than a quarter of a century. It was like meeting a woman one might have loved and going swiftly by with no backward glance; and coming back after a long time to find her the mother of nine children.

I am sorry now, and yet not sorry. The memory of the morning and afternoon was burned deep, and no amount of idle staring could have more surely perpetuated it.

We picked up our bicycles and packed our absurd possessions, then went into the hotel and drank as a stirrup cup a bottle of ginger beer each. There was magic in this mild liquid, or in the clear light that began to slant from the west, or in ourselves and our time of living, for we yelled and whooped all the way down the mountain, fleeing swiftly past our last night's camp and bursting out in a few minutes to where the main road collected our mountain tributary—and near where the ski lift began when I last saw Mansfield.

The ski lift, the great perilous trails, women as well as men on Mansfield in winter and in the full and triumphant flush of life—what would we have thought then of these glories?

We coasted through Stowe village and down the almost continuous descending grade into Waterbury, and now we saw in the late afternoon only our familiar hills and farms, closed in, protective, shutting out the larger world. This was the Vermont we were accustomed to. How could we deal with miracles?

It was still light when I wheeled my bicycle sheepishly into my grandmother's yard. My mother, my aunt, my sister and my grandmother, in turn, wanted to know what was the matter. Had something happened? Was anybody hurt?

No, I said, nothing, nobody. We just thought we'd come home.

The three older women smiled hardly visible smiles. I could see that they had not been too confident of our woodsmanship. I see now that we were then between two worlds: the days and real memories of the pioneers, when a boy of eighteen would have thought nothing of lying out all night alone to kill a deer in the morning, were gone entirely; and today's revival of outdoor learning had not arrived.

Other persons smiled, too, when we told our stories and made our explanations, but the brief glory of that mountain expedition stayed with me—inside me, for any mention of our truncated adventure brought jeering queries as to what it was that had scared us out of the second night.

I had still a year to stay in Waterbury, but now I was more restless than ever before. I had to see the Rockies and the Great Plains and the Sierras, the shore of the Pacific and the Alps and a slice of the Andes before I stopped being restless.

And then I didn't stop being restless.

There was a world visible from the ridge of Mansfield into which one would yearn all his life to travel, but could not travel, not ever in this too-real world.

CHAPTER FIVE

―――――――・◆・・◆――――――――

But Don't Let the Bell Turn Over

1

BEFORE I sold myself down the river to work in Harry Whitehill's ink-and-paper plantation I did a few other things to earn an honorable penny or two. One of these jobs was janitor of the Congregational Church. I already knew how to sweep and dust and I soon learned how to operate the furnace which to some degree kept the congregation warm in winter.

I have stood in front of that furnace many a time, pulling the chain that opened the draft to make the heat come on stronger or that throttled the heat down if the congregation seemed to be reasonably well browned on both sides. I knew a boy who pumped the organ in the Methodist Church, but I never had any such luck; nobody asked me to pump an organ, not ever.

The best I could do with the furnace in the basement of the Congregational Church was to pretend I was running a locomotive on the Central Vermont Railroad (this delusion, that it was fun to be a locomotive engineer, lasted me well into my middle teens) and that some girl of about my own age was admiring my skill and courage—possibly peering at me from the front end of the baggage car, which was about as close as she could have come. Boys of that age nowadays would borrow the family car, and also the girl, and flights of fancy would not be necessary. My way was safer but not so much fun.

By the time I was well into my junior year in high school, of course, I sneered at such nonsense. The locomotives, I mean, not the girl. I was still glad that girls existed.

But I couldn't sneer, and still can't, at one of the other functions of the janitor of the Congregational Church, which was to sound the bell for services. A church bell could be heard all over town. I remember the pride with which I once left the high school, duly excused, in the middle of the afternoon session, and went down to ring the bell of the Congregational Church for some kind of special service.

What kind of special service? Who cares now? If it was a funeral the sorrow is all gone out of it now. If it was a wedding the grandchildren are growing up.

The thing that entranced me and gave me delusions of importance was that about fifteen minutes after I moved modestly out of the classroom of the High School there would be a tumult of bells audible from the direction of the village —and that would be me, myself, speaking. Even though I wasn't too impressive when I had to recite in front of my fellow students I could ring bells as well as any young man of my age in that section of Vermont.

There are two main divisions of bell-ringing, aside from the Swiss variety. Tolling was easy, and doubtless still is. You pulled a little rope and the hammer hit the side of the bell. Tolling was for when the service was about to begin, or when somebody was dead. And a dead man could do it, with hardly any practice.

Ringing was different. Ringing demanded skill and experience. I learned about ringing church bells from a venerable predecessor who seemingly ran the risk of getting his beard caught in the rope and being hauled up to high heaven before he was quite ready.

"Anybody could toll a bell," said Mr. Calderwood. "A baby could toll a bell if it could get hold of the cord. Ringing is something different. You do that wrong, just once, and the whole town knows about it." Mr. Calderwood fixed me with his Ancient Mariner's eye. "You get the feel of it," he continued; "if you don't get the feel of it you better get a job chopping wood. What you got to do is to stand that bell almost upside down, but not quite. The risk is, if you stand it up too straight it turns over. Then what do you get?"

"I guess it doesn't sound well," I said.

"It sure don't," replied Mr. Calderwood. "I see you're getting the idea. It don't sound good. You got to let go just before that happens. You got to get the feel of it."

"How do you do that?" I inquired solicitously.

"Practice," replied Mr. Calderwood. "If I had my way nobody would be allowed to ring a church bell in this town unless he had practiced in some other town. And the same with the other towns."

"Then somebody would always be ringing church bells wrong somewhere," I suggested. "Even here."

Mr. Calderwood scratched his head. "I suppose so," he admitted. "Maybe a man who wants to ring a church bell should ring a cow bell first. He might learn something, because a cow is a real intelligent animal, and not the way some people claim."

Mr. Calderwood considered the matter for a while. "You listen to the way church bells are rung around this town," he pursued, "and you'll get the idea. The Methodists are no good at all—too tinny, and they don't give a damn how it sounds to anybody but Methodists. Catholics are too slow and solemn—you never get a laugh out of a Roman Catholic

Church bell. The best you can say about them is they hardly ever turn a bell over. It's the Methodists that do that, mainly. You get a Methodist bell-ringer feeling religious on a Sunday morning, and he sounds like a green fireman ringing the bell when a freight engine is backing off a siding."

I laughed politely. "Maybe fireman is the right word—."

Mr. Calderwood didn't laugh. He seemed to think there was something irreverent in my comment.

I changed my course. "When you hear them all together on a Sunday morning," I said, "they sound pretty good. Seems to me—"

Mr. Calderwood snorted. "It seems to you, does it?" he inquired. "My opinion is that the way things seem to you when you're as young as you are can't matter much." He relented at the expression on my face. He put a large hand on my left shoulder. "I'll tell you, Rob," he said. "Don't keep 'em too warm or they'll complain you're wasting the coal. And don't let the heat go too far down or they'll all have colds and blame it on the minister. And don't let the bell turn over when you ring it."

I said I wouldn't, and I almost never did, during the brief interval when I was ringing the bells of the Congregational Church, and of course before Harry Whitehill took me in thrall and started, almost without realizing it, as I believe, to make me a newspaper man.

I had some good times being janitor of the Congregational Church. Once Joe Smith and I took turns going up into the pulpit in the empty auditorium and delivering sermons that would have shocked that good and patient man, the Rev. Kellogg.

At about this time Mr. Kellogg organized a boys' club, which met regularly at the members' houses. It was his duty, and he did.

2

Mr. Kellogg seemed to have an urge to organize things. I think now that he felt he had to justify himself against the Methodist preacher, who put a good deal of revivalism into his sermons and prayer meetings, and the Catholic priest, who had a good deal more authority over his flock than Mr. Kellogg could hope for.

Unlike Mr. Blake in Williamstown, Mr. Kellogg didn't get involved in doctrinal disputes. He didn't have to. There were very few Congregationalists in Waterbury who gave a hoot in hell (as we used to say) for doctrine as doctrine. They liked their church but they used it first as a social outlet and only after that, usually when they were sick or scared, for religious solace.

There was nobody in Waterbury who passed judgment on Congregational ministers with the final authority that George Ainsworth possessed in Williamstown. What we required of a minister was that he should be interesting. I think Mr. Kellogg realized this demand and worried about it, because he wasn't sure just how interesting he was.

When we met at Mr. Kellogg's house, or at the house of one of the members of the boys' club, we played games, had candy-pulls, sang songs, indulged in what may have been uplifting conversation, and once, as I remember, experimented with an old-fashioned recording phonograph. Mr. Kellogg spoke the Lord's Prayer onto the cylinder (because it was a cylinder in those days) and the machine prayed it back at us.

One of the boys said afterwards that this was irreligious. "A machine can't pray," he protested. "He shouldn't have done it. He should have read a poem or something."

I think we wanted Mr. Kellogg to be a little sterner and more austere than he was. He on his part, I am sure, was

convinced that in order to get on with boys and be a good
influence a minister had in some degree to turn himself into
a boy.

Another thing Mr. Kellogg did was to improve the equipment for holding sociables in the church basement, and it
seems to me we had more oyster suppers, sugaring-off parties,
chicken-pie dinners, and ice-cream festivals after he came to
Waterbury than we had ever had before. The church hadn't
been a club-house in the old days, but the venerable persons
who grumbled about this were too tired to make much of a
fuss about it.

When Mr. Kellogg preached he came out strongly for good
behavior, mother love, conscientious citizenship, and the kind
of public reform a Vermont Republican could support without being partisan enough to scare off the Democrats. Most
of the Democrats, of course, belonged to the Catholic Church
and a few to the Methodist Church, but if they wanted to
join the Congregationalists we tried to keep the door open.

Mr. Kellogg liked to quote Tennyson, and did it very well.
What I know about flowers in the crannied walls I learned
from him. On rare Sunday mornings he would give us a bit
of Browning, perhaps the less pessimistic portions of "Pippa
Passes."

I wondered sometimes if I would have been a better boy
if I had been a Methodist or a Catholic, but I didn't experi-
ment to find out—one didn't if one's ancestors had been
Congregationalist. I looked at Father Ryan with some awe,
though he was a pleasant, hearty human being—and nowhere near so worried about anything as Mr. Kellogg was.
Mr. Whitehill would trade jokes with him now and then,
and if Father Ryan came into the office to say that his parish
had raised enough money for some new pews and electric
lights throughout the church Mr. Whitehill would act as
pleased as he would have been if the Methodists had got the

new furnace they had so long needed.

For myself, I steered clear of the emotional side of religion. I wanted to think my own thoughts and endure my own hopes and fears. And into that strange adolescent world, so romantic and so troubled, Mr. Kellogg did not dip. For one thing, he was too busy organizing his successful church and its activities.

Once, when an evangelist came to town and we had some revival union meetings with the Methodists, I was afraid I would "get" religion, as though it were chicken pox; but I didn't, though I was ashamed to stay seated when the visiting exhorter called on all those who wanted to be saved to stand up.

Revival meetings were tough on Mr. Kellogg, and indeed on nearly everybody in our church, because we couldn't deny that we wanted to be saved, at the proper time and in the proper way, and, on the other hand, we didn't wish to make a display of ourselves in public.

I can't imagine Mr. Kellogg shedding his vest, necktie and collar in the pulpit on a warm summer evening and dancing around, and, as we put it, hollering. You didn't holler about flowers in crannied walls, or Pippa passing.

We did have in Waterbury a lot of variety. I remember one middle-aged man who had once had quite a prominent part in a religious movement, but had retired to Waterbury rather early in life. But all I recall about him is that he played the piano in public very well and that he wore on such occasions a dress coat with a long tail that hung clear to the floor when he sat down, creating the impression, if you looked at him squarely from behind, that he didn't have any legs.

There weren't many dress coats in Waterbury at that time. This one had two buttons at the back, which bobbed up and down with the music and helped keep one aware of the rhythm.

3

A Congregational Church in 1906, so it was argued in the circles in which I moved, could do anything its members wanted to that was not against the law. I once asked my grandmother if our church could worship the Devil if it wanted to. She said I was a sophist (I looked the word up later and didn't forget it) but the truth was, she admitted, that a Congregational Church in Vermont was about the most independent institution in the world, except for certain isolated savage tribes she had read about.

She added that our particular Church, or any similar church in Vermont, would hardly be likely to worship the Devil. She said it would make talk. But she added that this very independence made Mr. Kellogg's job a hard one. He— or he and his deacons, and they always listened to him because they regarded him as an expert—had to decide many things the Methodist minister and the Catholic priest both took on authority.

She speculated, wisely, as I now perceive, that sometimes this state of affairs worried Mr. Kellogg. She believed Mr. Kellogg tore around organizing things, both inside the church and in the village at large, because he wasn't quite sure where he stood.

"Do you suppose," I asked my grandmother, "Mr. Kellogg ever wishes he was the Methodist minister or the Catholic priest?"

My grandmother smiled. "I wouldn't be surprised if he did," she answered, "sometimes when he's entirely alone and nobody is even looking at the expression on his face."

"Aren't all religions right—in some way?" I asked. I'd been reading something about Buddhism and kind of liked it.

"Yes," said my grandmother. "I think they are, to some extent. But Mr. Kellogg couldn't admit that, and Father Ryan couldn't, and this new Methodist minister—they change so fast I've forgotten his name—couldn't. They've all got to go on being what they are—bless their hearts."

When Mr. Kellogg had got the church pretty well organized he helped with some other things that were going on. We had a sort of community club for a while, up over a store on the right side of the Main Street hill as you went down to the depot. Meetings could be held there and all groups and denominations could come, because this was neutral ground. I remembered when it was opened, though about all that lingers in my mind is that along with our lemonade we had the first sugar wafers I ever ate; I must have been hungry or something.

Mr. Whitehill also thought Waterbury should have a quick-lunch restaurant, with meals at all hours, in addition to the big hotel, the little hotel, and the miscellaneous boarding-houses. Mr. Whitehill said the idea of having to wait for fixed hours before being able to get anything to eat was old-fashioned. He said that, mark his words, people would be driving automobiles through Waterbury almost every day before long and wanting to get a little food in a hurry while they waited for the engine to cool off. And for a while, along about 1906, there was such a restaurant; then it died and some years had to go by before another appeared.

Mr. Kellogg helped in these movements. He was a good citizen and a good influence, even though some of the very elderly said they couldn't quite see the connection between the future life or the Sermon on the Mount and being able to get a steak at half-past three in the afternoon.

People of good intentions and serious purposes who were passing through Vermont often stopped to call on the Kel-loggs. Once he preached an entire sermon about a man who dropped off the train one day to talk with him about some good cause, and asked so many questions about Waterbury that Mr. Kellogg didn't know all the answers. Mr. Kellogg said we ought to know more about the place in which we lived. He looked thoughtful as he tried to hook this statement on to his text, but he managed it by saying that we ought to be truly grateful to the Deity for creating such a beautiful world, of which Waterbury was a small but not unbeautiful part, and then sailed into announcing the concluding hymn without ever stopping for breath.

Another of Mr. Kellogg's visitors was a Japanese, the first I ever saw. This alien from far away was standing with his host on the Kellogg lawn as I came by with the *Burlington Free Press,* and Mr. Kellogg introduced me. I believe I even wrote down the name and made an item of it, which pleased —and surprised—Mr. Whitehill.

I would have liked to talk longer with this Japanese. I think he was a convert and made a speech that evening at a prayer meeting, in which he told how quaint his country was and expressed the hope that it could be converted to Christianity before long.

In California two or three years later I found it was unwise to like the Japanese immigrants, who were thought to be threatening American ways and the American standard of living; and many years later it was, of course, unpatriotic for a while to say or even think anything good about the Japanese. But in spite of myself the tintype remained of this smiling young traveler standing in the sun on Mr. Kellogg's lawn. Maybe this is a final tribute I should pay to Mr. Kellogg, who did the best he could to bring civilization in Waterbury down to date. Mr. Kellogg was no mystic, no Saint Francis, no John Wesley, but he was about as full of good will as any man I ever knew, and his trouble may have been that he wasn't sure how to organize this good will.

Toward the end of my time in Waterbury Mr. Kellogg worked and worried so hard that he lost ten pounds in the course of a very few weeks and went hastily off to Colorado to rest and regain his health.

My Aunt Alice said she liked Mr. Kellogg, but what puzzled her was that a minister, who knew he was going to heaven when he died, should be so particular about his health. "It's different with the rest of us," said my aunt. "We can't be sure. But Mr. Kellogg, with such faults as he has, if any, has got a first-class Pullman ticket straight through, and to the right destination."

My mother protested that being a minister didn't make a man less human. She said Mr. Kellogg had indeed worked too hard and she was glad if the church was going to keep him on and make it possible for him to get well.

My grandmother said Mr. Kellogg would get well, all right. Mr. Kellogg didn't have consumption, that she knew. She and my aunt looked at each other when she said this, for each had lost a beloved husband by that disease.

And Mr. Kellogg did get well, in fairly short order. His pulpit was filled during his absence by a succession of preachers. One of these, one of the saintliest men I ever knew and also one of the dullest speakers, delivered a sermon in Waterbury once a year for the American Bible Society. He spent the whole of his time during most of his adult life preaching that sermon in various communities, but it never got any better, it never had any funny stories, it never produced a tear, it never took anybody's mind off thoughts of the approaching Sunday dinner and the Sunday afternoon nap.

However, Mr. Kellogg got well before I left Waterbury, and came back home, brown with the western sun, his moustache a little longer and more western in style, and some allusions to the Rocky Mountains and the simple virtues of western life that were quite stimulating after poor Mr. Eliot's Bible Society sermon. He preached to us about his travels in a way that enabled him to avoid the excessively emotional side of religion, and conveyed the impression that Heaven was a little like Colorado, only you didn't go there on the Burlington Railroad. There wasn't any one in town who wasn't glad to see him again.

He seemed a little more composed, too, and I don't recall that he organized anything after his return and before my own departure.

"I guess he's learned what Mr. Calderwood told me," I suggested one evening at supper.

The family asked what Mr. Calderwood had told me, and I explained.

"That's right," agreed my Aunt Alice; "he let the bell turn over that time. He'll have more sense next time."

"I sometimes wish," my grandmother began.

"Wish what?" asked my Aunt Alice.

"Never mind," said my grandmother. "Except that people shouldn't try to be what they aren't and can't possibly be."

"We expect too much of him," sighed my mother. "That's enough to wear anybody out."

CHAPTER SIX

The Pure in Heart

1

*W*HEN I think of Lewis Stillman, who clerked in Charlie Haines' grocery store, and who took orders in the morning by house-to-house calls, just the way Wallace Green did for the butcher shop, I would like to think of Lewis in his jovial and happy days. If I were able to do this, however, if he had been able to remain jovial and happy, this chapter would have been no more than a paragraph.

No housewife could help ordering just a little more from Lewis Stillman than she had intended, he was so gay and entertaining. I've seen Lewis stand in my grandmother's kitchen and flip a quarter up his sleeve, or somewhere, faster than you could see it go; once he picked a quarter out of one of my ears, and made me wish I had ducked and run, quarter and all, before he made the motion.

Wallace Green, who took the meat orders, was a friendly young man, too. He later married Belle Cooley, the milliner. Belle Cooley made hats for half the ladies in town during the feverish few weeks before Easter. But tragedy never touched Wallace Green. He and Belle came as near living happily ever after as any two persons could manage.

Most people would have said that Lewis had as good prospects as Wallace; and except for one thing he did have. The one thing was that he could not live up to his own ideal of purity.

So when I think of Lewis Stillman the first picture that comes into my mind isn't Lewis at all. Let me explain. Charlie Haines' store was on Stowe Street, on what I would call the south side of the block between Main Street and the bridge over the railroad tracks; it was just a step away from the Whitehill store and office, the home of the *Waterbury Record* and *Stowe Journal*.

Charlie Haines kept a horse, for delivery purposes, in a stable near the corner of Main and Randall Streets. You went out of the Haines store, turned left at the corner of Main Street, turned right at the foot of the hill, then turned right again to go into the house or stable.

Lewis didn't need a horse to carry him around when he took orders in the morning, the distances were so short, and at that time in Vermont men, and even women, had legs, two each, except in case of accident. Lewis looked after the horse and used the animal when he made his deliveries in the afternoon. The horse knew Lewis and must have felt friendly toward him. Who—or what—didn't feel friendly toward Lewis Stillman? I ask that question and then wonder about the answer. For someone did take the trouble to do Lewis an injury.

So what I like to remember is Lewis Stillman's flipping a quarter into my ear in my grandmother's kitchen, or seeming to do so. You don't pick your memories, but that is the one I would pick, so far as Lewis is concerned.

I would like also to think of the end of the story as the notice the *Waterbury Record* and *Stowe Journal* printed when Lewis Stillman and Linda Alberson were married. But that wasn't the end of the story.

I can remember the former Linda Alberson well enough, but only after her marriage. I can remember her, her suddenly lined lovely face concealed, yet not concealed, behind a heavy dark veil, fumbling her way into the *Record* office on a certain morning, and going back to Mr. Whitehill's den, her hands clasped beseechingly as she approached him. Even Justin Moody, who liked so much to gaze on feminine loveliness, kept his eyes down as she passed him, and did not speak.

And I can remember Harry Whitehill, moved beyond his customary poise, the not-too-easy tears forming in his pale blue eyes, coming to meet her, almost with tenderness.

But Lewis Stillman, Lewis the Debonnaire, Lewis the flipper of coins, the gay, the innocent Lewis, Lewis the man happily in love, wasn't there. He wasn't anywhere, any more.

What comes to memory when I think now of Lewis Stillman? A bleak late winter afternoon (and in beautiful, idyllic Vermont they can sometimes be bleak enough to thrust your heart down into your boots with foreboding), and Charlie Haines, bareheaded, without any coat, running wildly down the middle of Main Street toward Randall Street, and turning right at the bottom of the hill.

Charlie Haines paid no attention to me or to any one else. He was, as the whole town soon knew, occupied with a terrible event, a sudden, unexpected glimpse of hell.

2

Lewis Stillman had lived with his widowed mother before he married Linda, in a house on Main Street, not far from Stowe Street. He was a faithful son. People said, afterwards, that he never left home, not even after dinner in the middle of the day, without kissing his mother good bye.

Nobody said his mother was jealous of Linda. That was not the story. Nobody, then or afterwards, said a word critical of Linda, except maybe that if she could have forgiven Lewis for the offense he confessed to her, he might have been able to live. As to that, I could not judge her then and do not judge her now. Who could judge that strange and tragic loveliness, that passion for purity? She troubled me afterwards, in the nights, when I thought of so many things and persons, and the infinite woe of human life hung over me like a nightmare.

Mr. Whitehill never told me, in so many words, or in words intended for my hearing at all, what he learned in his conversation that day with Linda Alberson Stillman, the widow of the late Lewis Stillman. Nobody told me. Yet little by little the story became clear.

The trouble was that Lewis Stillman was an idealist, who believed with all his heart in virtue as he saw it, who longed to present himself, a shining and spotless knight, before the impossibly beautiful and virtuous lady who was destined to be his one and lasting love. When he found her he wanted to be pure in heart before her, and to deserve her—and let no one say that this could not happen in a prosaic small town in Vermont half a century ago.

But Lewis also wanted to come to Linda with evidence, already certain to himself, of his manhood. And this required the cooperation of the lady I have called Lilith in this book, Lilith, the giver of joy and death.

That was the trouble with Lewis, and with Linda, and also with the world.

I myself was pure, at the age I had reached. I could afford it, and I was. However, I do recall a young man, a little older than myself, who liked to discuss the question of continence. I believe he felt better if he discussed it, even though he didn't practice it. This young man said it was unhealthy for a young man to abstain from sexual relations. I replied firmly that it wasn't right, according to all I had heard, for unmarried young men and unmarried young girls to run around together, or stay put together, in a sexual way.

My friend, I regret to state (for he had many good qualities), laughed at me. It seems to me now, as it did then, that people were always laughing at me when I took high moral ground. He wanted to know where I had been all these years, and had I been weaned, and did I think it was wicked to steal green apples.

But Lewis Stillman, whatever he thought about green apples, had been confused about women. That was why he was dead.

3

There is no use any more in making a mystery about what happened. Lewis Stillman had spent at least one night in a Barre hotel, testing his manhood with the lady I call Lilith. The names were there on the register, for it never occurred to Lewis to invent a lie. The register read: "Mr. and Mrs. Lewis Stillman." Maybe these names, in Lewis' handwriting, turned Lilith into Mrs. Lewis Stillman. Naturally, this item would not have pleased Linda Alberson, when called to her attention.

But Lilith, as I understood her, was not disposed to make too much of technicalities. It was somebody else who did that, a nameless and shameless Somebody Else, who waited until Linda and Lewis had had their wedding trip—I think to Boston, where they inspected the Bunker Hill Monument —and then drew back her bow (it was a woman, I am sure) and sent the arrow home. The name of this criminal is not known. The best I can think of to say for her is that she, too, may have loved Lewis Stillman; if this is so, or even if it isn't, it is now too late to swear out a Mary Doe warrant against her, charging murder.

Lewis and Linda came back from their wedding journey, as all newly married persons must finally do. They loved each other, that I am sure of, and could have had children of

a creditable sort. But the truth or rumor disseminated by
Mary Doe, address unknown, made it certain those children
would not be born.

Now, when Lewis went to work, he not only kissed his
mother good bye, he kissed Linda good bye. The day came
when he kissed both of them a final good bye. What had they
had for dinner? What had they talked about, the three of
them? Did Linda already know something about Lilith?
Maybe she did. Maybe he had told her, so that when somebody else told her she would not be altogether startled.

And perhaps Linda, who was also pure in heart and deeply
in love, had refused to forgive her young husband at one
o'clock in the afternoon; maybe, at the same time, she had
decided to teach him a lesson in fidelity and then, at supper-
time, forgive him. Maybe.

At any rate, Lewis left the house in a mood of strange
hilarity, as though now there was nothing left to decide, nothing to puzzle over or worry about. He passed the time of
day gaily with one or two friends, who ever afterwards remembered the way he looked; then he went into the drugstore that was kitty-corner from his house near the intersection of Main and Stowe Streets.

Wilfred Grimes, the druggist, told how Lewis had come
into the store, how he thought him even more cheerful than
usual and had joked with him in earthy country terms about
his marriage. He recalled that Lewis smiled.

"You learn a lot you didn't know before," Lewis said, and
paused.

Wilfred waited for Lewis to speak. Lewis didn't. He didn't
seem sad, Wilfred observed afterwards; it was more as if he
were thinking of something else. Kind of absent-minded,
Wilfred said.

"We've got a new nerve tonic," Wilfred remarked after a
while. "A little alcohol in it to preserve it, maybe, but per-

fectly legal."

Lewis shook his head. "My nerves are all right," he answered, looking up thoughtfully. "Perfectly all right. I've got to go down and hitch up, anyhow." He turned as though about to leave. Then a thought seemed to strike him. "I almost forgot," he said. "Have to have everything the way it ought to be now—for Linda." Wilfred said Lewis almost choked on his wife's name, he seemed to love her so much he could hardly say it, but some people thought Wilfred may have remembered more than actually occurred. "It's an old house. I need some poison—strychnine I guess is what most people use—to kill a rat."

He looked Wilfred squarely in the eyes.

"You have to be careful with that sort of stuff," Wilfred warned him as he wrapped it up.

"Don't you worry," replied Lewis, who didn't seem nervous at all now, as Wilfred later testified at the inquest and to all who came into his store and would listen. "I can't afford to be careless any more now. My day for being careless is over now."

Wilfred nodded. "I guess that's so," he agreed. "When you're married you can't take the risks you used to."

Wilfred watched Lewis walk down past the soda fountain and out the front door. "I didn't dream that would be the last I'd ever see of him," he told everybody later. "Alive," he would add.

What Lewis did for purity and honor and love, as he conceived them, was to go down to the stable where the Haines horse was kept. There was a loft, above the level of the stable, where the hay was kept handy to be thrown down when the horse's day's work was over.

Lewis climbed up into the loft, without hitching the horse, and took the strychnine. Later I heard over and over again what happens to a man who takes strychnine, before he dies.

Why Lewis did not choose an easier death I don't know.

Or maybe I do know. Maybe he thought the method would speak for him and somehow extenuate and expiate what he took to be his sin: those moments when he lost himself in carnal ecstasy with the woman I have called Lilith, in the dingy, musty room in the Barre hotel where no questions were ever asked.

If extenuation and expiation were desired by some unmerciful, unfatherly God, He must have been satisfied. People said later that Charlie Haines' horse, after that day, seemed frightened of the stable, and kicked and plunged every time the young man who replaced Lewis Stillman in Mr. Haines' employ tried to tie the animal up for the night. The young man may have been nervous, too. Vermonters, then as now, sometimes deceived people by their calm exteriors.

The Waterbury Record and *Stowe Journal,* in pity for the young widow, suppressed most of the story. Mr. Whitehill wrote briefly that Lewis had died suddenly and unexpectedly, praised the dead man's character, mentioned the funeral and who was there and what the minister said, and gave the place of burial.

I would like to know what happened thereafter to Linda Stillman, in her vast lonesomeness, in the heart-breaking purity that had been thrust upon her. I would like to know if in the end she came to forgive Lilith—or herself.

All I know further about this matter is that Wallace Green's employer, Al Thompson, the butcher, went over to the drugstore on the day after Lewis's funeral. Al walked Wilfred Grimes down to the end of the room, where no customer could hear.

"Wilfred," he said, "don't you ever sell any strychnine to Wallace. I need him."

Sometimes when you can't shudder any more, and the weeping is finished, and there is no more screaming, you have to laugh.

CHAPTER SEVEN

———◄•••►———

The Wayfarers

1

MUCH OF what I knew about tramps in the early years of the twentieth century, when I was working for Harry Whitehill, I learned from the comic magazines of the day, such as *Life, Judge,* and *Puck*. The tramp, who seems to have appeared in American life during the depression of the early 'nineties, had become a figure of fun. He was in vaudeville in the cities, he did turns as a clown in circuses, then as now; finally, Charlie Chaplin, but that was later, immortalized a certain species of tramp.

But the tramps didn't show up in Vermont very often. Nobody who hated work, the way a tramp was supposed to do, would make a point of coming to Vermont. He might find work, and the tramp of the comic legend didn't want to find work. I don't say that there ever were many such tramps; the device some people in the early 1900's resorted to in dealing with unemployment was to pretend that men who were out of work didn't want to work.

So I don't know whether or not the two men, father and son, who ambled into Waterbury in the spring of 1906, were real tramps. They wandered down from Barre (perhaps they had passed through my old home town of Williamstown), got permission to sleep in somebody's barn on condition they didn't smoke, maybe paid ten cents each for the privilege; and then drifted around inquiring aimlessly for odd jobs. Maybe they chopped a little wood, though the best time for that was in the fall. Maybe they cleaned out a privy or two, though that was considered Asa Baker's monopoly. Maybe they handled packing-cases at the wrapper factory.

But they didn't work hard or continuously, and then they were not welcome. The town could have managed with another good carpenter, or even a plumber—though bathroom plumbing was at that time just dawning on us and was not considered a necessity, except for the rich to show off with. Sometimes there was extra work on the farms at haying or cornshucking times, but these didn't occur in the first flush of spring.

Quite a few upright and righteous persons around town said that this father and son ought not to be allowed to stay. They might commit a crime, it was argued. They might get drunk or annoy women or burn George Brattle's barn down or rob a freight car on the siding. They didn't do these things, as it turned out; the point was, they might have.

Mr. Whitehill and Mr. Moody talked it over in the store, and sometimes other persons came in and helped them talk. Mr. Whitehill said there never had been a day in the history of the United States when anybody who wanted a job hadn't been able to get one. Mr. Moody said times had really been hard in the 'seventies, and he had often wondered, but of course, he added, all that was changed now.

Mr. Whitehill said he had come to Waterbury when times weren't any too good, and without any money to speak of, and had made a go out of his newspaper business and some other things by hard work.

Mr. Moody could have said that Mr. Whitehill had married Mr. Moody's daughter and borrowed both money and credit from his father-in-law, but Mr. Moody didn't say this—not when I was within hearing.

I could see that Mr. Moody agreed with Mr. Whitehill about these and some other matters, except when they disagreed; but it was also true that Mr. Moody didn't care much for hard work; he could endorse work for other people but he didn't make a hobby of it for himself. What Mr. Moody liked to do, in the way of work, or in place of work, was to sit around the store, handing out philosophy or advice to anybody he judged needed any, waiting on a customer but not too often, and building up good will.

I was then still somewhat hypnotized by the philosophy of work, and I now believe—and even suspected at the time —that Mr. Moody was quietly amused by me. Mr. Whitehill and Mr. Moody were investors in the new wrapper factory down on the other side of the tracks, below where Little River came in, and Mr. Whitehill had at times permitted me to copy off the orders sent in by the salesmen to be filled. I was a little awed by the responsibility, and once I said to Mr. Moody that I guessed there would be trouble if I copied the orders wrong.

Mr. Moody said he guessed there would. Then he picked his teeth for a half minute or so and ran a disengaged hand through his side whiskers.

"But you won't get them wrong, Rob," he observed. "You're the kind of boy that works so hard you'll always have to work for a living." He motioned toward his son-in-law, who was out of earshot at the other end of the room. "You'll never be like Harry there," he went on. "You haven't the sort of brains that gets other people to do the work." I waited for him to continue, which, with a slight expression of alarm, as though he had already spoken too fast and too much, he did. "But if you weren't such a good worker, and didn't come from a good family," he concluded, "of course there wouldn't be a place for you here. This is how you have to begin. You may—" at this point he waved a grandly noncommittal hand

—"er—after you leave Waterbury—college, perhaps—grow up."

I then and there determined to grow up. It was only some decades later, and after trying hard, that I abandoned the enterprise. I wish I could explain this to Justin Moody.

2

What our wayfarers, the father perhaps fifty years old, the son of possibly half that age, liked about Waterbury we never knew. We never asked them. The scenery, as we natives believed, was good, but it was not spectacular; you saw the Hogback Mountains in the morning if it was clear, but not Camel's Hump or Mansfield; there were elms along the streets, and maples, too, but other villages were similarly supplied; the train service was fairly regular and reliable but they had not arrived by passenger train and would not, as we correctly assumed, depart that way.

I can't remember what they looked like. They did not, in fact, do anything to call attention to their personal appearance. They looked ragged, but so did many of ourselves when in working clothes; the blue jean was not yet in common wear. They looked dirty, but so did many a man who had been working on the highway or the railroad or in a blacksmith shop or on a farm. The father shambled when he walked, but so did some of the natives who were of the same age. The son had a way of looking sidewise at pretty young women, but he wasn't the first youth in Waterbury to do that. If anybody was annoyed by it the reason was only that he was a stranger and poor.

Mr. Whitehill, after listening to some of his customers and subscribers, and in view of the fact that this was a quiet period, agreed that something ought to be done and said he would take it up with the Sheriff, C. C. Graves. C. C., as it happened, was in Burlington for a few days, and Mr. Whitehill had to wait. When C. C. returned Mr. Whitehill thought it better to wait some more until C. C. dropped into the *Record* office, rather than going to consult C. C. or telephoning him.

As a matter of fact, there were only about a dozen telephones in town at that time, and a man felt the same hesitation in telephoning from the *Record* office to the depot, or Brown's Livery Stable, or the sheriff's office, that he might feel now in lifting his instrument off the hook and calling San Francisco from Waterbury.

When Mr. Whitehill did get in touch with C. C. the day was Friday. It seems that C. C., though in accord with Mr. Whitehill's opinion that we did not care to have tramps in town, had a respect for the letter of the law. He said you could not arrest a man if the man had done nothing that was against the law and was willing to work. Mr. Whitehill asked, how about men without visible means of support? C. C. replied that no man could make visible means of support out of cobwebs and moonlight; C. C., indeed, had at times a surprisingly poetic touch in his language.

However, C. C. added, he would speak to the wayfarers and warn them that if they did anything illegal they would be arrested, and that perhaps they should soon be on their way. There was Jonesville, for example, eighteen miles northwest of Waterbury. Why not try Jonesville?

C. C. called on the strangers down by the Little River bridge, below our house, on Saturday morning, and spoke to them, just as he had promised to do. By that time some timid ladies who lived on the north side of the bridge were going around by Maple Street to get to the Stowe Street stores, and making their children do likewise. In this way they ran no risk of harm from the two men, who were sunning themselves on the abutments and looking lazily at the water.

C. C. told them they should be careful and not scare

women and children. As he explained afterwards, they were good-natured and maybe surprised, and promised not to scare anybody at all, not even the sheriff. What were they doing on the bridge? Well, they just wanted to sit. C. C. couldn't suggest that they ought to hook on to the north-bound freight that went through in the early evening, for it was against the law to steal rides on freight trains.

C. C. whittled a stick he had picked up on the way down the street, and the older man said he was a good whittler —C. C., that is—and asked him if he had ever carved a ship to go in a bottle. C. C. replied, no, he hadn't, he wished he could do such things, and he judged it would be a good thing if the two were out of town by Monday, though he didn't know what law he would bring into play if they weren't. They thanked him, as he afterwards recalled, very politely.

C. C. went back up the hill to Stowe Street, and told Harry Whitehill about the interview. Harry told C. C. that he personally didn't wish to be hard on anybody, but that he thought we should be careful about the kind of people we allowed to stick around Waterbury. Harry said he would write an editorial about it for the next issue of the *Record*, which went to press on Tuesday. C. C. agreed that this might be all that was necessary. I think C. C., after some years as sheriff, usually with little to do, had decided that the less law had to be invoked the happier everybody was. He was for commonsense, which may have been where law started, anyhow. Though of course I wouldn't argue that it stayed there.

The two wayfarers came uptown Saturday night and bought some fishline and hooks. They said they might try for a perch or two. They were as polite as any two men on earth could be; everybody who saw them in the hardware store or walking quietly up Main Street and along Stowe

Street commented afterwards on how polite they had been.

They shouldn't have fished for perch or any other kind of fish on Sunday, of course. There could be no luck in such fishing, any more than in sugaring-off on a March Sunday, which was almost certain to be followed by the sugar house burning down—and at that, some oldtimers said the Lord was letting the sinner off easily.

The two men went down Main Street on Sunday morning, past the Little River bridge, and turned off to the left at a little body of water known as Butler's Pond. I judge this pond must have been at one time a loop of the Winooski River, and had been cut off by an act of God or by the railway embankment, which now ran just west of it. It was a deep pond, with shelving rocks on one side, and gravel and broken stone from the railway on the other side. I used to go there often before I started working for Harry Whitehill, but I never caught any fish there. I didn't try too hard. It was restful there.

You could sit on the slanting rock on the east side and look straight down, almost, into the water. Sometimes you could see clouds reflected there, and sometimes, if the light was right, you might see the quivering, luminous shapes of fish.

Some persons caught fish there, even though I didn't. The rocky bank was also a good place to sit and think about other things, the universe and subjects like that, and why girls behaved the way they did, and what one was going to do in life, assuming one had any say in the matter.

One could also listen to the trains going by, if one took the trouble to be there at the proper moment. They always whistled when they came past my grandmother's house, half a mile away, and were usually still whistling when they passed Butler's Pond; or going the other direction they would whistle at the Winooski bridge and stay with it as they came into the village. When a train roared and rattled past the pond, whistling like a drill-sergeant giving an order, or a bugle calling troops to mount and charge, and blowing out dark smoke that smelled like the perfumes of the meadows of heaven, it spoke so much of travel and far-off places that I got chills up and down my spine.

It was somber, there by the pond, too, and I don't know why. Butler's pond was not altogether a cheerful body of water. We didn't skate on it, for it was the sort of pond that would just love to open up and take a skater in.

But the wayfarers of whom I have been speaking could not have felt about Butler's Pond the way I sometimes did. The Sunday morning when they went there was clear and comfortably warm, with a gentle sort of breeze coming out of the East. As they sat there together on the sloping rocks of the east bank they must have heard the church bells ringing—the Congregational Church nearest at hand, and highest, the Methodist about a quarter of a mile further south, the Catholic another quarter of a mile south, or more. When all these bells happened to be ringing at the same time nobody within earshot could help feeling religious and wondering if he would go to heaven when he died, or somewhere else.

Some people said the father and son had been drinking before they went down to Butler's Pond to try for perch. This was a reasonable theory, for even the most upright Vermonters would often assume that the state prohibition law didn't apply to fishermen. And it was true that the wayfarers, in their subsequent haste to be gone, did leave an empty quart bottle on the shore of Butler's Pond. The two had brought along some sandwiches and an apple or two, and these were found, untouched, along with the empty bottle.

There was a sort of hurrying and a beating of wings over Butler's Pond that Sunday morning. Some matters that might have been attended to were forgotten.

We fished with worms in that part of Vermont. I never heard of anybody fishing with tied flies. The only exception was when you borrowed a rowboat and could move silently across the water. Then you had a float and a spinner, and when a fish pulled the float down you pulled the fish up and out. Maybe. This may not have been sportsmanlike, it may have been like shooting a fox, but it was handy. What we wanted when we fished was fish.

The two wayfarers, father and son, on this Sunday morning, couldn't use a float and spinner because they hadn't any boat. They seem to have sat on the shelving rocks and fished from there—which wasn't an especially smart thing to do if you expected to catch fish. It was smart enough, of course, if you merely wished to enjoy a warm spring morning without being asked by C. C. Graves or somebody else what were your visible means of support.

Tom Moran, section boss on the Central Vermont, happened to be walking track that Sunday morning, not because he had to but because he had some doubts about certain stretches of ties and rails. He could do this on Sunday, since he had already been to early mass. His son Johnny, a brilliant classmate of mine, later became a priest.

So Tom came along, not watching out for trains, because there were no trains to speak of on Sunday, and for Tom, never any unexpected trains. Tom must have felt relaxed and easy, too, as he came along the embankment on the west side of Butler's Pond. He was in a position to catch sight of the two men, the middle-aged man and the younger one, on the opposite bank, only two or three hundred feet away. His first thought was that they were wasting their time, and his second thought was that there was time enough that fine Sunday morning, and his third thought was, as he said afterwards, shaking his head mournfully whenever he told the story, that there wasn't any time at all left for those two.

As Tom looked he saw the older man, recognizable at that short distance because he was partly bald and the hair he did have was grayish, whip his pole out of the water, make a left-handed grab at the rock he was sitting on, and disappear without even time or breath to yell.

Tom waited a second to see if he'd come up, and he did, but he was screaming and splashing water and perhaps tangled up in the fishline. The son, a little higher up and a little to one side, watched all this, just as Tom did. "It was like they had been playing a game," said Tom later. "You couldn't believe anything could happen."

But the older man kept splashing and yelling, and Tom started to run the nearest way around the pond to help him if he could.

Tom was still scrambling around the end of the pond nearest the village when he saw both men in the water, and when he got there both had gone under. They were, it seemed to him, in a death grapple at the bottom. He tried to pry a rail off a rotten fence, but when he got it clear it was too late. Tom ran up to the road and yelled for help, but when two or three men from neighboring houses came running the wayfarers had finished their journey.

Tom and the others got them out at last, carried them up to the bank and tried to bring them round. Somebody sent for Dr. Janes, who ordered the spectators—half the village, it seemed at that time—to stand clear, but after a while gave it up. If anybody could have brought them back to life it would have been Dr. Janes, everybody knew that.

A small boy ran up Main Street with the news, and a little later I saw a flat-bottomed wagon, drawn by one tired-looking horse, go by my grandmother's house, with something covered by blankets in the back.

It's often what you can't see but have to imagine that's hard to look at, I thought confusedly—and in a way I was right.

Will Boyce, the undertaker, laid the men out and provided the plain coffins that the town would have to pay for, and they were buried at the edge of the cemetery. No relatives could be found. There were no mourners.

Some people thought this tragedy was a warning to the careless and ungodly. The two strangers had been fishing on Sunday, without going to church first, and maybe they had been drinking. Moreover, they wouldn't have been wandering around the country the way they did if they had been honestly trying to earn a living. At their respective ages they should have had wives, and the son could have had young children, and it did look as though they had abandoned them.

Mr. Whitehill said it was certainly an object lesson. Mr. Moody pondered the matter a little, and suggested that if C. C. Graves had moved them along on Saturday they might not have been drowned at all, or might have been drowned in a pond down Jonesville way. The Rev. Mr. Kellogg preached a sermon in the Congregational Church on the following Sunday in which he compared the dead men with the Prodigal Son and judged them with his usual kindness. He seemed to think they might do better in the future world than they had in this one, but I couldn't imagine anybody wanting to get drowned with that expectation.

All I could think of was the deep horror of that wagon coming slowly up Main Street, past my grandmother's house, with the huddled forms under the blankets. The picture haunted me for a day or two, and a night or two, and longer.

Then Tom Moran came into the office and got into a conversation with Mr. Whitehill and Mr. Moody. He had seen more of what happened than anybody else had. I hung around, listening. I wanted some sort of reassurance, for if two lives could be ended like that, with no meaning to them, on a fine Sunday morning, with the church bells ringing, what was life worth?

The thing was too casual, like stubbing one's toe or sprain-ing an ankle.

Tom Moran reflected for a while, and then aimed at, and hit, the handy spittoon.

"It all turns on one thing," he ruminated, "and that is, how did the young fellow get himself drowned? If he was drunk maybe he deserved it, though I like my nip well enough to be the last one to say it. But he didn't act drunk. I picked up the bottle they'd been drinking out of, and what it smelled of was coffee. Another thing—" Tom mused some more, pulled at his pipe, and spat again.

"Another thing," Tom went on, "is that that young fellow didn't fall in. When the old man came up, God rest his soul, yelling and kicking, the young fellow jumped in. There he was, you see, doing his best to save his poor old dad. And that wasn't the worst of it." Tom drew deeply on his pipe, choked and coughed till the tears came into his eyes ("They're making tobacco out of horse radish," he said).

"What was the worst of it?" demanded Mr. Whitehill, after a long wait.

"The damned fool couldn't swim," retorted Tom Moran fiercely. "He knew he couldn't help the old man. He jumped in, anyhow."

I drew a long breath that made the other three look at me. Suddenly the shadows of the tragedy passed. I seemed to be hearing a brass band playing, and the drums thumping, and seeing flags waving.

"There's a sermon for you," remarked Justin Moody.

"Maybe you could write it up, Rob," said Harry Whitehill.

"I'd like to," I said.

And now I have.

CHAPTER EIGHT

─••◦••─

An Equal Chance

1

I *SOMETIMES* think I know what Howard Bryant died
of. I know what Dr. Janes called it, but after a good
many years I still wonder. Howard was older than I
was. So was his sister Celia, whom I remember a little better
than I do Howard. Celia was a pretty girl, in spite of her
deep brown color and full lips. Why do I say, in spite of?
The deep brown color would have made her prettier and
the full lips more adorable for a young man who loved her,
and did not look on her as a problem that had by chance or
mistake become located in a Vermont town. In time there
was such a young man, I believe, for this is not a story about
Celia.

Our Vermont town was not entitled to have any race
prejudice—except, perhaps, the sad illusion on the part of
the descendants of the first settlers that the Irish, the French
Canadians, or the Italians were not quite as good as the rest
of us. For that matter, my father's Scottish birth was not to
his advantage when he first courted my mother—though that
was, of course, a long time before the period of which I am
writing.

But there was a good reason, a secular reason, why we
should not have any prejudice against Negroes. It was a
Vermont judge—and we were proud of him when we read of

him in the Vermont Historical Reader—who had to deal with the case of a fugitive slave in the late eighteenth or early nineteenth century.

The Southerner who claimed ownership of the slave brought documents into court. These were all in order. They showed that the man had bought his slave from somebody else, who had bought him from a third party. The claimant introduced these documents, and leaned back and laughed. These Vermont bumpkins, he seemed to think, couldn't answer that sort of argument.

You did not laugh at Vermonters in those days, nor in that court, nor perhaps even today. Not the real Vermonters, who are not precisely what the books and magazines written by outsiders sometimes say they are, but who do not gladly take arbitrary orders from anybody who walks in shoes.

The Vermont judge inspected the papers. "These," he said, "seem to me to be in good form as far as they go." He paused while the claimant reached for his hat and fingered the handcuffs in the lefthand, inside pocket of his frock coat.

"However," the judge continued, "they are not complete." He took off his glasses and eyed the slaveowner with a look that had some decades of history in it, present and to come. Then he rose, and his voice rose. He pointed an accusing, inquisitory finger at the litigant. "Have you," he shouted, "a bill of sale from God Almighty?"

That was how we and our predecessors in Vermont had felt about slavery. That was why Vermont never had to draft a single soldier during the Civil War. That was why the men of Stannard's Brigade, Dr. Janes' patients, country boys sick of war and sick for home, stood their ground on the final day at Gettysburg while the Confederate artillery pounded their positions, and then came down to deal with Pickett's equally brave—but, as we Vermonters thought, mistaken—men, in the angle of a blood-soaked stone wall.

They didn't know, and neither did most of us who later read of their exploits and saw their tattered battleflags in the State House at Montpelier, that Pickett and Lee, and all the great Confederate commanders, couldn't have won a skirmish with slaveholders alone. We thought every Confederate soldier had at least twenty slaves. And so, God forgive us and reward the slain, our forefathers saved the Union.

But this didn't help Howard Bryant especially.

2

I don't suppose anybody, anything we did, any historic heroism on Culp's Hill, Little Round Top and Cemetery Ridge, could have saved Howard Bryant or made Celia Bryant's life as easy as that of a white girl of her own age and generation. Not Horace Greeley. Not William Lloyd Garrison. Not even Abraham Lincoln, who so greatly suffered for the two causes he never quite joined or quite separated, the Union of these States and emancipation.

Howard Bryant and Celia Bryant should have been happy and all right in this town of ours in Vermont. Lem Bryant, their father, was no less a good carpenter and a quiet, pleasant, modest good citizen because of the fact that he was black. Mrs. Bryant I hardly knew, for she rarely went anywhere. I can understand that she loved Lem Bryant truly. She must have, for even after the Emancipation Proclamation and Appomattox, even in Vermont, through which there had run some lines of the pre-war Underground Railroad by which escaped slaves reached Canada and freedom, it was not expected or desired that a white woman should marry a Negro. I don't know that many persons would have said it was wrong, but they would have agreed that it was embarrassing.

But Mrs. Bryant—and I do not know her maiden name, nor of what stock or derivation she was—did marry Lem

Bryant. And I do not know how Lem Bryant, or the two of them, came to Waterbury. They were safe there, of course. No one would ever trouble them. The meanest rowdies wouldn't break their windows at night.

Neither would anybody, in those days, invite them to join one of the leading churches (though I think I should except the Catholic Church from this indictment); nobody would expect to see them at sociables, sugarings-off, picnics, and hay rides. Nobody would expect Mrs. Bryant, whatever her educational background, to become a member of one of the reading and study clubs to which most Protestant women belonged. Mrs. Bryant would be expected to be quiet and unobtrusive, which, God rest her soul, she was.

Lem Bryant wouldn't be asked to join anything, either. He could talk back to a white man if he wished—which he usually didn't—but he wouldn't ever be third selectman or timber-reeve or even fence-viewer.

But what about Howard and Celia Bryant? What share of the sin of being dark in color should they have to bear, in Waterbury, Vermont? For people in Vermont, being opposed to slavery, could not logically accept the theory that persons who had been enslaved, wrongly and by force, were thereby inferior—they and their descendants to the ultimate generation.

Celia came out of it with less hurt, less visible hurt, than Howard. I believe both she and Howard went to Waterbury High School. There was no reason why they should not. This was, however, a little before my time as a steady inhabitant of Waterbury and a sort of prenatal newspaper man.

Subsequently Celia worked for H. C. Whitehill for a while —this also before my time. Mr. Whitehill was broadminded; he was also practical. Everybody said Celia was a good girl, and she was. Mr. Whitehill, speaking of her, added something. He said he believed in equality between the races, any two races you wanted to mention. He also said that Celia was especially useful to him because she could go into the barber shop and one or two other places that were perfectly respectable, but where a white girl couldn't go.

I can't explain, in these enlightened days, why a white girl couldn't go into a barber shop. She can, now, and scandal will not point its ugly finger at her.

I can't even recall how women got their hair cut in Waterbury in 1905 and 1906. Maybe they just let it grow, but I don't believe so. If they curled it this was likely to be done at home, I think with hot curling irons; or they did it up with paper twills or something just before going to bed, and whatever the process was, there wasn't much of anything more respectable and proper than a Vermont lady in 1905 or 1906 looking after her hair.

But men didn't do their hair, or even their whiskers, in the same way. A barber shop was, therefore, a man's world. So it was useful to Mr. Whitehill that the state of interracial relations in Waterbury at that time was such that whereas a white girl couldn't go into a barber shop and ask for news a dark girl could. And Mr. Whitehill was admired and praised, and maybe got a credit mark in Heaven (though I can't vouch for that) because he gave Celia a job.

At any rate, Celia could go into a barber shop and ask the barber if he had any news. Often he did have news, for it was news when a farmer came into the village from Waterbury Center, or Duxbury, or Moretown, to do a little shopping. The farmer might have some information about his neighbors, too. At the very worst, he might produce or mention a big pumpkin or potato, and that was news. Or somebody was visiting somebody from out of town. Or somebody was building a new barn or getting in some new dairy equipment.

Celia could also ask the hotel clerk at the old Waterbury

Inn what was going on. The clerk might tell her a little more than he would have told a white girl. After all, you didn't have to be skittish with a girl whose skin was a bit darker than the average. The clerk and Celia could kid each other a little, as we used to say, for Celia had no dignity that could be lost. I mean she was permitted no outward dignity, no matter how much dignity—and I think it was adequate—she had in her soul. The people of Waterbury, without any intentional or conscious unkindness, had already classified Celia Bryant in such a way as to impair her dignity. Why wasn't she the same color as other folks, they seemed to be asking? Why wasn't she the same color as Ethan Allen?

Let Celia answer these questions, if she could. They were, however, unspoken and could not be answered.

Yet I don't suppose that Celia was different, inside, from the other Waterbury girls. Her color didn't strike inward. What must have struck inward was the reaction the color produced on other persons. She was a creature of her environments, just like a white girl, just like a white boy such as myself. It may not have seemed strange to her, or it may have seemed fantastic and bitter to her, that she could pick up news items for Harry Whitehill in places and in ways that a white girl couldn't.

She must have been clever. She must also have developed a philosophy of her own. In my brief memories of her she seemed more cheerful, far better adjusted (though we didn't use language like that then), than her brother Howard. Perhaps she had more of Lem Bryant's tranquil temperament, possibly, too, a little more of the quiet resolution that led him to accept the true love betwen himself and a white woman and, with that woman, to make the best life he could, in our comparatively sympathetic community.

I have been told that at one time Celia faced the problem of marrying a white boy and that she was advised by the

Methodist minister not to do it. In the end, she married a man of her own race, who was, I believe, a minister. If the children looked like Celia they would have been handsome.

Howard Bryant's story was different. He was always a good boy, just as Celia was a good girl. No doubt it would have been difficult for either of them to be bad, in the usual youthful way, in Waterbury.

Howard worked hard, and he never had an unpleasant word for anybody. But he was sad, inside. I knew this, even though I don't remember ever talking much with him.

If Howard had been as bright as he was and as white as most Vermonters were, somebody would have made it possible for him to go to Norwich University, the University of Vermont, or Middlebury College. Nobody did do this, and, happily or unhappily, this was before the days of athletic scholarships. When Howard Bryant went to college it was, I think, to Hampton Institute. Somebody in Waterbury helped him to go—maybe Dr. Janes; it would have been like Dr. Janes—but Howard didn't feel happy there. I suppose he experienced, for the first time, a sense of group segregation, and this felt worse than anything that had happened to him in Waterbury. He wasn't a group—he was a person, he was a Vermonter, he was Howard Bryant.

So he came home. Some critical townsfolk, mainly, I am afraid, the feminine ones, said they were afraid Howard was the restless type and would never amount to anything. I think they did honestly want him to amount to something, and they were also unconsciously ashamed of what the town had done to keep him from amounting to much. They were aware, just the same, of the irony of a Negro boy not having as much chance as a white boy in a town that had fought and argued so hard for freedom, and had thought so highly of the Great Emancipator.

It was true, of course, that we had some practical men

among us, even during the Civil War and the political warfare that preceded it. A Vermont Senator, coming from a Waterbury family, had voted for the Fugitive Slave Act, and had thus gone on record as being in favor of bills of sale not derived from God Almighty. Some of the older generation were still bitter against that Senator, who doubtless thought that by voting as he did he was helping to prevent a war.

But this difference of opinion as to what was right, under God, and what was expedient under the lesser gods of politics, wouldn't have made it seem right to return Howard Bryant into any kind of slavery. It didn't even make it seem right to deny him the opportunity that would take him out of the kind of servitude in which he existed, even in the first decade of the twentieth century, even in free Vermont.

The conscientious people of Waterbury really did have Howard Bryant on their minds. They wanted good things for him, even though they could not forget that his pigmentation was darker than theirs. There was a sort of appeal in his dark eyes that they could not respond to; and this he knew, even if they didn't.

The trouble with Howard Bryant was, he wasn't inferior, he was merely dark-skinned. He wasn't inferior—that was his tragedy.

What was Howard Bryant to do in Waterbury? Apparently, I don't know why, he couldn't be a clerk in a store; for no one, so far as I ever heard, suggested that. A clerk in a grocery store or butcher shop, for instance, somebody such as Wallace Green, could go round on foot in the morning and take orders—there weren't enough telephones to do it any other way. In the afternoon he could get out the wagon and deliver what had been ordered.

But he had to be at ease with his customers, not embarrassed, not worried. He had to be ready to exchange a bantering word or two—and know just where the bantering ought to stop. Howard Bryant couldn't do this, hadn't been brought up to do it, was too dark-skinned to do it, wasn't that kind of young man. Life was serious for Howard Bryant, just as it would have been for me if I had been Howard Bryant.

He could have been the ice man, who usually found out how much ice was needed by looking at the ice card in the sitting room window, and then filled the icebox, which was in the woodshed or barn. But this wasn't an all-year-round job. Even the aristocrats who took ice, my grandmother and aunt among them, didn't take it in winter. What was the use? Winter provided its own ice—too much ice.

So being an ice man wouldn't have been a career for Howard Bryant. He might have become a carpenter, as his father was. I don't know why he didn't try it, unless that he didn't want to try anything merely because he was dark-skinned; unless he wanted to be a free-born American, as Mr. Jefferson and Mr. Lincoln seemed to have intended for everybody. He couldn't become a ditch-digger or common laborer, though we had some need for them; God had committed the social error of making Howard too intelligent for such jobs. For the same reason, he couldn't, or didn't, go in for being a section hand on the railroad.

The jobs that would have been open to him in Waterbury just weren't up to his abilities. Even the white boys of old stock around our town found it easier to go away for a job than to try to make a go of it in Waterbury. Except when they were farmers' sons and could take over the land when their fathers quit; and even then, farming in the first decade of the century seemed to have no great future in our part of Vermont.

But what if Howard Bryant chose to look for his fortune elsewhere? He wouldn't look for it south of the Mason and Dixon line, for he had been brought up to be free and outspoken, just as the Declaration, the Bill of Rights and some other documents indicated. He knew, or soon found out, that he couldn't move to a Northern city and have an equal chance with a white boy of his own age and education—the documents didn't cover that point. He hadn't any money with which to go into business, for Lem Bryant earned just enough to keep the family going—in which respect he was like the white carpenters. He hadn't any influence, big or little, to help him along.

I think many Waterbury people really worried about Howard. I know my grandmother, mother, and aunt did, for they talked of him, and perhaps gave me some of the ideas I have just been trying to express. Everybody wished Howard well. Everybody would do anything and everything for Howard, except admit in their secret hearts that he was precisely as good and as worthy of consideration as a white boy of his own age and gifts.

He must, indeed, have been on Waterbury's mind. He must have created what later came to be known as a sense of guilt among us. I imagine there were some persons who were on this very account the more critical of Howard's ways and attitudes. It would have been much simpler, from one point of view, if when Mr. Lincoln freed the slaves Lem Bryant hadn't married Howard's mother, or the family had gone to live somewhere else—in Rutland, for instance, or in St. Johnsbury, or even in some other state.

We all approved of Lem's being free, but there were those among us who would have preferred that he be free somewhere else, where we wouldn't have to be so concerned about Howard.

I never talked much to Lem. I was too young for that. I just passed the time of day with him, as I would have done with any other adult I met on the street.

3

Somebody finally decided—maybe it was Mr. Whitehill, that voice of conscience, at times, in our community—that the best thing Howard could do would be to become a Pullman porter. There were seemingly good arguments for this, and I shouldn't wonder if Mr. Whitehill, in his kindly way, didn't call Howard in and explain them to him. One argument was that Mr. Lincoln's son Robert was then running the Pullman Company, or had been, or something like that, and it was thought that in giving jobs to Negroes he was doing what his father would have wanted, and not just solving a difficult labor problem.

At any rate, Howard Bryant was persuaded to become a Pullman porter, and his Waterbury friends breathed sighs of relief. Howard would travel around and get to see faraway places. What fun—I almost envied him. This was all the easier because I had never been in a Pullman car and thus didn't know what porters had to do and what the traveling public felt free to say to them.

The Central Vermont line ran right behind my grandmother's house, even though we were on the correct side of the tracks, and I supposed that Howard Bryant, rumbling north to Montreal or south to Boston or New York, would be happy.

Howard wrote irregularly to his parents and Lem was not communicative about him. Lem said that Howard liked being a porter all right. He said that Howard sent a little money home sometimes, and he seemed proud of that fact. Howard got around on different runs, as far west as Chicago and as far south as New Orleans. He didn't like it so much down south, Lem said.

Then one day Howard reappeared in Waterbury. He had never been talkative, the way Negroes are supposed to be, and now he was less so than ever. Some people thought he took after his mother more than after Lem, except in the matter of color, and his mother was a silent woman.

Howard did say he was taking a little vacation. He said you needed to rest up after traveling around so much, you didn't get much sleep on trips, and as often as not there wasn't much time between trips.

But Howard didn't go back to his job. After a while word leaked out, mostly through things he didn't say and Lem didn't say, that Howard hadn't liked the porter job. For one thing, he didn't like to be talked to the way white men talked to Negro porters. He didn't like to be jolly when he didn't feel jolly, just for the sake of a bigger tip.

It dawned upon the town that Howard Bryant's career was again a problem. Mr. Whitehill talked about it to me. "He could do some of the things you're doing," he mused.

That was true. Howard could have swept out the store and shop, fixed the fires in cold weather, carried the papers, run the presses and gone on errands. He would have done it for less than the six dollars a week I was receiving.

"But not quite all," Mr. Whitehill pursued. "I don't suppose he could write as well as you do. He couldn't have covered that investigation at the Asylum, the way you did." Mr. Whitehill chewed some more on the cud of his reflections. "There's nothing like an old Vermont family, even if you're not rich," he concluded, "and that is nothing against your good Scotch father." He shook his head soberly. "I don't hold Howard's color against him. God made him that way."

"With some help from Lem," put in Mr. Moody, who had been listening.

"I'm in favor of everybody having an equal chance," Mr. Whitehill said, "but I'm disturbed about what's going to happen to Howard Bryant. He doesn't seem to realize his—his limitations. I guess we'll have to think up something else. He can't just be allowed to drift."

"I guess not," I agreed. I thought it was about time for me to say something. "He seems kind of unhappy."

"We're lucky to be white," Mr. Whitehill resumed. "We don't always realize our own blessings, even in Vermont. You ought to think of that sometimes, Rob, when—well, sometimes."

I saw Howard Bryant a few times after that. He would walk up North Main Street from the small house where his parents lived, drop in at the postoffice, make a small purchase for his mother at the grocery store, maybe go down to the depot and watch a train come in. He was friendly, but he said little, to me or to anybody else so far as I knew.

He seemed more shy, somehow, than when he went away. He had appeared to feel, all along, that he shouldn't be too friendly with white girls or women, and now he hardly looked at them, even when they spoke to him.

"I don't know what's got into Howard Bryant," my aunt complained one day. "It's almost impossible to get more than two words out of him."

"Poor boy," said my grandmother. "Poor boy. After all the fighting, too." It was as though she were summing up swiftly in her mind the long crusade against the iniquity of slavery, all the sorrow, pain, and hate; and as though she were wondering what this anguish had accomplished, in the town of Waterbury, Vermont, for Howard Bryant.

"I know," agreed my mother. "I think that experience hurt him, somehow."

Howard didn't go back to the Pullman Company and he didn't seem to be looking for a job around town. Maybe he did a few things—helping his father on some easy work, mowing a lawn, chopping wood, things like that, that didn't last and didn't lead anywhere.

Dr. Janes said that Howard had let himself get run down,

so that he couldn't shake off the typhoid that had fastened itself on him. Dr. Janes never talked much about his patients, and he didn't talk much in this case, but when he said Howard had let himself get run down I knew what he meant. Everybody knew. There wasn't anywhere for Howard to go but where he went, there wasn't anything for Howard to do but what he did.

A less sensitive young man might have managed the situation better; he might have adjusted himself to the way life had dealt with him; I remembered a jolly, swaggering young Negro I once saw in Montpelier, handling baggage at the Wells River depot, who had certainly done just that. But Howard couldn't. He couldn't swagger. He couldn't be an end man in the minstrel show of daily life. He wanted to be what he was, not what his color was, and people wouldn't let him. Not quite. Not wholly. Not even in Vermont, from which so many men had gone to lay down their lives for freedom.

I've often wondered what the people of Waterbury could have done and didn't do, or what they did that they might have avoided doing, to save Howard Bryant from defeat. But there was a gap between the Bryant family and the rest of the town, and no way to bridge it. The Ladies' Aid of the Congregational Church sent a committee to call on Mrs. Bryant during Howard's illness, and some things for Howard to eat, only, because he was so sick, he couldn't eat them.

Our cemetery extended over a ridge back of the Congregational Church, running over toward the river. The older families had plots large enough to serve them for several generations in that slowly growing community. Newer families had to bury their dead along the edges, where the land began to slope down toward Winooski Street.

There were houses on this, the northwest side, as there were on the southeast side. The creamery, too, was just under the edge of the cemetery hill, and you could take a short cut past the tombstones to reach it, from the *Record* office and the other shops and stores. It seems to me I'd seen Howard Bryant down by the creamery once or twice. Any boy or young man, of whatever race or color, with nothing much else to do, would visit the creamery occasionally. I don't know anything much more fun, in the factory line, than watching butter made or milk in process of being pasteurized; except, perhaps, Bert Demeritt's corn-cannery, which I wrote up once for the *Record;* it made me hungry just to watch the corn going into the cans.

Howard's grave was down by the creamery. I came on it by accident one day, not long after he died. I hadn't gone to the funeral. I didn't like funerals—never had, indeed, since I went to my step-grandfather's, a man I had been fond of and didn't want to think of as being dead. I hadn't realized, before that, that dead people didn't look like people—they looked like images made out of wax. I couldn't understand why the undertaker—it wasn't Will Boyce then—was so proud.

I knew that Howard Bryant couldn't have looked like an image in white wax. He wouldn't have wanted to, for he had pride in himself and in his race. But he wanted to live, too, I knew that, if only he could have found out how.

There were a few flowers on his grave, and a wreath. But it had rained since the funeral, and no turf had yet been laid, and the earth that lay over the coffin was muddy.

CHAPTER NINE

Death of a Lamplighter

1

*D*URING my last year in high school a professor from
Middlebury College traveled through Vermont, talking with members of the senior classes. This man
came to Waterbury and three or four of us went down to the
Waterbury Inn to have a chat with him. He was a pleasant
person, possessing a classical education and trying to interest
others in his own brand of culture. That was what Middlebury had to offer at that time.

Earl Boyce said he was going to Norwich University to
study engineering. Joe Smith, whose father was the proprietor, with Jim Somerville, of the hardware store, said he
was going to the University of Vermont, at Burlington, and
he, too, as I recall, planned to study engineering. Electrical
engineering, maybe.

As for myself, all that I positively knew was that I didn't
want to study engineering of any kind, because solid geometry was about as much as I wanted to cope with, and to hell
(I still feel that way and I do hope the sentiment is not
subversive) with calculus. So I had little to say.

My very silence, as I think, caused the professor to look
at me hopefully; he may have confused blankness of expression with indecision. No doubt he hated this job of going
around soliciting students. No doubt he would have liked it

better to be alive today and have the job of eliminating students who shouldn't go to college at all. Still, in 1906 or thereabouts, I was his meat. I really wanted a classical education, without much notion as to what I would do with it when I had it. Newspaper work was in my mind, but what I knew about newspaper work in its larger aspects wasn't enough to put in a canary's ear.

"I'm glad you know what you want to do," the professor began, addressing Earl Boyce and Joe Smith. Incidentally, he was wrong. Both Earl and Joe went into business after graduation, and, as far as I know, never did a lick of engineering after they had their diplomas in their hands.

"I'm glad you've made up your minds," the professor went on. "It shows you've done some thinking." The professor had a small, well-trimmed beard and I respected him for that and because he seemed to be in the camp I preferred. He paused, reflected and resumed. "However, I think you should bear in mind that the way things are going now, the way young men such as yourselves are picking their future careers, there will be about as many engineers—especially electrical engineers —a few years from now as there are electric lights." He smiled, as with a pleasant memory. "Or gooseberries on a gooseberry bush," he added. He continued, more seriously. "I won't say electricity is a passing fad. What I mean is, electricity isn't the only thing in the world. We still need well-rounded men and women."

What I really wanted, at that time, I began to think, was to be a college professor, like this one. Some of them, I had been told, got fabulous salaries, maybe as much as three thousand dollars a year, which worked out at ten times what Harry Whitehill was paying me; and of course there would be the long summer vacations.

Earl and Joe said they would think it over, which meant, as the professor instantly recognized, that they weren't buying his goods. I merely mumbled. The professor looked at me, but dubiously. He seemed to be thinking, is this all I can winnow out of the class of 1905 at the Waterbury High School?

The professor was wrong about the demand for electrical engineers, and engineers in general. Half a century after my brief encounter with him, I learn that my native land is in grave danger because it hasn't enough engineers.

The professor can't look reproachfully at me, of course, because he can't possibly be around any more, not in this world. I didn't become an engineer and I didn't go to Middlebury until I traveled there twenty-one years later to make a speech full of good advice—I forget just what—for the young of that year.

On the other hand, I contributed nothing toward the electric light, nothing toward the H-bomb.

2

Whether or not there were engineers enough to provide one for each electric light, there were soon plenty of electric lights. I do not say that the kerosene lamp or the candle was better, though a good kerosene lamp, well-shaded, its wick well-trimmed, was as good and soft as anybody could desire.

And I don't know, and don't contend, that the Waterbury lamplighter, when we had one, was any happier than other men. I would rather have been that lamplighter, at one time, than anybody else except a railroad man, but the choice was not offered me. The lamplighter himself may have liked lighting lamps because he had been doing it so long, and maybe associated it with his lost youth and what he thought had been simpler and happier days.

The lamps descended North Main Street at suitable intervals, and there was one near the front of the steps of my grandmother's house at Number 27. The lamplighter, with his stepladder and some sort of ever-burning torch, came along just before dusk or just after dusk, winter and summer, spring and fall, and lighted each lamp separately. You could detect his progress down from the intersection of Stowe Street and Main Street by the glow he left behind him. Sometimes he also came through in the daytime, filling the lamps with kerosene when they needed it, and trimming the wicks. Once in a while I came upon him very late at night when he put the lights out. The village didn't figure that any law-abiding citizen had much need of street lights after midnight, and it would have been foolish to keep them on for the convenience of the non-law-abiding.

He must have heard the river rushing as he worked, at certain times of the year, and especially during the spring floods, when the ice had just gone out, and it was of course the river that finally put him out of business. The river had begun to provide light for Waterbury before I left the town forever. This was the meaning of the dam at Bolton Falls, below the Lover's Leap—it seems to me, sometimes, that almost all the Indian maidens prior to the coming of the white man must have perished by jumping off cliffs into rivers because of frustrated mating impulses. The dam turned generators to produce electric power, and the electric power illuminated Waterbury.

The day came when Joe Smith and I, in the dusk of a summer Sunday, sat on the top of the Split Rock, looking westward and northward across the valley in which the village lay, and saw it blossom with light in the fraction of a second.

"It would take Old Man Durbridge an hour to do that," I commented.

Joe sniffed thoughtfully. "It saves a lot of walking," he said. "I wonder what he does now. I wonder what he did with that damn little ladder of his he used to carry around. I wonder why they never put cleats on the lamp-posts, so he wouldn't have needed a ladder."

"Should have thought of it sooner," I retorted. "He could use it to pick apples. There aren't any electric apples, not yet."

Joe picked up my figure of speech. "There will be," he re-marked. "You just wait. They'll be picking apples by electricity before long."

"I wonder what Old Man Durbridge will do now." The thought troubled me. Everybody liked Old Man Durbridge. He just fitted into what he had been doing.

"He won't work in the powerhouse," said Joe. "That's certain."

He was right, of course. Old Man Durbridge never did get a job in the powerhouse to make up for the one he had had looking after the kerosene lamps along the Waterbury streets. During the brief remainder of his life he did odd jobs, of which there were always some for a man willing to work hard for ten cents an hour.

It wasn't until long afterwards that I learned the words for what happened to Old Man Durbridge. He was a victim of technological unemployment, so it was explained. He had specialized in doing something that nobody wanted done any more.

But we were proud of our new electric street lights. They semed to me much more beautiful than the sputtering arc lights which I had seen for the first time riding down from Williamstown on the train past the grimy back streets of Barre, in the drabness of a midwinter late afternoon. The arc light was hard and sinister.

It was not until after I had left Waterbury that my grandmother's house had electric lights. By that time, she, a child of the candle-lit early nineteenth century, had gone to where there was another kind of light.

3

Mr. Redmond was the engineer in charge of the powerhouse that supplied light to the Insane Asylum before we had electricity in many houses in the village. At the time of which I am thinking the Asylum wasn't hooked on to Bolton Falls power. It operated on coal.

Mr. Redmond's powerhouse was a neat affair, inside and out, in spite of the nature of its fuel. I recall going in there with Joe Smith and taking a look around, with Mr. Redmond doing the honors. Mr. Redmond didn't agree with the Middlebury professor. He said there was a great future for electric engineers, indeed, all kinds of engineers. He pointed to his young assistant, who was paddling around in rubber-soled shoes, with a wiping cloth and an oil can.

"See George there?" asked Mr. Redmond. We saw George, and Mr. Redmond continued. "He's on his way. He's learning it from the ground up. That's how I got my start. Books are all right. I've read a lot of books myself, about electricity and generators and wiring and design, and all that. But you can't really know much about those things until you see them in action."

I knew something about electricity, too, or thought I did. You took some iron in a kind of horseshoe shape. Then you wound some wire in coils and revolved this wire inside the horseshoe. Then you connected the stationary parts and the revolving parts with brushes, and off came your electricity.

"But how do you begin?" I asked, just to keep Mr. Redmond talking.

"Every piece of iron," said Mr. Redmond proudly, "has some residual magnetism. That is enough to get the operation started. It builds up." He wiped his hands on a rag. "I never dreamed of doing anything like this when I was a kid, and we used to play with those horseshoe magnets. Sometimes we'd rub a needle on one of them, and if you floated that needle in water—and you could, if you were careful, because it had a film of air around it—the end of it would point north."

"Which end?" asked Joe Smith.

Mr. Redmond glared at us impatiently. "It's not a laughing matter," he replied. "The north end, of course." He waited for another irreverent interruption, and continued. "The time is coming when electricity will be the only power there is. It will run everything—automobiles, railways, machinery. There's the Conley boys fooling around with gasoline engines. They'd do better to build generators."

"But doesn't there have to be something to turn the generators?" I asked. "The way you have here. Steam."

Mr. Redmond shook his head. "Waterpower," he replied. "Waterpower. Let Nature do the work while we take it easy. Harness all the rivers we have in this country and we won't need coal any more."

We couldn't argue such points with Mr. Redmond. You could look across to the Asylum and see all the windows brilliantly lighted with the electricity Mr. Redmond was making. It almost made it worth while to be just a little crazy (this was, of course, before it turned out we all were) to be so beautifully illuminated.

"You can walk around and look at things," Mr. Redmond said in his kindly way. "Only don't step off the rubber mats. Rubber is a non-conductor of electricity."

I thought then, and I still think, that there has never been any machine lovelier than a steam locomotive, a heavy one for freight or a light one for passenger hauls; and I didn't then know that the steam engine belonged to a vanishing race and would be in my lifetime a sort of museum piece, or an object for a reservation or a zoo, like the buffalo and the Indian, and no longer of any interest to the Baldwin Locomotive Works.

But I also liked Mr. Redmond's generators, or dynamos, as we used to call them. They were slick and smooth, like water running swiftly through a gorge. They made no noise, except a kind of whisper. There was strength in them but it didn't snort, chug or puff.

"That's the power of the future," said Mr. Redmond. "Clean, tidy and quiet. You boys will live to see it sweep the country."

In a way we did, and in a way we didn't. I'm glad Mr. Redmond did not live long enough (though no doubt he would have liked to) to learn about atomic power. It would have confused him. Mr. Redmond's power at least had no "half-life," as the scientists put it today. It did its work and departed.

4

The truth is that atomic power confuses me today about as much as electric power confused Old Man Durbridge. Mr. Durbridge had worked his way up in the street-lighting business. In the beginning he had been allowed to go around with an older journeyman lamplighter and carry the ladder. Then he had risen to a point where he had been permitted to clean the lamps, trim the wicks and fill the reservoirs with kerosene, all by himself. Then he had become the chief lamplighter after the older lamplighter had resigned or died— and in Vermont we didn't resign, we died.

Mr. Durbridge talked to me about his occupation, at about the time of his changeover. I suppose I was writing something about it for the *Record*, though Mr. Durbridge was not prominent enough in Harry Whitehill's eyes to get more than two or three sticks of type. I always learned more on such occasions than I could get into the paper. And sometimes I think people would tell me more because I asked few questions than they would have if I had been primed like a district attorney.

"Kerosene lamps," Mr. Durbridge began, "were what you might call a modern improvement after not having any lamps at all. People had candles, of course, and you might stick a candle up at the corner of Main and Stowe Streets, in a lantern frame, but you couldn't count on its being there, lighted, half an hour later. That was the trouble with candles."

"It must have been unpleasant," I ventured, after the silence had grown embarrassing.

Mr. Durbridge snorted. "What was there unpleasant about it?" His thoughts seemed to go a long way back, where I could not follow. "People knew enough then to stay home," he resumed. "At night, I mean. There was plenty to do at home at night. Or wait for a full moon. Speaking of full moons, it reminds me—."

"Yes," I breathed, getting out my notebook, which I rarely used because people didn't—and don't—talk so freely and so well in front of a notebook.

"Never mind," said Mr. Durbridge crustily. "You're too young to understand."

"But you liked the kerosene lamps when we got them, didn't you?" I asked.

"I was young enough to like anything," Mr. Durbridge answered. "They could have fed me castor oil and I'd have liked it and asked for more. That's how young I was. And all the girls were pretty. I guess they look that way to you, don't they?"

"Some," I confessed.

Mr. Durbridge laughed. "You're getting old before your time. Or the girls are getting plainer. What were we talking about?"

"Kerosene street lamps," I reminded him.

"That's right." Mr. Durbridge's face lighted up. "I thought being the lamplighter would be the grandest job there was. So I followed Old Man Bilton—that was what they called him, he was so old, even then—around until he sort of took me on and showed me how. He'd been in the war, and had rheumatism and a wooden leg, and they took him on partly on that account, though I must say the wooden leg made it hard for him, sometimes, to climb up that ladder, especially in winter, when it was naturally slippery. But a man who'd been in the war wouldn't be scared off by that."

"The Civil War?" I asked.

Old Man Durbridge looked at me indignantly. "The Civil War?" His voice rose to a sharp question mark. "I was in that one myself. I am referring to the War of 1812. The second time we licked the Britishers. Old Man Bilton—of course he was, as you might say, Young Man Bilton then—fought under Tom Macdonough at the Battle of Plattsburg in 1814. That was a little before my time, of course." He smiled reminiscently. "He was old-fashioned, if ever a man was, but when he saw that the selectmen wanted to light up the streets at night, when everybody by rights should have been in bed, he fell in with the idea."

"I guess you don't think the new electric lights are as good as the old kerosene lights," I suggested.

Mr. Durbridge cleared his throat noisily. "As good," he repeated. "They're better. Of course they're better." He was silent for some seconds, and I waited. "They're better if you want to go out in the front yard and read the *Waterbury Record* in the middle of the night. It all depends on what you want." He devoted some more time to meditation. "Look," he resumed, "things could have gone on well enough here if we hadn't known there was any such thing as an electric light. We had good kerosene lamps on our streets, and they were well tended, summer and winter, if I do say so. Electric lights are better. Sure, they're better. You can see more. But is anybody any happier? You tell me that."

"I see what you mean," I said.

Mr. Durbridge sniffed. "If you do," he retorted, "you're smarter than most young folks of your age. What you want is change, change, change. A man learns to do something—works hard at it, tries all the different ways of doing it, to see which is best. Then nobody wants him to do it any more.

That's me. My trade is looking after street lights, with wicks and kerosene, one light at a time. What do I do now? Mow lawns in summer. Shovel snow in winter. I carpenter some. Dig holes in the ground and fill them up. Don't get me wrong. I'm all for progress. But I was better off before there was so much progress in my line of work."

Mr. Durbridge glared at me, or rather he glared through me at the whole spectacle of modern life in Waterbury. A gleam came into his eye. "And if you get a big wind or ice or heavy snow," he declared triumphantly, "your electric lights go out."

"Didn't you ever have trouble with the kerosene lamps?" I asked.

"Yes. One at a time. Not all of them at once." Mr. Durbridge sighed. "I've got to do a small paint job for C. C. Warren," he said, and rose to go. He paused and threw over his shoulder the last words I ever remember hearing from him. "Odd jobs," he said. "Nothing permanent."

5

Mr. Durbridge was a widower, with no near surviving relatives—at least, none that came to his aid when he had to stop working. So he went downriver to the poor house, where I never saw him, and after a short time there died.

"Rheumatism," I heard Dr. Janes tell Harry Whitehill. "A touch of pneumonia. Trouble with the heart."

"What kind of trouble?" asked Harry Whitehill, who was always interested in other people's diseases.

Dr. Janes eyed him thoughtfully. "A broken heart," he said, "though that is not the medical name for it."

"I didn't know he took it so hard," commented Mr. Whitehill.

Dr. Janes nodded. "He didn't know it, either. That's the way with people sometimes." He started to leave and then turned back. "It wasn't the lights so much. It was not being wanted."

Mr. Whitehill thought the matter over after Dr. Janes went out, and that was when he suggested that I find out what I could about Old Man Durbridge, being a sort of expert in the subject because I had interviewed him, and write a paragraph or two about him. Unlike the hunted criminals sometimes advertised, Mr. Durbridge was worth a little more dead than alive.

"Oldtimer dies," said Mr. Whitehill, thinking in headlines. "Well-known citizen of Waterbury will be missed. Something like that. Lamplighter saw kerosene take place of candles and electricity take place of kerosene. You might blow it up a little for the *Free Press*, too. They like that kind of stuff. Don't mention the poorhouse, though."

I didn't mention the poorhouse.

On the day after the funeral I came past the Asylum power plant as I delivered my papers. I stopped for a moment and listened to the soft whir of the machinery, and then I looked at the hospital buildings, shining in the dusk with the light Mr. Redmond was producing. Mr. Redmond, torch bearer, bringer of light, Mr. Redmond and his brethren in countless towns and cities, in many countries, illuminating the dark earth. I thought I might make a poem about Mr. Redmond, but I never got around to it. For one thing, the rhymes were hard.

In fact, I couldn't truthfully have sung the ballad of Mr. Redmond after another short interval, for the little powerhouse he had operated had to give way to the cheaper hydroelectric power from Bolton Falls, that came so silently up the river.

Mr. Durbridge was obsolete. So, in time, was Mr. Redmond. I hope they were able to compare notes in some bright skyland, for, since they were both in the lighting business, they had much in common.

CHAPTER TEN

The Four-Dollar Necktie

1

THERE WERE two Irish girls whom I associate with the office of the *Waterbury Record* and *Stowe Journal*. One, whose name I don't remember, must have been about twenty-one years old in 1906, was gay and pretty, and spent her working hours upstairs over the store operating the telephone exchange.

Sometimes I had occasion to go up there, and then I could look at her, which was a pleasure. She was the one who offered me a dime to go call somebody to the telephone, and I paid her the supreme tribute of refusing the dime. I can still see her puzzled look; being a modest girl, she never suspected that for me it was well worth a dime just to see her and hear her voice. I do not know what she did with the dime the company had authorized her to bestow on me. Maybe she put it in her hope chest.

I could hear this fascinating creature's voice whenever I picked up the phone to call the depot or Brown's Livery Stable or some other address important enough to be on the line. We did not give numbers in those days, much less did we dial; we just said in so many words that we wanted the funeral parlors or the Insane Asylum or some other cheerful place, and that was what we got. We had to turn a crank to get any results at all, but for robust country people, only two or three generations removed from the pioneer stage, this was not too great a hardship. And it was no hardship at all to listen to this Irish girl say, what number, please, or good morning, or how do you like the weather today?

I was fond of this girl, possibly, because I saw her so seldom. The other Irish girl worked as a typesetter in the *Record* office, was maybe in her middle twenties and was no doubt just as pretty as the telephone operator. The difference was that I saw Mae O'Reilly every day, whether I wanted to, or she wanted to, or not. Being the romantic type, I could not romanticize a girl or woman who was always around. As far as Mae was concerned, I was a cub not yet dry behind the ears, a competitor in the sense that I also set type, and at times a nuisance that made funny sounds, whistled, pied type, and didn't respect my elders.

In general, I could not regard Mae O'Reilly as an iridescent dream, and a good deal of the time she pretended she wished I was somebody else.

I do not mean to say that our printing office was not a happy one, at times. We had our moments of extreme good humor. I remember when we all got to singing a refrain that Walter Robinson had dredged up from somewhere:

> My mama told me, if I were goody,
> That she would buy me a rubber dolly;
> But when I told her, I loved a soldier,
> She would not buy me that rubber dolly.

But on her best days Mae O'Reilly just barely tolerated me —or forgot all about me. She wasn't in the mood that year to be patient with immature males. She was beginning to worry—she wouldn't need to now, and that is a sign that the world has improved—about being in her middle twenties and not yet married. She didn't wish to spend her life setting type, she wanted to have a husband and a few babies. And she thought, wrongly, that Walter Robinson, Walter Sheldon and I doubted her feminine charms because she was not, in fact, married.

I can understand Mae's state of mind. I could, even then. But she teased me, and as far as I was able I teased her.

2

How Mae got into the job of setting type I don't know, but I suppose she needed the money, couldn't find a position in the drygoods store, didn't want to be a hired girl, and had enough education—probably a high-school diploma, the same as myself—to qualify. She didn't try to do reporting, as Celia Bryant, the colored girl who had once worked for Mr. Whitehill, had done. I don't know why. Maybe Celia, who did it well, had taken the bloom off that job for her.

Mae sat on a stool, like most other printers, and picked the type out of the case. I don't think she worked on job layouts and other fancy stuff; I believe she set straight matter, eight point with one-point leads, for the weekly issue, and distributed the same after it had been used.

Mae was a good Catholic and a good girl, and I suspect she was a good deal more refined than the rest of us around that shop. Not that we were often obscene—we were merely vulgar.

Mae maintained her dignity even when a tramp printer with a red nose and a wealth of off-color stories wandered in, as they did in those free-and-easy times, for a spell of work. A tramp printer was by no means a tramp in the strict sense of the word, but he did like to move around, and most of those I saw during my *Record* days also liked to drink. Getting a drink in Vermont in the old state prohibition days was, of course, an adventure. This was before national prohibition came and went. Tramp printers could get drinks in Vermont in 1906 if they believed alcohol was good for their health. Otherwise they had no truck with the stuff. The dilemma was not too painful. Most tramp printers in 1906 did think alcohol kept their diseases down, and proceeded accordingly.

The result was that tramp printers lost, at times, a good many of what later came to be called their inhibitions. I have seen them try to make up to Mae O'Reilly and even attempt to persuade her to go to a dance with them, but never with any success. She did not, and she told them so, regard their presence in the *Record* office as a formal introduction.

There was a story in our shop, and I suppose in every such shop in the country, about the self-proclaimed tramp printer who was hired to distribute type, and did so. The only trouble was that after his departure for Capetown or Melbourne, or wherever it was he was going, it was discovered that he did not know where the letters went.

Mae O'Reilly had her own thoughts and her own plans. She wouldn't have anybody think for a moment that she was in any need of masculine society; she could have such society whenever she wanted it; she had, in fact, a beau who was ready to marry her at the drop of a hat, but she wasn't quite sure he was what she wanted.

Naturally, this situation gave Mae O'Reilly some confidence in herself. Or it seemed to do so. She looked about the office at Walter the foreman, who was earning twelve dollars a week, and the other Walter, his assistant, who took home eight dollars every Saturday night, and expressed no mating interest in them; she looked at me and murmured words of sympathy for the unfortunate woman who would be so foolish as to have me when I grew up.

Her emphasis on the fact that I still had to grow up did not endear her to me, for I did not then comprehend that being ungrownup is the happiest state there is. My Aunt Alice used to say, when I spoke of looking forward to this or that, "Rob, don't wish your life away; try to make out with what you have."

I wasn't important in Mae O'Reilly's eyes, I was so young and perhaps (this I can face after all the years) so unpromising. She would have liked to call me various names that would have hurt my feelings, but, being a lady, she could not.

I do wonder, however, why she didn't give more attention to Walter Robinson, who could have supported a wife on his twelve dollars a week, and Walter Sheldon, who a little later married a girl from the wrapper factory and became a fireman on one of the branch lines of the Rutland Railroad.

Walter Sheldon had a cow, which, believe it or not, a man could have in those days, even though he lived in a sophisticated town like Waterbury, Vermont, and spent most of his daylight hours being a printer. I wish I knew why he had a cow, for this would be almost enough of a topic for a novel: for example, young Vermonter with cow marries girl who doesn't like cows; crisis arrives, will boy give up wife or give up cow? I think Walter Sheldon gave up cow, for female Vermonters at that time were realistic and firm and took no nonsense from male Vermonters.

But when Walter Sheldon was on his honeymoon, he still had his cow tethered in the yard of his former boarding-house in Waterbury, and he left this animal to me to chaperon. I do not mean that I took the cow with me wherever I went, but I did feed her, and would have milked her except that she was at that moment dry.

I therefore took a great deal of trouble, on the day the *Waterbury Record* and *Stowe Journal* went to press, during Walter Sheldon's honeymoon, to stop the press, and for a run of one (1) copy insert a paragraph reading substantially as follows:

Last Saturday a cow belonging to Walter Sheldon, an employee of this newspaper, now on his honeymoon as stated in
our social columns last week, escaped while being fed by Rob L.
Duffus, also an employee of this newspaper. Mr. Duffus pursued
the animal vigorously, but without success. When last seen Mr.
Sheldon's cow was trotting over the Winooski bridge of the
Central Vermont Railway, shortly before the arrival of the
Boston-Montreal express. We extend our sympathies to all concerned.

If Mae O'Reilly had known about this nonsense she would
have cried out against its silliness. But she never did know
about it, nor did Mr. Whitehill or anybody else except Walter
Sheldon and myself—and probably his bride.

I asked Walter after his return from his wedding journey
if he had received the marked copy. He said he had. But he
didn't laugh, not to any great extent. His mind at that moment was on his young new wife and his projected career
with the Rutland Railroad, and not on his cow—and the
faithful creature was, indeed, by some miracle of genetics
which I do not pretend to understand, bellowing to be
milked, on the boarding-house's side lawn, when Walter
came back with his bride.

Walter milked her then and there, or tried to, or pretended
to. The cow, I mean, whose name was Hortense.

3

If Mae O'Reilly had ever wanted Walter Sheldon, which I
doubt, she couldn't have him now; and she had never seemed
to care too much for Walter Robinson, the foreman, who
earned twelve dollars a week, as I have mentioned, had a
little moustache, liked to look at pretty girls, and was slightly
undersize.

But the only difference I noticed in Mae, as the time went
by, was a somewhat sharper temper. On the whole, the
temper was becoming to her, as it often is to young women

(though I well know this is a dangerous thing to say), and she looked prettier when she was angry than when she was serene.

It was at about the time of Walter Sheldon's marriage, however, that Mae began to talk about her suitor. Naturally, this suitor was not one of our native-born and native-bred Waterbury boys. If he had been there would have been no mystery about him, and Mae, with her Celtic background, needed mystery. Mystery made a better story, too. So it seemed that Mae's suitor was a traveling salesman, a drummer. What he sold she never said. Maybe it was drugstore stuff and maybe it was drygoods and maybe it was lumber or shingle nails. Whatever it was, it had to be romantic (maybe it was horseless carriages, maybe it was baby-carriages), because Mae let it be known that her suitor was not only rich by Waterbury standards but was also of the romantic type.

As soon as Mae let out this information we in the composing room, the two Walters and myself, had to make a little fun of her. She retaliated chiefly, as it still seems to me, by making fun of me, as the most vulnerable of the lot. She said I had no right to talk about other young people's boys or girls, because everybody knew I had no girl of my own, and never would have unless I took a bath now and then and learned to do something more than grunt when I met one on the street and didn't have that kind of ears; in fact, she almost convinced me that I ought to take to the woods at once and become a hermit.

All this time I really liked Mae O'Reilly, in spite of her scorn for me, but the situation was such that I could never admit it. I didn't love Mae O'Reilly—that emotion, if such it was, was saved for one, or maybe two or three, of my contemporaries on the female side; and I had some sort of feeling for the woman I call Lilith for quite a while, but as I have indicated not so much in the daytime as when I woke up in the middle of the night and couldn't go back to sleep again for a half or a quarter of an hour.

Mae said her suitor would drop in at the office some day, and we would all have a look at him, and see if he wasn't all she said he was, and if he wasn't she hoped to drop dead then and there. Walter Robinson said if she really meant this he'd be glad to do his part, assuming that whichever way it turned out there would be no hard feelings.

Mae said he lived in Montpelier when he was at home, but he wasn't at home much, because he was always traveling; she said he came of a solid old family and was intelligent and highly educated; and she nearly tore Walter Sheldon's left eye out when Walter asked her if he was solid between the ears and if he traveled so much because he didn't like his wife and children. He hadn't any, Mae cried, making a pass at Walter's left eye; he never had had any.

And, said Mae, calming down a little as Walter said he was only fooling and offered to get down on his knees and apologize if that would make her feel better, her suitor, whose name was Albert, wore four-dollar neckties.

Well, this was enough, and more than enough, to floor the usual sort of Waterburyan in 1906. I have tried to translate a four-dollar necktie of that year into a corresponding necktie in New York City, Miami or Palm Springs in, let us say, 1960. The inflation of the currency might make a four-dollar necktie in 1906 worth five times that much in 1960.

So, in the language we talked in the *Record* office in 1906, Mae O'Reilly had a suitor who had the equivalent of what we would call today a twenty-dollar necktie. To put it in another way, a girl who had in 1906 a suitor who wore four-dollar neckties was the equivalent of a girl today who has a suitor who has a car that takes three minutes to pass a given point, will not fit into any private garage east of the Mississippi River, produces only five miles of travel for each gallon of gasoline, and can't be parked anywhere; a motor car to be proud of and wondered about.

So if Mae O'Reilly was speaking the truth, she was quite a lot superior to the society in which she found herself when she came to work; she was socially superior to the two Walters, even though they earned a little more than she did, and she was at least equal to my snobbish self, who had respectable Vermont ancestors on one side, a Scotch father on the other side, a shy and unsociable disposition and two ears that could only be useful in a following wind; I could never tack with them when the wind was unfavorable.

Mae O'Reilly had a beau, the beau wore four-dollar ties— what answers could there be to that argument?

There was but one answer, and in this both the Walters and myself joined: let Mae O'Reilly produce the suitor and his four-dollar ties. We would believe him when we saw him. Meanwhile we would not apologize for the fifty-cent ties or the twenty-five-cent ties or the no ties at all that we habitually wore.

A thing called a stock came along at about this time: it took the place of a collar and a tie and looked horrible. It wound around a young man's neck, and supposedly saved laundry bills, for you could wear a shirt with collar and cuffs separate a lot longer than you could wear a shirt with both attached; and if a stock got dirty you could reverse it, with the dirt inside and the clean part, such as it was, outside.

I didn't wear a stock. I never wanted to, though a young man named Merton Patterson did wear one, and people said what a fashionable young man Merton was getting to be if he would only fix his finger nails and wash behind his ears.

I didn't wear a stock. I never wanted to. Nor did I, for many, many years aspire to a four-dollar necktie.

4

I wish I could say that Mae O'Reilly finally brought in her suitor, four-dollar tie and all; but I am trying to be truthful, and though this is a struggle I shall keep on trying. Some very interesting things didn't happen that year, and this was one of them. I never saw Mae's loved one, though I did hear descriptions of a person supposed to be him, himself.

We tried to pin Mae down. We said that the man we believed to be her suitor had a handle-bar moustache (and this meant something in the days when the upper classes still rode bicycles), that he wore a turbulent black- blue- white- and pink-checked coat, that his shoes came to points so narrow that he could split wood with them, only he was too lazy, and that we wouldn't dare look at his necktie for fear of damaging our eyes.

We made a brave show. Yet we were not as sure as we sounded. For all we knew, Mae might really have accumulated a male of some size and resources. Girls did. You never could tell.

When I came in from my paper route the two Walters would often ask me, in chorus or separately, "Did you see him?" Or, "Did he get off the train, like everybody expected, and what did he look like?" They wouldn't say whom they meant by who, or him, but Mae knew. Mae would get swiftly pink, and she would set type at a great rate—though not as accurately as usual. And once, when Walter Sheldon had been especially inquisitive, she pied a whole galley of type— which, when type is set one letter at a time, by hand, is no laughing matter.

Time went by, weeks and months of it, and the joke at last lost its flavor. Mae went on sticking type, for which, I suppose, Mr. Whitehill paid her a little less than he did me —maybe he paid her five dollars a week. And perhaps part

of the slight animus Mae O'Reilly showed toward me was
that just because I was a male I got more than she did, just
because she was a female. I know she put up with me better
when I was a high-school boy getting two dollars a week
than when I was a graduate getting six.

So Mae continued with her work, and sometimes we were
all quite jolly, up there in the *Record* office, especially that
last summer, with the windows open and the smell of decaying oranges, bananas, and various elderly vegetables
floating up from the back yard of Charlie Haines' store. I
shan't ever smell a rotten orange, to the end of my days,
without thinking of the summer of 1906—even though I don't
always want to.

Then one day, without previous notice to any of us, though
she must have dropped a word in Harry Whitehill's ear, Mae
O'Reilly disappeared. At first we supposed she was sick, but
in a day or two, when Mr. Whitehill brought in his first social items for the week, we learned the truth: Mae O'Reilly
was either worse than sick, or better than sick, depending
on one's point of view; Mae O'Reilly had got married, in
Montpelier, and changed her name to Mrs. John B. Carnahan.

We all received invitations to the wedding, though they
arrived several days after the event. We also got invitations
to call at the Carnahan home, which we couldn't conveniently
do, because it turned out to be in Boston.

Mr. Whitehill hired a series of tramp printers, some of
them sober, and finally a new girl; but this came so late in
my postgraduate year that I can't remember the new girl's
name; all I know is that our office conversation was polite
and distant; she merely swept in and out (and a girl really
could sweep around at that time, skirts being where they
were), and if I did any heavy chores for her in the course
of a day's work she always murmured a thank you. That was
all.

But I often thought of Mae O'Reilly Carnahan and her husband, and wondered if he were the one who wore the four-dollar ties, or if anybody on earth except millionaires and kings wore such ties; and whether you could see them in the dark.

Since then I myself have owned four-dollar ties, mainly those given me at Christmas or on my birthday, but nobody makes an issue of it.

———◆◆◆◆▶———

CHAPTER ELEVEN

To Get Rich, Invent Something

1

*H*ARRY WHITEHILL was a business man who always tried to make a profit on each deal. Justin Moody was also a business man, with the same impulse, but it was Justin who said to me: "You'll never be a business man, Rob—you haven't the gumption for that. You're the dreaming type. Why don't you invent something? That's the way to get rich."

I had no especial interest in inventing anything, but I gave this suggestion some thought, for I did have an interest in being rich—that is to say, in being rich enough not to have to bother to get rich.

"A labor-saving device," Mr. Moody went on. "Like Thomas Alva Edison. The phonograph or the motion picture, for example. This is an age of miracles, Rob." He chewed musingly on his after-dinner toothpick. "I wish I was a young man again."

"I'd like to," I agreed, "but I can't think what."

"That's the advantage of being young—and busy," said Mr. Moody quickly. "You can think while you're sweeping out and while you're carrying the papers. That's the advantage of it, you can do two things at once." Mr. Moody reflected some more. "It's a great help to have a—a good job," he concluded, "and still be able to look forward toward the future."

I was never able to follow Mr. Moody's advice; I just wasn't bright in that particular way. I had young friends who were far more inventive than I. I worked with one of these while he built what I suppose was a practicable ice-boat. The only trouble was that after the boat was built, with an outrigger, sails, rudder, and all, we didn't dare sail it on the Winooski River and there wasn't any pond near by large enough for our purpose.

On another occasion, before I took service under White-hill and Moody, this boy and I built a treehouse, and then planned to dam a neighboring brook, construct a small water-wheel, buy a little dynamo, some wire and a tiny electric globe and light the treehouse with electricity. We actually did create a water-wheel—a turbine, strictly speaking—or rather my friend did while I stood around and egged him on. The trouble was, we were never in the treehouse at night. There were some other difficulties, too, I forget just what; and before we could solve these we had grown up to a point where treehouses seemed childish.

It was a good treehouse, though, while it lasted. It was all the better because we discouraged intruders by climbing up a nearby sapling and then lassooing the main tree, revers-ing the process when we climbed down.

But all this was before I became a printer and journalist and put away childish things.

2

I knew another young man, possibly three or four years older than myself, who was not content with dreaming and planning, nor with constructing artifacts he couldn't use. Dean Fullerton procured and assembled an awe-inspiring electrical contrivance that would throw a spark across an in-terval of several inches. I saw this machine at work. Why Dean didn't kill himself by accident I don't know, but he never did.

Marconi had sent the letter *s* across the Atlantic four or five years earlier. I suppose what Dean was after was to make that spark of his do some useful work, and maybe carry messages. I don't know that he actually invented anything, but he was the stuff of which electrical engineers are made. Losing track of him, I have since wondered what use he made of this early experimenting.

The truth was, just as Mr. Moody said, that this was an age of invention. The primitive automobiles, already trundling around our streets occasionally and scaring horses, but not yet in such numbers as to create a traffic problem, reminded us of that.

I rode in C. C. Warren's automobile a year or so before I left Waterbury; you got in at the rear and the apparatus chugged like a battery of field artillery. One of our townsmen, a traveling salesman of some note, had a steam-driven car; it was convenient, he said, because it never took more than fifteen minutes to get up steam, and you could be eating breakfast; and though the boiler was directly under the driver's seat in that model it was never too hot, except in summer, when the weather was too hot, anyhow, and so what difference did it make?

This man swore, up-down-and-sidewise, that he had run off the road on a curve below Waterbury, turned a complete somersault, landed rightside-up, and gone on driving. Nobody could prove this hadn't happened. I have seen the actual curve on which the accident might have taken place; it was rugged, even for 1906.

At about this time Thomas Alva Edison, Mr. Moody's hero, was reported to have said that he proposed to invent a small, cheap, lightweight storage battery that would drive a horseless carriage for hours on end. But he never did.

Similarly, but with less hopeful results, a great scientist did some figuring and wrote a magazine article explaining that flight in a heavier-than-air machine was mathematically impossible because the weight of the necessary power plant would always exceed the lift you could get out of the power the plant would furnish.

The Wright Brothers evidently did not read this article, for they went ahead, produced an airplane and flew at Kitty Hawk—and this while I was still in high school.

The secret of flight, of course, as the Wright Brothers worked it out, all unknown to Harry Whitehill, Justin Moody, and myself, was partly an ingenious set of controls and partly an improved gasoline engine.

The gasoline engine interested me because at that time there were living and working in Waterbury two brothers, Fred and Erwin Conley, who had taken over an old foundry and were actually making gasoline engines in it. I know this, for I went to the foundry many a time, even when I should have been carrying my papers, and saw them do it.

3

The Conley factory would have interested me even if it had been making nothing more exciting than flatirons. The Conley brothers had a furnace in which they cooked their metal, a spout that they tapped whenever they thought the stuff was ready to serve, and molds into which they poured the thick, fast-reddening slush.

They knew their trade well, no doubt having learned it before they decided to apply it to the motor age. They were brawny men, though Fred was tall and Erwin was chunky— or the other way around. Either one of them could have tossed me out the door with one careless gesture if ever I had gotten in the way; therefore I tried not to.

So they set out to make gasoline engines. I don't know why they did this, or how they expected to make money out of it. They couldn't invent a new kind of gasoline engine—or could they? They couldn't make as good an engine as the ones that moved even the earliest motor cars. But maybe that wasn't what they needed in their business. Maybe what their customers wanted was not perfect gasoline engines but cheap power.

I wonder about all this. Were the Conleys just a few years too late? Or a few years too early? Did they have in mind an engine that would be better than those commonly in use, and maybe, some day, good enough to make an automobile travel?

The fact is, they were making stationary, one-cylinder engines, the simplest kind of gasoline engines a man could conceive and manufacture, simpler and less costly than horses.

I cannot explain what drove them, except some version of Justin Moody's theory that the way to get rich was to invent something. Maybe they bought some of the smaller parts, and merely manufactured the base and the cylinder. What came out of their shop was, at any rate, an engine that turned a wheel and produced power.

In those days, as maybe now, people spoke learnedly of one-cycle, two-cycle and four-cycle engines. The one-cycle engine's balance wheel went around once for every explosion, whereas in the four-cycle type you had to wait for the explosion. This was what I was told, and if any reader knows better I hope he won't tell me.

With a Conley engine a man could saw wood or thrash something—oats or wheat or something like that. The minute such engines got into general use the ancient horsepower devices could be discarded—and I don't suppose any horse ever minded being thrown out of employment in this fashion.

And a gasoline engine didn't eat anything when it wasn't being operated. This was something that appealed to thrifty farmers in Vermont and other states, who did not then stop to think that a gasoline engine did not enrich the soil with its excreta while alive or with its bones when dead. I can see now that in witnessing the Conleys at their work I was observing a revolution as important as the one that C. C. Warren had a part in when he rattled along Main Street in his four-cylinder Lucifer Tornado, or whatever the name of the creature was.

However, the Conleys weren't so much interested in causing a technological revolution, I judge, as in making some money. They had the eager look of men who have stumbled on something that may give them power or wealth, or both. They worked hard and fast, and even longer hours than were customary in Waterbury at that time.

They sold their engines as fast as they could make them. Often they seemed to be racing against time. I have seen Erwin Conley at the railway station applying a finishing coat of silver-colored paint to an otherwise completed gasoline engine. Some of our townspeople wondered if the inside of the thing had been finished off as hurriedly as the outside. I don't think so; I think the Conleys did a good job with the mechanism and added the silver-colored paint as a kind of flourish; they had a quiet sort of exuberance about them, and at the time they had reason for it, for they did seem to be on the make.

It was a dingy old foundry they had, but sometimes it glowed with more than the red fire from the furnace.

4

In 1906 the spectacle of the Conley brothers making gasoline engines was taken for granted in Waterbury. People had to work, and this was the kind of work the Conley brothers did. At this late date I begin to wonder how many Conley brothers, or a reasonable facsimile thereof, were at work at that time in the United States, how many hundreds, how many thousands.

I also wonder why it is that the Conley brothers never got

into the papers to any extent, except perhaps the *Waterbury Record* and *Stowe Journal,* whereas Henry Ford and a few others did get in.

Maybe the Conley brothers didn't want success as fiercely as Henry Ford and the others did. Maybe they were good mechanics rather than aspiring business men. Maybe that was their weakness.

But how can I know that? How can I guess what was in the minds of the Conley brothers in 1906? How can I deduce what they said to their wives when they went home at night, an engine or two finished during the day, a new order or two on the books? Did they sit in silence, as so many hard-working Waterbury men did, until their appetites were satisfied?

Did it ever occur to them that with a little more capital they could enlarge their operations, hire more helpers, turn out more engines, make more money?

I think it must have. But the Conley brothers were not the kind that liked to sit in an office keeping records, or walk around a plant giving orders, while somebody else did the manual work. The Conleys liked to get their hands into things. They liked to pour their own molds. Maybe they even liked to be grimy and tired at night; that instinct had been bred in the bones of Vermonters for some generations.

Possibly it was for some such reason as this that the Conleys weren't much heard of in the remarkable days that were to come. They had their brief and not conspicuous hour on the stage—and then they vanished. They financed no Peace Ships, did not set up to be authorities on economics and sociology, did not change the customs of a nation, were never feared and never hated, nor did they run for office.

There may also have been another reason. One day late in 1905 or early in 1906 something happened to one of them, I think it was Erwin. I never learned quite what it was. Dr. Janes certainly knew quite what, for he was called to have a look at the injured man two days or so after the accident, when Erwin's backache didn't get better.

The upshot was that Erwin Conley had to take life easier after that. He went on living, but he couldn't handle heavy weights any more. People said he had hurt his kidneys, or something else inside him, when a heavy mold toppled over and pinned him against the wall. He had a misery, as the old-timers used to put it.

Erwin wasn't a man to complain. He did what Dr. Janes told him to do, but he didn't go around feeling the small of his back and making excuses for not working so hard any more. There were farmers and others that would do that, maybe sitting around Charlie Haines's store during working hours. But not Erwin.

I think now, though, that Erwin had been the driving force in the partnership, and that after the accident he didn't have so much energy, physical or the other kind. Fred was as strong as ever, but Fred depended on Erwin's ideas and initiative.

The Conleys went on making gasoline engines, as I could tell from seeing them ready for shipment at the railway station; and though Erwin may have had a weak back after the accident, he was never too weak to put on silver-colored paint while waiting for the train to come. The engines, as often as not, still went by express, which showed what the demand for them was.

But the Conley engines remained in the stage of evolution they had reached before Erwin's mishap. I had hoped, in my innocent way, that the Conleys might some day blossom out into making automobiles, or at least automobile engines. But they never did, and they never got rich. There was something wrong with Justin Moody's formula. They had certainly invented something, but still they weren't rolling in gold. They went to and from work wearing old clothes, like the rest of the population.

Yet except for the trifling obstacles and mishaps mentioned

there might have been a Conley Horseless Carriage running around Waterbury about the year 1906 or 1907. There were quite a number of such vehicles on the market, and any up-to-date young man had to know one from another, just by looking at the pictures and without reading the print.

But the Conleys never made one. They were a little like the characters in the "Elegy in a Country Churchyard," though I didn't catch this connection until somewhat later. Theirs were the hands the rod of empire might have swayed, though it was happily not true that chill penury repressed their noble rage and froze the noble current of their souls.

They did pretty well by Waterbury standards, even though all they did was to manufacture one-cylinder gasoline engines. They never crowded out a competitor, never betrayed their friends, never set up to be potentates and oracles, never could afford cast-iron dogs on their front lawns.

Nor were they responsible for those noises that sometimes keep me awake at night when I try to sleep in a big city, or a small city, either. Their invention, if they really made one, does not hiccough at me or burble in my ear when I wish to think of something else. It sings a quieter and pleasanter song.

I shall remember them, however, as often as I think about Waterbury during the years 1905 and 1906. I shall hear their engines being tested, and sounding something like this: swish, swish, swish, CHUG, swish, swish, swish, CHUG.

They were the makers of a miracle, but it was a small miracle, and I suppose I am the first, and perhaps the last person to write even a brief and inadequate biographical sketch about them.

I don't believe they would have desired to be either Thomas Alva Edison or Henry Ford, or both. They just wanted to go on with their work, which, for a time, they did.

Swish, swish, swish, CHUG: such was the song their engines sang, and there have been more discordant songs.

CHAPTER TWELVE

Lady, by Yon Rising Moon

1

I DON'T KNOW whether this is a love story, or not, though it seems to me that if it is not a love story the parties most concerned and their next of kin put themselves to a great deal of unnecessary inconvenience. You couldn't go wrong in Waterbury, any more than you could in that other Vermont village I knew so well, without literally everybody knowing about it, talking about it, and making it their business.

It was easier, of course, in Waterbury than in Williamstown, for Williamstown was on a branch line, whereas Waterbury was on the main trunk of the Central Vermont; and Williamstown was much smaller than Waterbury. Perhaps Waterbury was more sophisticated than Williamstown, even though it wasn't Babylon.

At any rate, it was generally said and believed that Mrs. Susan Ransome, a widow who owned a house not far as the crow flies and the wind blows from my grandmother's house, was seeing too much, under imprudent and (as the real gossips may have hoped) improper circumstances, of Philemon Edgehill, a lawyer, married, with two children. Philemon went to Susan's house, remained there an hour or so, and came out. Philemon went to Susan's house two or three times a week. He then went back to his office and thence to his own

(162)

house. People were sorry for Mrs. Edgehill. They also wondered what he saw in Mrs. Ransome.

Mrs. Ransome didn't print an explanatory notice in the *Waterbury Record*. She sued nobody for slander. Her side of the story, nevertheless, leaked out. What she was understood to have said was that after the death of Mr. Ransome, who had been a reasonably prosperous lumber merchant, she had needed legal advice, and that Philemon had provided it. Philemon used also to recommend investments. Mrs. Ransome said it was more convenient for her to have Philemon come to her house than for her to go to Philemon's office.

If Mrs. Ransome had been bedridden this explanation would have been more favorably received by the guardians of Waterbury's morals. But Mrs. Ransome wasn't bedridden —not in that sense, anyhow, as one local commentator expressed it—and she often went up to the postoffice or stores or down to the railway depot, just like other women of her not too advanced age.

By this time I had heard of Romeo and Juliet, and, I believe, of Aucassin and Nicolette, Tristan and Isolde, Abelard and Hèloise and a dozen or so other famous lovers. But I did not think of Susan Ransome and Philemon Edgehill as being in the same category. I would have started an epic love poem on the slightest provocation, but not about Susan and Philemon. I believed in frustrated love because it was so beautiful and because there were no grocer's bills.

I now try to look at Susan with the eyes of an adolescent boy and also with those of a, let us hope, more mature observer. The boy did not ordinarily see Susan Ransome as an object of men's desire (she was not the Lilith image of my young dreams); the belated observer, far beyond the deadlines on this particular bit of news, now realizes that she was a blonde gone prematurely white-haired but with a regularity of feature and an expressiveness in the eyes that such a man as Philemon Edgehill might have found irresistible.

The boy thought of Susan as Mrs. Ransome, and does to this day; he thought of her as kind, generous and humorous; he wondered why it was that his aunt, mother and grandmother were so unwilling to discuss her; he wondered, also, why it was that she was a member of no church and of no social groups, and why we never called at her house and she never called at my grandmother's house.

My mother, aunt and grandmother never objected to my running errands or doing other work for Susan Ransome when she would pay me for doing so. For a while, prior to my entry into Harry Whitehill's demanding employ, I carried milk to her house from Dr. Janes's dairy. Once I spent a long, happy morning digging out her front walk and side entry after a snowstorm, and to this day I thrill at the thought of the forty cents she paid me; I would have accepted a quarter with gratitude. She smiled at me, too, not in any enticing way, not in the fashion in which a middle-aged woman can sometimes try her weapons on a boy, but gently, purely, and understandingly.

I liked Mrs. Ransome. I still do. I think she could have told me things about life that would have been useful—things that women in another position could not have told me. She never did. But I retained my fondness, and I think she knew it. Indeed, I hope so.

When I met Mrs. Ransome on the street she greeted me serenely, and I made a gesture to lift my cap, as though I were a cavalier sweeping the mud or dust of the street with plumes—though I don't believe it looked that way from the outside. But I never talked much to her. She remained a kind of stranger in that otherwise friendly town.

What was there wrong with Mrs. Ransome? The reply, when I asked this question, was always given indirectly. We should have sympathy for Laura Edgehill, I was told. Yet the truth was, we didn't see Mrs. Edgehill in our house, either, for the Edgehills were Methodists—not our adversaries, to be sure, but not in the secure and sensible Congregational circles in which we ourselves, the old families, moved.

Mrs. Ransome couldn't make Philemon Edgehill come to her house if he didn't want to. I wondered then, a little more than I do now, why it was he did want to. For it certainly wasn't a handy thing to do. There must have been some dividend in it to make him take the trouble. And to make him do the damage to Laura Edgehill that he knew he was doing. In short, he was a lazy man going to a lot of trouble, and he was a kind man causing pain.

2

I don't know precisely what a lawyer found to do in Waterbury. We had a few crimes, but not of the sort that were profitable to lawyers. Elderly persons made wills, business men executed contracts of various sorts, Harry Whitehill bought and sold land at a profit—always at a profit, trust him for that—farmers who didn't approve of hard work mortgaged their holdings, and sometimes somebody sued somebody.

Waterbury was in Washington County, as was Montpelier, the State Capital. This fact made it necessary, as well as pleasant, for a Waterbury lawyer occasionally to travel the twelve miles to Montpelier and there tangle with the city slickers.

He traveled them on the train, as a rule, for even though there were a few automobiles in and around our town, it would not have occurred to Philemon Edgehill, or any other man who had an appointment, to jump into a Stanley Steamer and steam away to Montpelier. If the Steamer blew up, the lawyer would not only be in all probability scalded and fractured but also late for the hearing and deprived of his fee.

The lawyer went on the train, that is what he did. That, no doubt, is what the possibly romantic, maybe philandering, certainly indiscreet Philemon Edgehill did. Why didn't he maintain a lady in Montpelier, if he had to maintain a lady somewhere? The answer seems to be, romance.

And yet, nobody is less like a figure of romance than a good lawyer, and I am sure Philemon Edgehill was a good lawyer, for if he had been an inadequate lawyer people wouldn't have so generally overlooked his social frailties. What I now assume is that Philemon Edgehill was a man of parts, a man, perhaps, who would have gone far in a community where there was more distance for a man to go.

Mrs. Ransome may really have called in Philemon Edgehill in the first place to settle questions arising out of her husband's will. Mr. Ransome's lumber business may have been, though I doubt it, too complicated for a woman to understand. The reason I doubt it is that my mother, my maternal aunt and my maternal grandmother never had any difficulty in understanding anything in the business line that was presented to them.

My grandmother, who in her young womanhood had taught school, used sometimes to catch sight of the town alcoholic weaving down Main Street on his way home. He used to do this on Sunday, after church, but nobody ever supposed he had actually been to church. My grandmother said she couldn't understand why the Lord should take so much trouble to keep Joe Simpson (which not only wasn't his name but didn't even faintly resemble it) from falling into barbed-wire fences or off bridges, but Joe never did; the Lord must have sent at least one of His apprentice angels along to keep an eye on him, so my grandmother thought. If the apprentice angel could protect Joe from disaster maybe the angel could be given more important work later on. Or maybe Joe, who was a good-hearted man when sober and not really mean when drunk, had some importance in himself. Maybe it was worth while to keep him out of fatal harm. My grandmother might reason that way, or might understand if I did.

My grandmother, however, was not a sentimental woman. She could sympathize with Joe, but she also believed that it was a strange thing that he should be permitted to vote, whereas she couldn't, nor could my mother or my aunt.

My grandmother, and also my aunt, did have advisers on their modest financial problems, but they called them in because they were experts, and not because they were males.

Maybe Mrs. Ransome started out the same way. Maybe she first summoned Philemon Edgehill because he was a lawyer believed to be skilled in estate matters, and then discovered, too late or just in time, according to one's point of view, that he was also a man.

Nobody, certainly, would have thought of Philemon as a man a woman would sacrifice everything for, nor of Mrs. Ransome as a woman for whom a man would give up or risk domestic happiness. Neither of them suggested blank verse. She was handsome but not in her first bloom, not trembling with a budding love; he was under medium height, adorned with an unimaginative moustache, under a short nose; he was beginning to grow bald; he had no flourish about him; he could not win one's passing attention by a twisted saying or an aged anecdote, the way Justin Moody could.

I could imagine men of Justin's type, if not precisely Justin himself, calling on some forbidden lady after dark, and making that lady, for a while, forget reality. But not Philemon Edgehill. Not, to this day, Philemon Edgehill. And yet, what happened, happened, whatever it was.

It was romance, indeed, for which I myself in my more than typically dumb adolescent way was seeking; I sought it all the more because I was so conspicuously unable to take a step toward it among the realities of my life; I sought romance when I shoveled coal into Harry Whitehill's heating plant; I sought it when the telephone operator upstairs in the *Record* building that Harry owned offered me the authorized ten cents for calling somebody to the phone, and I, because she was so pretty, so beautifully Irish, though I didn't tell her so, refused it; I sought it all over town, and tried to be enduring and valiant in case I found it and had to justify myself. For I believed one had to earn romance.

I read of it in Shakespeare and in Dickens, I detected it in poetry of a certain sort, Tennyson's verses included, I felt its nearness when the moon came over the Hogbacks and when the soft spring winds preceded the glimmering dawns in March; but I didn't see it, at least not until chance forced it upon me, in the apparent relationship of Mrs. Ransome and Philemon Edgehill.

But the very nearness of this phenomenon made it difficult to accept. When Tristan betrayed his king to woo Isolde, the episode, as I read about it, was admirable and lovely; but when Philemon Edgehill was late for dinner, as people said he often was, and the fried chicken got dry, and poor, tired Laura Edgehill sat by the stove thinning out the gravy with her tears, and that was what people said she did, and she was a good cook, too—that was not romantic.

I didn't suspect that sometimes, perhaps always, somebody got hurt wherever there was romance, and perhaps, as the older folks implied, it really wasn't worth the bother.

At this distance in time I understand that a lawyer in a country town must find some source of illusion; it may be sex, it may be drink, it may be fishing or getting ready for fishing, it may be playing cards and gambling, it may be going into politics and getting sent to the Legislature; but there does have to be something to take the lawyer's mind off being a lawyer in a country town—or in any town, unless he can somehow find in law a game and lure to keep him salty and passionate.

I ask myself, what did Philemon Edgehill have? He had a practice that kept his family well-housed, well-fed and well-clothed; he had a wife who may have cared little for him when he was readily available but who made appropriate noises and gestures when he was not; he had, in most regards, the respect of his fellow citizens.

"Don't you ever be like Philemon Edgehill," Justin Moody remarked one day as I came in from my paper route. Justin liked to unload a little philosophy on me when I was not too busy.

I gazed at Mr. Moody in surprise. Philemon Edgehill was the last man I would have expected to be like.

"Get married and stay married," pursued Mr. Moody. "Don't go running around like a tomcat after the tabbies."

It hadn't occurred to me to do either of these things. Marriage was something that would happen to me some day, I believed, like losing my hair or teeth or having colds in winter, but I didn't contemplate it.

I didn't even contemplate marriage with any of the numerous females I so ardently admired when I was seventeen and eighteen. I was never convinced that I would get anywhere if I asked anyone of them, let alone more than one, to be my lawful wedded wife.

"If you behave yourself," Mr. Moody was continuing, seemingly intent on making a good man out of me without further delay, "people won't talk about you the way they talk about Philemon Edgehill."

"I hadn't thought of that," I replied. I really hadn't. I didn't want to be or resemble Philemon Edgehill.

"You'd better think of it," Mr. Moody declared severely. "Now's the time to think of it, when you're young and innocent. Didn't they tell you, up at the high school, what makes babies?"

"That's in physiology, I guess," I replied. "I couldn't get to the physiology class because it came before I finished my paper route." My youthful pride brought a flush to my ears, for I believed Mr. Moody was making fun of me. "I guess I know, though," I said. "We boys talk about such things."

"And we girls, too," snickered Mr. Moody. "Only not when we boys are around. But you youngsters don't always understand how easy it is to make a baby you don't really need, when it's almost as if you were thinking of something else." He sighed heavily. "If you work hard enough," he resumed, with a swift change of manner, "you won't have to worry about babies. That is why I think you will be grateful to Harry Whitehill and myself after we are both gone." He inspected me contemplatively. "From all I can hear," he proceeded, "you're not much of a hand with the girls."

"I guess not," I conceded.

Justin Moody smiled wisely and shook a forefinger at me. "Don't you worry," he said. "You'll get over it. The thing to worry about is when you aren't afraid of girls. I would like to say to you what I would like to print in the columns of the *Waterbury Record* and *Stowe Journal* if the law allowed. I would like to say, look out, young man—girls will produce babies on the slightest provocation—and then where are you? I'll tell you where you are. You're out of town and not having any mail forwarded, or you're married when you'd rather not be."

"I guess that's so," I agreed. I knew of cases where the baby arrived a surprisingly short time after the wedding.

"You're a shy boy, Rob," continued Justin Moody. "At the same time you are able right now to produce babies if things happened that way. If I were you I'd stay shy for a few more years."

Justin Moody stroked his long burnsides in a characteristic

gesture. I wondered if he had ever been a shy boy. I also wondered what would happen to him, even now, if he ever crossed the path of Lilith, the town sorceress who had already caused one man's death—and maybe two. Even at his age, I thought—and he seemed as old as the hills.

"But," said Mr. Moody, "when you stop being shy get ready for trouble, a lot of it and for a long time. All the rest of your life, in fact. As I have often said to you, Rob"—and he often had—"man is born to trouble as the sparks fly upward." He looked so sanctimonious and self-satisfied as he said this that I could hardly imagine trouble that would really trouble him.

"I guess if people really love each other—" I began.

"It happens," Mr. Moody agreed. "I don't know as I ever saw it happen—outside of my own marriage, of course—but it can."

"Thank you, Mr. Moody," I said, after a pause.

"Not at all," Mr. Moody replied. He cleared his throat. "I guess you'll want to be getting on with your work," he said. "Nothing like work to keep your mind off those things. A good deal of work and outdoor exercise. Makes you sleep like a baby."

I would have liked to sleep like a baby until eight in the morning, or later, instead of waking up like an adolescent, in the employ of Moody and Whitehill, at half-past five.

But I went without further comment into the printing office and there fed some picture postcards of Lake Champlain into our smaller job press, at the rate of about eighteen hundred an hour. I pretended there were Indian canoes passing up that portion of lake shown on the picture side of the card. I imagined the Indians had a better time of it paddling canoes around than I did feeding cards into the job press.

I also thought of Mrs. Ransome and how she must have looked as a young girl when Mr. Ransome, the successful

lumber merchant, came courting her, and what they said to
each other; and whether Mr. Ransome and Mr. Edgehill had
looked alike, and what Mrs. Ransome and Mr. Edgehill did
when they had finished talking in the privacy of Mrs. Ransome's front parlor about Mrs. Ransome's investments.

3

I never found a completely satisfactory answer to my questions about Mrs. Ransome and Mr. Edgehill. I never found
answers to most of the questions that came to me during my
uneasy adolescence in Waterbury. I did, however, notice
what went on. I noticed it without trying, in the exercise of
my daily duties. I was supposed to distribute the out-of-town
newspaper morning and evening, and I did. And I was supposed to distribute one of my newspapers, the *Boston Globe*,
to Mrs. Ransome. I was supposed to throw it far enough up
on her front porch so that it wouldn't get rained on or snowed
on. I was supposed to do this, and I did. I was not supposed
to watch the comings and goings of Mrs. Ransome's visitors.
But I did. I couldn't help it.

I would occasionally meet Mr. Edgehill as he came out of
Mrs. Ransome's house. He did not come bounding out; he
walked with a sedate middle-aged step, and I noticed that
if he hurried a little he soon grew puffy. He did not look
ecstatic, nor desperate, but on the whole a little worried and
a little sad, as though he had eaten something that disagreed
with him.

He did not seem embarrassed if he encountered me, but
greeted me in an absent-minded way. It was just as though
he had come upstreet after the mail instead of downstreet
to talk over investments, or whatever it was, with Mrs. Ransome.

He wasn't Romeo at all, and I couldn't make him seem to
be so. Indeed, I hardly tried. Even William Shakespeare

couldn't have done much, I thought, to make Mr. Edgehill resemble Romeo. Who had erred, Mr. Edgehill or Mr. Shakespeare?

One evening Mr. Edgehill was coming down Mrs. Ransome's front steps as I arrived with the *Boston Globe*. He took the paper from my hand and carried it back to Mrs. Ransome, who stood looking after him in the open doorway. She thanked him, but he went away without another word that I could hear.

But I remember best a moonlit night when the town was deep in snow and tingling with cold. Mr. Edgehill passed me that time without noticing me. He had a sort of droop in his shoulders and the collar of his overcoat was turned up. He looked cold.

I wasn't quite at Mrs. Ransome's porch, and I saw her, half in profile, gazing after Mr. Edgehill's retreating form. He hadn't looked back; I wondered if she wanted him to.

I stopped. Somehow I didn't want to interrupt her, though at another time I might have gone forward and given her the paper. With the moonlight almost as bright as day on her, or so it seemed, she suddenly wasn't the daytime Mrs. Ransome at all; she was a lovely young girl again, her head held high. She seemed for an instant to be about to call after Mr. Edgehill, and her arms might have been reaching for him.

Then she clasped her hands swiftly over her breasts, in what I now believe the most beautiful of feminine gestures and must have so felt it to be then, to remember it so long. Yes, whatever the truth might be about Mr. Edgehill, I realized, Mrs. Ransome could have been Juliet.

After the door closed I took the paper from my bundle and slid it quietly across the porch, as though Mrs. Ransome were sleeping and I didn't want to wake her up.

Next evening she must have been on the lookout for me,

for she came to the door. "Rob," she said, "you gave me the *Boston Journal* instead of the *Globe* last night. Don't you ever do that again!" She laughed, and I knew she wasn't really angry at me.

But I promised I'd be more careful after that, and I was.

CHAPTER THIRTEEN

———◄••►———

Over the Hill to Waterbury Center

1

A T *ABOUT* this time I took refuge in culture. I did this, I suppose, from that excess of energy which might make a modern young man drive a hotrod car or spend his evenings with his peers down at the drugstore. But I don't really know why I wanted so much to be cultured—I just did. I think the dream of culture took the place of the dream of martial glory that I had had at an earlier stage in my evolution.

I read everything readable that I could lay hands on in the Waterbury Public Library, which then occupied one room (up over the bank, I believe) and was open once a week under the direction of one of my mother's old friends, Alice Smith. Alice Smith was the still-sprightly wife of the admirable "Arv" Smith of Smith and Somerville, hardware merchants, and the mother of a friend of my own, Joe Smith. Mrs. Smith suggested books to me but didn't pressure me. In this respect, she was a model librarian.

I read the whole of the *Lives of the English Poets.* I read *The Rise of the Dutch Republic.* I read almost all the plays of Shakespeare, though there were passages in some of them that I did not consider proper. I read G. A. Henty, but this was for fun, and Lewis Carroll, also for fun, and the boys' adventures of Castleman. I read the poetry of William Cullen Bryant, Henry Wadsworth Longfellow and John Greenleaf Whittier, partly because I liked it and partly because, like the sulphur and molasses we used to take in spring, I considered it good for me. I read more of Tennyson than I had to in high school, and a bit of Browning. I read Gulliver's Travels, not learning till later that it was a bitter satire on the human race; I read some of Stevenson; I read *Robinson Crusoe* and *Swiss Family Robinson;* I read a good deal of Dickens and Thackeray; I read until words should have dropped out of my ears.

It was my belief that at some future time, later defined as entrance into the freshman class at Stanford University, professors of literature would stand aghast at my learning. They never did, though some of them voted later to bestow the Phi Beta Kappa award on my brother and myself.

I tried to write some poems, not one line or word of which, I am happy to say, has survived. And once I met a real poet —or so I considered him, and this was just as good.

If I had been a real reporter, as I much later, to a certain extent, became, I would have been disillusioned about culture—or I would have pretended to be, for we journalists are really the most ingenuous of created beings. But in 1906 I was not a real reporter, I was an imaginary reporter, often dispatched to cover events that Harry Whitehill would not otherwise have considered worth covering. If he gave me an evening assignment he did not stand to lose much, for I was not paid to work in the evening. I loved to work in the evening on assignments interesting to me, but that was just Mr. Whitehill's good luck.

It was in this connection that I went to Waterbury Center in the spring of 1906, or thereabouts, to cover a lecture and reading by Will Carleton, the author of "Over the Hill to the

Poor House" and many other popular poems. This was after dark. It was quite an assignment, as I saw it, for it meant that Harry Whitehill was willing to pay the ten cents each way that it cost to go between Waterbury and Waterbury Center on the electric railroad. This was, I imagine, my first journalistic expense account. It gave me ideas which decades of experience could not erase; I still hope, after all these years, to be called into some discerning editor's office and asked to go to the Mountains of the Moon and charge everything, including the necessary snake-bite cure, to the paper.

But Mr. Whitehill did, I believe, give me twenty cents, to go and come on the electric cars. And twenty cents to Mr. Whitehill in the year 1906 was the equivalent, psychologically if not quite financially, of twenty thousand dollars today. Mr. Whitehill might make a lot of money in a short time but he did not throw it away at the same rate. He couldn't. That was not the way he had been brought up.

So there I was, a cultured young reporter—the way I looked at myself—assigned to go up to Waterbury Center on the electric railroad and report about a lecture and reading by a famous poet named Will Carleton. I was, for the evening, in the dark, a sort of dramatic critic. I was a hell of a young reporter, a Richard Harding Davis just out of the egg. I was, as we used to say, full of beans.

I should mention at this point that going up to Waterbury on the electric railroad, which continued from there to Stowe, was something of an exploit. A few years earlier the only way to get to Stowe, or even to Waterbury Center, if you didn't care to walk and couldn't afford a carriage (and there was a song about that which I hope somebody will ask me about some time), was in a stagecoach. I have seen that coach waiting for a train at the Waterbury depot. All it needed to make it really atmospheric was an Indian ambush up in the hills.

A year or so after my first sight of the stage I saw a parade on Stowe Street in Waterbury; this was in the dead of winter and the parade consisted of sleighs plastered with signs advocating and announcing the electric railroad. I remember the parade passing in front of the *Record* office, though I didn't work there then, and everybody hooting and hollering (as we said the word) and tooting on horns. A person would have thought that America had just been discovered or that the sap beer had been kept just long enough.

So there was an electric railroad, the stage went where all good stages go, and Stowe, which had some busy woodworking factories, could be reached easily in January, as well as in other months. However, few people who didn't have to reach it in January cared to do so.

Have fun in winter after the age of eighteen? The very thought, in that day, made people's blood run cold. Children slid down hill on sleds and barrel-stave jumpers—I had done that myself in more callow years—but they didn't ski. Grownups stayed indoors all they could, and if they went outdoors they made the worst of it.

But on the day I mention, which was the spring of 1906, the electric railroad that ran through Waterbury Center to Stowe was in the prime of life, and in the soft darkness I rode up to the Center.

I hadn't particularly noticed the only other passenger until he asked me if this was in fact Waterbury Center. I said it was, and he thanked me, and then I realized that I had touched the coat-tails of fame—this was Will Carleton himself, the poet, the lecturer I had come so far to see and hear.

2

I should have said, as soon as I recognized Mr. Carleton, "My name is Duffus and I am the correspondent of the

Waterbury Record and *Stowe Journal,* and how do you like Vermont, and what made you start writing your poems, and which of them is your own favorite, and is there anything I can quote you about, or on, and would you like to give the *Record* and *Stowe Journal* a sort of special message, an, as it were, exclusive?"

I don't know what would have happened if I had said something like this. Perhaps I would have realized that I was indeed a newspaperman. Perhaps the human interest story I would have written would have impressed Mr. Whitehill, who might have overruled Mr. Moody and raised my pay from six dollars a week to six dollars and seventy-five cents, or even seven dollars (but here I am indulging in the dangerous habit of daydreaming) a week. But I didn't say it. I didn't say anything. Mr. Carleton eyed me as though he would have been grateful for human company of any sort. Then he went forward and talked about the weather with the motorman. The motorman knew about the weather because he had been born on a farm near Mount Hunger and his grandfather had been able to predict rain several weeks ahead. That was what he told Mr. Carleton. The motorman said the weather was too good to last.

I examined Mr. Carleton carefully, even though I didn't interview him. He was at this time in his early sixties, which isn't young and isn't old, but often caused people to conserve their energies. Mr. Carleton, and I don't blame him, was not that night in a mood to pick up a new character for another poem. I don't believe he would have considered a motorman poetic, anyhow; a motorman or anything else, it seems to me, only begins to get poetic when it begins to get scarce.

When the trolley car stopped near the Seminary Building in which the meeting was to be held I waited for Mr. Carleton to get off, and then I got off. If I had written *Thanatopsis,* and I really had tried to write something even better than that somber masterpiece of a sixteen-year-old boy, I would have got off first.

So I followed Will Carleton into the former Seminary Building, which was, after a fashion, even more historic than Mr. Carleton.

Vermont in those times had a good many seminaries—or rather seminary buildings, for many of them, like the Green Mountain Seminary at Waterbury Center, had been emptied by the rise of the free public high school. Montpelier Seminary and Goddard Seminary at Barre were among the survivors. Some seminaries became junior colleges or even full-fledged institutions of the higher learning, but that was a long time after Will Carleton lectured in Waterbury Center.

I wondered that night, as I had before, what the Green Mountain Seminary had been like in its prime. It was a four-story brick building, in what I might venture to call Vermont Gothic, with well-worn stairs, and I pictured to myself the young people of a generation back running up and down those stairs. Were there shy young men then, and pretty girls to whom they hardly dared speak? What had become of all the shouting and the laughter?

I wished Mr. Carleton had written a poem or two about this subject, but as far as I knew he never had.

He had, however, written quite a few other poems that were eminently suitable for the thirty or forty people who had gathered to look at him and hear him. I don't know what they paid for this privilege, for I was enjoying that delightful journalistic immunity that enables one to walk in free where others have to dig into their pockets, or to walk in where the general public can't go at all.

I knew Mr. Carleton was a real poet, and not a make-believe one, for my grandmother had an illustrated volume of his poems and I had read them thoughtfully. I wish I had that volume handy at this moment. I find in looking back through various books of quotations that some of the fragments included in them bring back overtones of the whole. What these fragments can't bring back is my youthful conviction that if words are arranged in regular lines in a printed book they are poetry.

I believe "Over the Hill to the Poor House" was as well-known a set of verses as Will Carleton ever did. It broke my heart, and I suppose everybody else's, because it was a sort of tribute, in reverse, to mother love. Then, to make sure our hearts didn't stay broken, Mr. Carleton did a sequel, entitled, "Over the Hill *from* the Poor House."

Another that sticks in my memory was "Betsy and I Are Out"—and that had a surprise happy ending, too. From an old grammar-school reader I pick an aphorism that has clung long in my memory, though I had forgotten it was Carleton's, and didn't really need it, either: "Boys flying kites haul in their white-winged birds; You can't do that way when you're flying words." Will Carleton wrote about such simple things as leaving the "old house" (not the poor house in this case); about how money isn't everything; about the church choir and the new organ, which Waterbury folks could easily understand; in short, he was somewhere between the author of "Way Down East" and the author of "David Harum"— which, incidentally, I remember when it was first published.

Will Carleton could have been a novelist, I imagine, if the thought had occurred to him, and there would have been a little wholesome acid in his novels in addition to the sugar. He might have done well on radio if he had been born at the correct time, or on television, for he was a handsome man even after sixty, when I saw him, and had a pleasing voice.

I don't know just how he was getting along financially when he came over the hill to Waterbury Center that night to read his poems and talk about them. I felt then, and of

course am sure now, that if he could have filled a big hall
in Montpelier or Burlington, or better yet in Boston or New
York he wouldn't have traveled to the forlorn, semi-aban-
doned Green Mountain Seminary to talk to three dozen people or so, at least one of whom had come in on what show
people call an Annie Oakley.

But he was a good trouper and he did his best. I sat up
near the front so as not to miss a word, and I made notes of
what he read. Of course he read both of the poor-house
pieces, the first with enormous pathos, the second with a practiced rising lilt at the end. I suppose he also read "Betsy and
I Are Out," and the others I have mentioned. So there I was,
listening to a man who was speaking words that he himself
had written and that had been printed in a book. Could I
ever do that?

It hardly seemed possible. It was a kind of magic. Yet, behind the magic, he seemed sad and tired.

I began to wonder what it would have been like to hear
other famous writers: Shakespeare, Milton, William Cullen
Bryant, John Greenleaf Whittier, people like that. I thought
to myself, there must have been a time when Mr. Carleton
had gotten part way through "Over the Hill to the Poor
House," and not all the way through, so that nobody but
God and Mr. Carleton knew the rest—and maybe not even
Mr. Carleton, for he doubtless had to figure out what he was
going to say, just the way I did when I myself wrote what
I called a poem. There was the matter of getting a rhyme,
for instance; sometimes you had to choose between saying
what you really wanted to say and getting a rhyme that
would fit. As an amateur poet who had once tried to rhyme
bargain with chagrin, I knew the pitfalls.

But I speculated how it would feel to have written a few
poems, and have had them published in a book, and then get
up on a platform before an audience—a larger audience, I

would hope, than the one at the Green Mountain Seminary that night—and read them. Would I like that, or wouldn't I? Would the fun of being famous and rich outweigh the misery of having to speak in public? Or would I get used to it and not mind any more?

How did Will Carleton feel, deep inside, where nobody but himself ever went? You couldn't tell how Mr. Carleton was feeling, for he had the instincts of the stage and acted out each line and character. I saw him eyeing the audience soberly as he was being introduced, though I can't recall who did the introducing, but after that he went sailing up into the poetic clouds.

I imagine he thought his own verse was pretty good. I don't believe he ever wrote down to his public, or ever talked down to it when he did lectures and readings. He had a true, honest and homely character that suited the generation, the culture, and the place. He knew the life and the language of the people he was writing about and talking to. He wrote for the purpose of communicating, and not just to let off steam —though this was a distinction I had not then heard of.

He probably also made poetry pay, or had done so once. I hope he did, even if not that evening at Waterbury Center.

I am being as reasonable and detached as I can about Will Carleton, just as I would be about James Joyce if the years and other circumstances had considered to bring him to Waterbury Center in the spring of 1906 to read some of his poems for an approximate gate receipt, as I figure it, between ten and fifteen dollars. Will Carleton had something to say to the people to whom he wished to say it. James Joyce had something to say, too, I imagine, but Will Carleton didn't require footnotes. If a person couldn't understand Will Carleton the best and kindest thing to do was to carry that person gently back over the hill, from the Green Mountain Seminary at Waterbury Center to the Waterbury Insane Asylum.

I myself, at about the age of eighteen, understood Will Carleton, every word of him that I had read and heard. You couldn't get tripped up on double meanings, or ciphers, or mythological allusions, or Freudian undertones (and of course I hadn't heard of Dr. Freud at that time) when you studied Will Carleton.

Yet I believe, now, that Dr. Freud would have been interested in Mr. Carleton, if the two could have met and exchanged data. And I suspect that Dr. Freud might have concluded that Mr. Carleton was a well-adjusted American male (there was no doubt about his maleness) who had unhappily lived into a period when there was a declining market for his wares. Let us suppose that a man is well adjusted to the fireplace business and that the fireplace is displaced —dare I say, disfireplaced?—by the Franklin stove. It isn't the man's fault that this happened. Maybe he wouldn't even be normal, in the eyes of the late Dr. Freud, if he didn't experience a certain amount of early morning depression.

I didn't do any supposing, or conscious imagining, on the night Will Carleton spoke at the Green Mountain Seminary at Waterbury Center. Mainly, even at the age of eighteen, a journalistic fledgling with the moisture still damp on my pitiful wings, with many a weary year to go before ever I dared to call myself by that noblest of occupational titles, a newspaperman, I wanted to get a story out of Will Carleton. I wanted to, but I didn't, not really, not till now.

I felt that there was a story, and a story behind the story, but at that time I could not have written it, even if Harry Whitehill would have printed it. What Harry Whitehill wanted, and got, was a glowing description of a lecture that never occurred and a lecturer who never existed.

The program was over at last. I would have been willing to have it go on for another half hour, but of course Mr. Carle-

ton had been paid—and that night so poorly paid, so tragically underpaid—for the exact hour and a half he gave us.
A half-dozen of those present came forward to speak to him
when he had finished. They brought something an author
doesn't always receive, a testimony to the truth of what he
had been saying and reading. It was true, all right; it was in
a tongue understood of the people.

I felt then, I know now, that he had touched the chords
of life in New England small towns. I am not sure that he
himself, that night, in the face of that tiny audience, knew
how much and how well he had done. He hadn't any reason
to, that night.

But for one thing he had somehow managed not to disillu-
sion that boy who had read Shakespeare and Milton so
eagerly, who knew that "Over the Hill to the Poor House"
was not as good as Shakespeare or Milton, but who knew
also that the man was real and honest at heart. If that was
the way Will Carleton impressed me I am sure he struck
others similarly. He was maybe corrupted by his own facility
and by such commercialism as was available, but he had the
makings of a folk poet.

I wish I had been able to say these things to Will Carleton,
but I couldn't find the courage or even the words to say what
came into my mind at the time. I didn't think that anything
the young apprentice reporter from the *Waterbury Record*
and *Stowe Journal* could dig up would seem important to
such an important man. I was wrong, of course, and if Mr.
Carleton were within hearing, which he isn't, I would tell
him so.

The Green Mountain Seminary was lit by kerosene lamps,
for I don't believe the electricity from Bolton Falls had been
brought in there at that time. The lamps had a smell of hot
metal about them, produced by the tin reflectors. They also
had wicks, and the janitor, who could not have made much

money out of the Seminary job, had to trim the wicks. Therefore he was clearly impatient to get the meeting over and
let the speaker and his audience disappear. Fortunately for
the janitor, Mr. Carleton had to catch the last trolley to
Waterbury, just as I did. Today somebody would have run
him to the train or to Barre or Montpelier, or maybe Burlington, but in the spring of 1906 nobody was going to hitch up
a horse when a shiny new electric railway, the transportation
of the future, was available.

So Will Carleton and I were again passengers on the
trolley, with the same motorman and the same conductor
and perhaps one or two other passengers. I paid my ten
cents and I assume Mr. Carleton paid his ten cents.

Nobody said much on the short journey to Waterbury depot. Will Carleton sat with his chin on his coat collar, maybe
meditating a new poem and maybe, as I also suspect, wondering how fame came and went. He didn't look famous, he
looked discouraged.

At the end of the line I crossed over to the station platform behind the poet. The time was a little before eleven, a
late hour for me. I had wondered whether or not Will Carleton would spend the night in Waterbury, at the Inn. He
wasn't going to. He was going to take the midnight train,
he was going to escape, somewhere, into a world where hundreds and even thousands of people waited for his slightest
word.

He came into the yellow light of the waiting room, and I
came behind him. It was quiet in there, except for the click-
ing of the telegraph instrument in the little office, where the
agent was talking to somebody, or just listening, as he had
often explained to me, to what was passing up and down
the wires. I thought there could be a poem about that.

Will Carleton paused, looked around him and sighed. I
wanted to tell him something, I hardly knew what or why.

His eyes rested on me with a question in them, and I had to say at least a word or two. "Mr. Carleton," I began, "I enjoyed your lecture. I'm from the *Record.*"

"Oh, one of those newspaper fellows?" He smiled gently. He had been a newspaper fellow himself, when not writing or reading poems.

"I want to be, some day," I replied.

He shook his head deprecatingly. "Don't," he said. "But if you do I wish you luck."

"I'm sorry there weren't more people there," I continued. The poet's eyes lighted up briefly. "You were good to tell me," he said. "I never know, these days." He sighed deeply. "These days," he repeated. "Thank you, son."

I turned awkwardly away, but I looked back. The singer of country joys and of happy endings had sunk back into his hard seat, waiting for the midnight train. He looked as though he had gone over some melancholy hill from which he knew he would never return.

CHAPTER FOURTEEN

◄••►

Harry, Won't You Speak to Me?

1

*W*HEN John Franklin took the money from the bank he may have thought that if he borrowed it for a few days or weeks he could make more money with it and put it back. Doubtless he became frightened when he lost the first lot he stole, and then threw in more in order to get things straightened out right away. He didn't mean to keep the money, of that I am sure; he just meant to use it for a while, the way people did when they borrowed it in the usual way. Doubtless he lay awake at night, for many nights, and sweated the whole thing out.

I think he must have done this, for when I first heard the story I put myself imaginatively in John's place, and did some sweating myself. What would it be like, I wondered, to be a criminal and have jail waiting for me?

John, so they said, had been playing around with a bucket shop. What a bucket shop was I didn't know, except that it didn't have anything to do with buckets. I did know that people who played around with bucket shops hoped to get rich, but usually didn't. The theory was, and this much I understood, that you put money in stocks or whatever it was when they were low, and then sold when stocks or whatever it was were high. Harry Whitehill did that with land, and bragged of it, and praised himself for it, and so did everybody else who had the chance; I mean, they praised and admired Harry Whitehill and then tried to be as smart as he was. But bucket shops were not quite so respectable, and stealing from a bank was bad.

John Franklin was an extremely pleasant young man. His family background must have been good or he would not have worked his way up to be cashier of the Waterbury Bank and Trust Company. Everybody liked John Franklin. Everybody predicted a brilliant future for him. George Reynolds, the president of the bank, was getting along in years. When Mr. Reynolds—which was what we called him, not using his first name unless we knew him well—retired, John Franklin might succeed him. For this John would need a bit of money to invest in the bank's stock, but he might save some of that and give his note for the rest; it was his character that was important.

From today's high plateau of prices and salaries the bank presidency wasn't much of a plum, but it had honor and respect and enough to live on connected with it. We respected bankers more than we did lawyers, almost as much as we did doctors, and a good deal more than we did the general run of business men.

The president of the bank was almost as good as Senator Dillingham, in the public estimation, though of course not so famous outside of Waterbury. He deserved it, too. George Reynolds, it was generally agreed, down to the day of his death, wouldn't have stolen a pin—if he had found a pin on the sidewalk in front of the bank, which was on the right hand as you came up from the depot, he would have taken it inside and waited for somebody to claim it. Or maybe he would have advertised it in the *Record*.

George Reynolds was a man I revere to this day, for his native intelligence, his built-in integrity, and his total inability to do anything wrong. I can shut my eyes and see him in his old age (as I did some years later): white-bearded like an Elizabethan statesman, dignified, kindly, full of wisdom even after his memory began to fail.

The only fault Mr. Reynolds had, so the Waterbury community at last concluded, was that he was too trustful of young John Franklin. Mr. Reynolds had children of his own, and he seemed to add John to the collection. He looked on John with a protective and paternal eye. He never seemed to have for John the envy that the elderly and aging often do have for those who are expected to succeed them.

And John Franklin appeared to return the affection. I never went into the bank to deposit or take out cash, but sometimes I entered to hunt, in my mild way, for news, and I saw the two men, the old and the young, together. They liked each other, that was evident. They also trusted each other, which was also evident.

I suppose the fact that George Reynolds trusted him was the final twist of the thumbscrew when John Franklin lay awake, in the treacherous darkness, hoping that better news would come from wherever that bucket shop was, and wondering what he would do if it didn't.

My grandmother, mother and aunt, when all had been finally revealed, said that John Franklin had been unkind to Mr. Reynolds, whom they knew and loved, but that John couldn't have thought this up all by himself. They said there must have been men in town—and they mentioned names —who encouraged poor John to take the money, and told him how to work it, and hoped, in some way I didn't understand, to make a profit out of it.

Though I will not use the names, even now, as I write some of them are still in my mind. They were not bad men. Some of them gave a large part of their time and strength to the service of the town. What they hated, I imagine, was to see money invested at four, five or six per cent, which was reasonable and safe in those days, when you could make a killing in the market and double your investment overnight. Maybe. Theirs was a sort of New England thrift gone wrong.

We were getting into the day when muckrakers were taking a long look at American business and finding much of it unethical. At about this time, in fact, Theodore Roosevelt was romping around in the Presidency, the American socialists were considered foolish but as harmless as gazelles, we hated anarchists because one of them had shot McKinley but we didn't know what they were, and there was a kind of unrest that may have upset a good many men in Vermont who always voted Republican, but were not quite sure, in 1906, ridiculous as it may now seem, that this was the best of all possible worlds.

There was one New York financier who wrote a number of scorching articles about Wall Street for a muckraking magazine. He seemed, for a while, to have reformed. Once he was traveling through New England on a special train, and Mr. Whitehill sent me down to the depot to cover an announced stop at Waterbury. Unhappily for me, he passed up the stop. The train flew through Waterbury like a bat out of hell, and I had no interview with whoever it was. I can't recapture the name.

The circumstances were such, however, that borrowing a little money illegally from a bank may not have seemed altogether wrong to some of our local citizens, especially since they honestly hoped to pay it back. So John Franklin did "borrow" the money, and took the rap for it.

The local citizens remained local and did not take the rap, unless it was a sort of punishment for them to be talked about behind their backs in unflattering ways. There wasn't any proof against them, at least not any proof that was brought out in the trial. And it was true in Waterbury in 1905, as perhaps it is in some communities today, that the real crime isn't in what you do but in going to jail.

John Franklin went to jail.

2

We didn't have the kind of courts in Vermont then, and perhaps don't have them today, that ask why a crime was committed. What the court asked in John Franklin's case was whether a crime had been committed.

To say that older men who were pleasantly entertaining themselves by putting their money into the bucket shops persuaded John Franklin to put some of the bank's money into the same game didn't really answer the question, why? If the older men thought it worth while to test John Franklin on this point they must have detected some weaknesses— some reasons why—in John himself.

For the life of me, on the facts I knew then and know now, I am not sure what John's weaknesses were. I can guess that he liked to dress well, but that didn't take much money in Waterbury in 1905. A clean collar and an occasional shoeshine, applied at home, were all that was really necessary; and the higher the collar the more stylish the wearer seemed.

I can also guess, and maybe I am getting closer to reality, that John liked to be with some of the older men in town, and was flattered when they began to pay attention to him and sometimes ask his opinion. I assume that his origins were modest, because if they hadn't been I would have known his pedigree right back to the settlement of the town, at the end of the eighteenth century, right after the War of Independence. He might have come from Mad River or Bolton or Underhill or Stowe, or some such place or region. His name—his real name—suggested that he was of native stock, but even native stock ran to seed sometimes. Maybe John's stock had run to seed, and then was sprouting again.

Maybe John had been taught, in Sunday School or at his

mother's knee, that it is a good thing for a young man to listen to the wisdom of those older than himself. Maybe he believed in miracles; maybe he thought that if solid citizens were willing to discuss with him the facts of life he should listen; maybe he had been persuaded that the Waterbury Bank was too conservative in its investment policies; maybe, as his ambition grew, he saw himself an important figure, first in Waterbury, then in some larger community.

I can't recall a thing about John's personal life. He went about town smilingly greeting people he knew, which was almost everybody. He attended the Methodist Church, I think, though he didn't sing in the choir. No doubt he boarded somewhere, as a young man in Waterbury without any family had to do. This may have been at the Waterbury Inn, but I don't think so; the Inn came into his life later on.

There were several boarding houses in Waterbury. I recall one that was run by a most respectable widow named Mrs. Lee. The only thing I ever heard about Mrs. Lee that made me glad I didn't board in her house was that when she made one of her excellent rice puddings with raisins in it she bit the tips off the raisins in order to get the seeds out. She was reported to have remarked that she did this in order to spare the boarders' teeth. Later, of course, some genius contrived to do it by machinery, but Mrs. Lee didn't bother with that kind of labor-saving.

I believe there was another boarding house on the same street, but I never cared much for that one, either, because it was said that a woman had worked herself to death there sewing for a living, night and day, and that her ghost, having got the habit, came back there nights; and you could hear the poor thing running the sewing machine. I never actually heard this, but I thought I did, and that was just as bad. Maybe John Franklin was also afraid of ghosts of one sort or another.

John may also have boarded in one of those eating places where the robust and pretty farm girls who worked in the wrapper factory took their meals. If this were the case he might have been attracted to one of those girls, and eager to make money in a hurry and marry her. If one of them had become pregnant with his assistance the case would naturally have been simpler, but I never heard anybody mention this possibility; and in the Whitehill store and shop I did, first and last, hear a good deal.

My mind also goes back to the woman I have previously mentioned as Lilith, who seemed to go away after each tragedy she had caused, but who also seemed to come back from time to time. My mind dwelt a good deal on Lilith.

It is unfair to the memory of John Franklin—for though he may still be alive I imagine he is dead—to say that Lilith induced him to take money from the Waterbury Bank and invest it, if that is the right word, in a bucket shop. Yet I prefer to think of John as suffering for the love of a woman, even a bad woman, than as being hoodwinked by a group of middle-aged males who wanted to take a flyer in the market at somebody else's expense and risk.

But when John Franklin was tried—in Montpelier, not in Waterbury—no mention was made of Lilith or of any other woman, not even of a pregnant farm girl from the wrapper factory.

We did those things in a delicate and tasteful way in Waterbury, and I suppose throughout Vermont, in those days. To have opened up the whole case of John Franklin might have carried us beyond the bounds of propriety; the grand jury and the prosecuting attorney would have had to turn too bright a spotlight on an entire community, on all its standards and all its hopes, on the Vermont Character itself.

The Court had to stick to the personal guilt of John Frank-

lin, who had done what was against the law and had to be
punished in order to discourage other young men from doing
what was against the law. Lilith did not figure; she was not
in the indictment.

John Franklin, therefore, was duly tried, on the abundant
evidence that he had taken money from the Waterbury Bank,
and not on any data as to causes for his act, whether personal
or of wider application. The available evidence was enough,
and he was duly convicted. Because he was such a pleasant
young man, and truly sorry that he had inconvenienced the
bank's trustees and depositors and made it necessary for the
admired, respected, and completely honorable bank president to resign, John received a light sentence. It was, as I
recall, a year in the State penitentiary.

Some middle-aged citizens of Waterbury may have
breathed a sigh of relief when the verdict was rendered
and the sentence announced, and no embarrassing evidence
called for. I don't suppose Lilith breathed any kind of sigh,
for she was probably off on a new pursuit by this time—if,
indeed, and to be fair to her, she had ever been on the trail
of young John Franklin.

John Franklin thereupon disappeared, for a while, from
Waterbury. We heard that he had been given a job in the
bookkeeping department of the prison, and everybody
thought how pleasant this was for him, because he wasn't
really wasting his time.

3

The year that passed after that was as short as most years
in Waterbury, no matter how long it may have seemed to
John Franklin. The bank got a new president and a new cashier. People said that the new president wasn't any more
upright than George Reynolds—nobody could have sur-
passed Mr. Reynolds in uprightness—but that he was a heap

tougher. As for the new cashier, he was also newly married, lived on his salary, such as it was, and was not too respectful of those of his elders who believed in bucket shops. When I went into the bank after that I always felt like a suspicious character. The place just wasn't as homey and easygoing as it had been.

I don't know whether or not the bank's depositors lost anything, in the long run. In the end they may have been paid back, for although an individual Vermonter might now and then go wrong Vermont as a whole did not go wrong; a debt was a debt, and except for legal bankruptcies all debts were paid. John Franklin couldn't pay the money back, of course, because he didn't have it—the men who ran the bucket shop had the money, and didn't see any reason for giving it back.

So the year went by, like all years, rapidly for some, slowly for others. It was, I believe, one of my slow years, so much happened to me, yet I waited impatiently for it to end.

I used to try to imagine what it was like for John Franklin to wake up in prison, after dreaming, maybe, that he was free and guiltless again, and going into the wood for mayflowers with some girl he loved; I wondered what it was like to wake up and be a prisoner and have to take orders, I wondered how it hurt, and where.

I gave a good deal of thought to John Franklin. I reflected that if the bucket shop had bucketed up instead of down John might have been a well-to-do man and put the money back into the bank and kept the profit, and been much respected. I wondered if there had ever been a cashier in the Waterbury Bank, or anybody else in Waterbury, who had taken such a chance—and won instead of losing. And if some men had done so, did the fact that they won instead of losing make them honest men?

I thought about luck and what it did to people. This was

wrong of me, because I had been told, in school and elsewhere, that if I behaved properly and did my work well, and
thought of my employer's welfare rather than my own, I
would probably rise in the world.

Some Waterbury boys had, indeed, risen in the world. I
recall one former Waterbury boy named Dan Richardson.
He had gone into some enterprise in some big city where his
abilities were soon recognized, and when he came back for
a visit to Waterbury—usually about once a year—people
said, look at Dan Richardson, he has a ten-thousand-dollar
salary. To make the story even better, Dan was an agreeable
man—and, as I subsequently noted, being modest and agreeable is one of the ways in which some men get ahead in the
world, whereas the other and often faster way is to be im-
modest and disagreeable. So everybody liked Dan, in spite
of his being so rich. People said he was the same old Dan he
had always been. The only thing he wouldn't do, and this
might have given us something to think about, was to come
back to Waterbury and settle down at twenty-two dollars
and fifty cents or so a week.

There were other Waterbury boys who had risen in the
outside world. One of them, Guy Boyce, had gone to work
for the Vermont Marble Company in Proctor, and had done
well. Other Waterbury boys followed, often with Guy's generous help and encouragement, but not all of them had the
patience to wait and grow up with the company. One of
these, my brother William, may not mind my saying that he
went to California, worked his way (as I did, imitating him
as well as I could) through Stanford University, and eventually became a college professor—a good one, as many dis-
interested persons said.

John Franklin might have risen in our Vermont world, or
the outside world, but what happened to him was that he
went down in the world. It seems to me now that his trouble

was not that he was deliberately sinful but that he was imprudent. Was he more wicked than the Waterbury boys who made good, or was he merely less wise?

However, for being sinful or for being imprudent or for not having the advice he needed at the time he needed it, John paid the due penalty, and put in his year in the bookkeeping department in the State Penitentiary. What would he do at the end of that year? Everybody asked that question. Why not go out west and start all over again? One could still do that, or so we thought in 1906. And it would have been less embarrassing to his friends.

But John Franklin didn't go west—not at first, certainly. He came home. How can I make plain to anybody today what it was that made John Franklin come home? Waterbury was a town much more worldly wise than my former town of Williamstown. It had an insane asylum, as I have said, it got the Boston newspapers as well as those from Barre, Montpelier, and Burlington, it had, in one or two houses, even before I left, modern plumbing, complete with a wire to pull, it had a good high school, and, again before I left, it had electric lights in the street and in some houses.

But it remained Waterbury, a town with traditions and legends and people who wouldn't lightly abandon their old friends, and because of this and in spite of everything else, John Franklin seems to have loved his home town. He came back after his term in the penitentiary, just as Harry Whitehill, an adopted resident, remained in spite of his encounter with Lilith, or whoever she was.

4

John Franklin came back, with what misgivings I don't know. The proprietor of the Waterbury Inn apparently believed that John had learned his lesson, and it was announced quietly, in a carefully buried item in the *Waterbury Record*, that John would be desk clerk at the Inn. The desk clerk's main function was to be pleasant and remember names, and John Franklin, in the old days—the days of a year and a half earlier, before he had even been suspected of embezzling the bank's funds—could do both these things. It was a natural gift with him, though not especially useful in the State Penitentiary.

The Inn's customers would include some regular boarders, such as the granite-cutter who took the *Boston Globe* and the *Boston Journal* but never paid for either of them except after weeks of pressure. They would include some drummers—many more of them, of course, than used to come to my former home village of Williamstown. In summer a few vacationists might arrive, but not many.

Mr. Whitehill tried to build up the vacation business in and around Waterbury. One thing he did was to get out an illustrated booklet for which I wrote the text. I hope no copy of this document survives, for my recollection is that the language was of the finest tradition of the Grub Street hacks of the middle eighteenth century. I know I assured the possible (but improbable) readers that Waterbury was a fine spot for the ornithologist, the horticulturist, and the ichthyologist (yes, I did—the words come back to me sometimes on nights of sleeplessness and guilt), and I might as well admit that I stated that our sunsets were unmatched elsewhere in the world.

My booklet caused gentle mirth in some of the newspapers with which the *Record* exchanged, and it may have been at about that time that I decided that possibly short words and uncomplicated sentences (not always short ones) were best. But I may have had something to do with helping the Inn's business; I may have made some strangers wonder what was going on in our little community, and whether our publicity was being written inside or outside the Waterbury State Insane Asylum.

I suppose John Franklin settled down at the Inn as soon as he returned. There wasn't anywhere else for him to settle down. I saw him before Mr. Whitehill did, as I came through the Inn one afternoon on my way up from the depot with the Boston papers.

John Franklin smiled at me, a twisted kind of smile, and looked at me, and then looked away. I was as much embarrassed as he was, though I hadn't stolen any money from the bank, and hadn't been in jail.

"How are you, Rob?" he asked.

"Fine," I said.

"You've been growing," said John, a little more easily.

"That's what they say," I answered. I studied the registration book, turning it around to read it. "Any items today?" I asked, for this was my duty.

"I've taken this job over," said John hesitantly. "If you want to print it."

I nodded. "Of course we do. Mr. Whitehill mentioned it." This wasn't true. Mr. Whitehill hadn't mentioned it, not to me. "Is there anybody from out of town?"

"There's me," John retorted, with a sudden savagery that died down immediately. "Maybe some others."

He turned the book around and studied it in his turn. Somebody came in at the front door, and I saw his face turn red. I knew the sensation, for pretty girls always brought out this symptom in me, and the prettier they were the deeper the hue.

It wasn't a pretty girl this time, though. John could deal with a pretty girl as well as the next man. At least, he had once been able to, before his trouble.

I went along back to the *Record* office. Next morning Mr. Whitehill came in, mopping his forehead, though it wasn't an especially warm spring day. "Guess who I saw just now," he said to Mr. Moody.

"President Roosevelt," replied Mr. Moody, who was in a happy mood. "President Roosevelt out hunting bears."

Mr. Whitehill did not laugh. "John Franklin," he replied. "I was coming over the Stowe Street bridge, and there he was, sort of strolling along." Mr. Whitehill gasped as though he were out of breath. "I was thinking of something else," he went on. "And, anyhow, I thought John would be down at the Inn, not up this way. So I was just going by, and he spoke first."

"What did he say?" asked Mr. Moody, picking his teeth thoughtfully.

Mr. Whitehill's voice trembled. He spoke slowly. "He said, 'My God, Harry, won't you speak to me?'"

"So you did?" Mr. Moody gazed reflectively out the window, spat daintily and smiled at some lady going by, I didn't see whom.

"I did," replied Harry Whitehill, almost defiantly. "I'd have felt like a skunk if I hadn't."

The two men looked at each other for a long moment, as though they were sharing a secret they would not reveal to me.

"Damn it," cried Mr. Whitehill, "there've been days in this town when I'd have been grateful to have Joe Simpson speak to me, drunk or sober." He needn't have indicated a choice, for Joe was never sober, except when his supplies gave out.

"I guess you knew how he felt," commented Justin Moody, his eyes resting expressionlessly on his son-in-law's face. "However, you never robbed the bank."

"I never had the chance," said Mr. Whitehill slowly.

"Not directly," mused Mr. Moody, looking out the window again, and absentmindedly flapping a hand at a friend.

"He paid for what he did," said Mr. Whitehill. "I'm not going to keep on dunning him." He turned and retired to

(201)

his little office, hustling less than usual.

Sometimes I felt that Harry Whitehill was a fake and a make-believe, for all his blarney and all the courage he had shown after that early disgrace. But on this day of which I am writing I thought he was something of a saint and a hero, too, which perhaps he also was.

As for John Franklin, he didn't stay at the Inn long, nor long in Waterbury. I wish I knew the rest of the story.

CHAPTER FIFTEEN

A Walk Through the Woods

1

*O*NCE during that last year in Waterbury a young traveling man representing a new sort of educational institution, the correspondence school, came into the
Record office. After placing an advertisement, he caught
sight of me and a gleam came into his eye.

Harry Whitehill explained why I was there and mentioned
that I had just graduated from high school. "Just the man I
want to talk to," said the salesman.

I liked being called a man, for I wasn't yet sure on that
point. "I'm going to college," I said.

"A laudable ambition," the salesman acknowledged. "However, while you're waiting . . ." He unfolded an imposing
set of documents. He could, he said, make me an engineer, an
architect, a certified public accountant and I don't know what
else—maybe a sea captain or a lawyer—in a few easy les-
sons.

I said I wanted to be a journalist, and did his company
have any courses in journalism? Some of his joviality immediately vanished. His company couldn't make a journalist, though he had to admit, standing there as he did in the
presence of a successful newspaperman, that mine was a
lofty ambition. If I changed my mind and decided to become
one of the other sorts of characters he could pick out of his

hat I could still let him know.

Strangely enough, it did not then occur to me that when I gathered items for the *Record,* or reported a basketball game for the *Burlington Free Press* (I almost always pointed up my otherwise dull stories by accusing the visiting team of playing rough), or attended an inquiry at the Insane Asylum, or dropped in awestrusk and tongue-tied at some bereaved home to find out dates of birth and marriage, surviving relatives, nature of illness and plans for funeral service and interment, I was after my fashion studying journalism.

The same with town and village meetings; or the railway accident when the freight train plunged into the washout, with four men riding in the engine cab; or a lecture or two, as when Senator Dillingham visited Alaska and came home to tell us all about it; or what might be called a rudimentary form of dramatic criticism, which consisted of saying good things about traveling minstrel shows or stock companies in return for advertisements and free tickets.

I remember more about these things than I was ever encouraged to write about them. I listened carefully to the oratory in the Town Hall, and it wasn't much, if any, worse than some I later heard in Congress.

I saw the dingy finery of parading troupers along our two principal streets and in spite of my theoretical craving for a wandering and adventurous life found pathos in it—they were so shabby and so brave.

I wrote a column about Senator Dillingham's Alaska speech, most of it in direct quotes, without making a single note—I was too modest to attract attention to myself in that way—and the Senator came into the *Record* office next day to tell Mr. Whitehill and myself that he liked it. And I remember when the Senator was re-elected and in writing up the celebration that followed I managed to suggest that in another two years or so he might become President. (He did not.)

The wreck stayed a long time in my memory. In fact, it is still there, in a series of vivid mental photographs. I remember what the shapes of the dead men looked like, laid out under blankets in the railway station, and the sorrow of the wet clothes they had worn, carefully wrung out and piled on the benches beside them. They would have new clothes to be buried in. The station agent had said that the undertaker had given directions that under no circumstances were the coffins to be opened—so why did it matter? But it did matter, I could see that. The wives would want to know that their men, though dead and mutilated, had been treated with respect.

Not so many hours before, after the all-day and all-night rain, the four men had been warm and cosy in the cab, and then the engineer, and the other three of them, must have looked for a long moment at death as the locomotive rounded a sharp curve in a deep cut and there was roaring brown water where track should have been.

The rear brakeman, lonesome in the caboose, knowing only that the train had suddenly stopped, ran back with his lantern and his fusees to flag any possible train behind. After a long wait he walked forward, beside the cars, not on their tops, to see what the matter was.

Some things I saw and thought about and did not write about. I rode in the cab of the wrecking train to where the four men had died and the one man had survived, and I saw the locomotive and a tangle of freight cars in the gorge, and on the other side the rest of the train, waiting with a kind of confident animal patience, like cars in a safe and humdrum railway yard, to be hauled away.

How could I write that for Harry Whitehill? I couldn't, of course. Maybe I couldn't have written it at all, for anybody. Maybe then I could merely feel it, as I appear to have done.

A big wrecking-foreman, losing patience with the time it took a workman to saw off the end of a rail and make it fit into the new piece of track, snatched up a giant sledgehammer and with one blow struck off the half-sawed piece of metal. He was showing off, but it worked.

There was a sort of fury in the way the wreckers did what they had to do, with oaths I never heard before but, I suppose because their friends had died, without laughter.

Toward sundown on the day I am speaking of, the engine of the wrecking train ran down to Waterbury station, and again I rode in the cab, just as I had once done, eight years ago, with Mr. Webb of Williamstown. But I was eighteen now, not ten years old, and the engineer, deep in whatever thoughts railway men have about fatal wrecks, was not in a playful mood. But he didn't have to worry about his signals and right of way; there would be no trains that night coming down from Essex Junction and no train, except the kind of train that is made of mist and memories, coming up behind from Montpelier Junction. The wrecking train had that division of the Central Vermont that night all to itself, and nobody spoke of ghosts, not that night, in that cab.

I would have liked to write all this for Mr. Whitehill and the *Record*—or for somebody, somewhere, to get it out of my system, to forget those huddled bodies under the blankets, and the wet clothes piled beside them, and the imagined sound of weeping. But that wasn't the way the game of journalism was played at that time in Waterbury. It couldn't be. There was no room for the whole truth. So what I wrote was something like this:

A Central Vermont wrecking crew has been at work clearing the track and building a new bridge at the site of the recent fatal wreck below Middlesex. Service is expected to be resumed next week. The promptness with which this work has been done has caused favorable comment.

As will be seen, I editorialized the news, which was wrong by standards I later learned. But I was, all unbeknown to myself, studying journalism, and after this long time I write another portion of the story. I would have made it longer and more detailed, but unfortunately I cannot offer it to Mr. Whitehill or to the *Record*, both being dead and gone.

The widows I never saw but of whom I thought for a long time afterwards, especially at night, will have forgotten by this time, too.

2

The town was just the place in which to study journalism. The town was full of stories. All towns, then as now, are and were full of stories, some of which can be printed and should be, and others of which cannot and should not be printed. Mr. Whitehill, like all good editors—and in his way and in his day he was one—was careful about the latter. It was from him I learned that what has not been published can be published, but that what has been published can never be unpublished, not to the last day of earth's history.

If an early-morning caller went to see a middle-aged friend about some business, and the friend, opening the kitchen door, lantern in hand after doing his chores in the barn, clutched his throat and tried to say something, and then pitched forward dead at the visitor's feet the essential facts might be recorded. But what were the essential facts? What had the dead man been trying to say? Could it have been a message to his mother, with whom he had quarreled about some property and hadn't spoken to for three years? The *Record* would not speculate about such matters. It would, however, mention that the mother was at the funeral. A little later the terms of the will might be published. And that would be all. The realities of the story would run from lip to ear around the town, but never would they be seen in cold type.

If a well-known business man drove his horse onto an un-protected crossing of the electric railroad that ran to Stowe, and this man was killed, the fact would be stated in the *Record* and *Stowe Journal* but no puzzling questions would be asked—not in print. It happened to be an open crossing, with wide visibility in both directions.

If anybody built a house, or an addition to a house, or so much as a chicken coop, that was news and would be pub-lished. Behind this incident might be new money from some-where—an inheritance or unexpected prosperity in business or the kind of lucky gamble Mr. Whitehill indulged in when he bought land from a native and sold it to some characters from Boston. But the *Record* wouldn't be curious as to where anybody's money came from.

Will Boyce, father of my good friend Earl Boyce, built a house with a regular flush toilet in the bathroom. He could do this because he was a successful furniture dealer but more particularly because he was a diplomatic and well-liked un-dertaker. The new house was news, but nobody would say in print that Will would have had to wait a while longer if it hadn't been for the deadly epidemic of grippe and pneu-monia that swept the town that winter. We had to have an undertaker, and Will Boyce was a good and kindly one, whom we all trusted to treat us fairly in our hour of need. Of course he had to charge for what he did so well, and what many men wouldn't have liked to do, and nobody begrudged him his new house with the flush toilet.

So there was news always happening, some kinds of news getting into print and others, usually far more interesting, being kept carefully out of print. I learned about journalism from both kinds of news.

What I liked best to write was what I later learned were called feature stories or human-interest stories. I don't know

why it was, but I didn't do many crime stories. I don't recall
being in court to take notes on a criminal case. I knew the
sheriff's name, but I don't remember the name of any judge.

Much later in my career I learned a little at first hand
about civil and criminal courts, but I don't think I even
heard about a divorce case in Waterbury. Waterbury people
usually assumed that once they were married they stayed
married, whether they liked it or not, until death did them
part.

As for the general run of legal doings, I often heard one
man say to another, "I'll have the law on you," but it wasn't
often that anybody did.

But human interest existed in Waterbury, as it did, and
does, everywhere that human beings draw out their troubled
and picturesque lives.

3

On South Main Street, on the northwest side, not far from
C. C. Warren's General Grant mansion and the Insane
Asylum, there stood in 1906 one of those nondescript frame
houses which weren't ugly and certainly weren't beautiful.
This one had been built after the waning of the jigsaw period
and was therefore pleasantly plain in its outlines, but it had
been built too late to catch any colonial or early Republican
influence, and therefore had no particular character. It resembled, in a fashion, the simple, unspectacular people who
lived in it.

It possessed a front porch extending across the whole
width, with the front door on the right and the curtained
windows of the parlor on the left. A stranger wouldn't have
remembered it fifteen minutes after he saw it for the first
time, and few of us would have noticed if it had been removed overnight and another building substituted for it.

Yet it came to have, for me, a kind of romance—not the

romance I felt inherent in a house where a certain extraordinarily pretty girl lived with her extraordinarily ordinary parents, but a romance arising out of a true story. A little story, indeed, without surprise or suspense, but one I never could forget.

I had gone to this house on an assignment from Mr. Whitehill to get some information about the golden wedding anniversary of the couple who lived there. The year was as I said, 1906, and therefore the original wedding must have taken place in 1856.

I am not sure of the couple's name, but I will call them Wilson for convenience. I seem to recall that Mr. Wilson was a carpenter, or had been during his working days.

The Wilsons were not, at any rate, prominent citizens. Such prominence as they had would have come from being married so long and having enough to live on in their old age. Mr. Whitehill said he wished I would find out something about their golden wedding anniversary. He said he thought this would please them and their friends, and it wasn't everybody who stayed alive and married that long. He thought this small item wouldn't take enough time to make me late for my paper route, or with the work he had laid out for me to do when I got back to the *Record* office.

I don't know how much time it took, but it was a time I still live over now and then.

Mrs. Wilson came to the door when I rang, and I explained why I was there. She was a faded woman, with dim blue eyes and white hair, smiling uneasily, so that for once it was I who was free from embarrassment and the other who was under some constraint. People just love to talk about themselves, Mr. Whitehill frequently assured me. They also hate to talk about themselves, I concluded; each wishes to make a picture and each is afraid he'll say or do something that will blur and soil the image.

I tried to reassure Mrs. Wilson, as she stood holding onto the door jamb. "It's about the golden wedding anniversary," I explained. "Mr. Whitehill wants to print something about it."

The pale blue eyes brightened. "About us? We wouldn't care for anything like that. We're not very interesting." But she evidently did want something like that. "He's in the sitting-room," she went on. "He isn't doing much these days. He's feeling poorly. He'll have lots of time to talk to you."

"I want to talk to both of you," I answered quickly.

Mrs. Wilson shrugged her thin shoulders and led me into the other room. Mr. Wilson, smoking his pipe, greeted me amiably. They looked a little alike, I thought. "You'll excuse me," Mr. Wilson said. "I've got some rheumatism. It's hard to get up."

"I guess we're neither of us as spry as we used to be," observed Mrs. Wilson. She dusted imaginary dust from a chair with the end of her apron and motioned me to sit down.

I asked a few diffident questions, which had at least the merit of not scaring the Wilsons into silence. When and where had each been born? How had they met? What was the name of the minister who married them? Where were their children? One or the other answered without hesitation all the questions except the last. On this one they paused.

"Well," Mr. Wilson finally replied, "you see, there weren't any. Mother here—" He used the word with a touching inflection.

"I wasn't well—" Mrs. Wilson began and stopped.

He reached over to pat her hand. "I'd rather have you, if the choice had to be made. And I guess it did. The doctor said so."

"Was it Dr. Janes then?" I asked.

They both nodded. "That was before he went to the war. He was a very young man then." Mr. Wilson glanced at his wife. "But we trusted him, just the way folks do today."

"He's our doctor, too," I said.

A silence followed. "There's happiness and unhappiness in being married fifty years," Mrs. Wilson volunteered, as though the thought had just struck her. She glanced sidewise at her husband. "Isn't there, David?"

He nodded. You couldn't put this sort of thing into the *Waterbury Record,* I knew, but it was real.

"Jennie," said Mr. Wilson suddenly, "do you remember our wedding trip?"

"Do I?" The sheen of an old mischief came over her face. "Would I forget?"

Mr. Wilson turned to me. "I bet you couldn't guess where we went."

"Boston, perhaps," I hazarded.

He chuckled. "I thought you wouldn't. We went to Niagara Falls. Lots of young married people did in those days. Everybody on the train seemed to know we were just married. Funny, isn't it? They always do."

"They wouldn't have if you'd behaved yourself," retorted Mrs. Wilson, smoothing down her apron.

"What's the use of being married if you have to behave yourself?" He glared at her with mock indignation. "What do you suppose I married you for?"

Her eyes shone softly. She didn't look old at all, if you didn't scrutinize her too carefully. "Do you remember?" Her voice was soft, and she seemed almost to have forgotten my presence. "We got off the train, somehow, at a little station, and they said Niagara Falls was a mile or so off, through the woods."

"We were young then," said Mr. Wilson. "Young and foolish. We had a couple of valises along and—" He paused. "What did we do with those damn valises?"

"It didn't matter. We didn't care." Mrs. Wilson grew

younger and younger as she spoke, as though there were a magic on her. "My best dress was in one of those valises, but we didn't care. We could hear the Falls roaring."

"We were young then," Mr. Wilson repeated. "We just took hold of hands and walked through those woods. Nice open woods, maple and beech and some softwood, spruce and all that."

"There was a squirrel we stopped to watch," put in Mrs. Wilson. "It was real cute. It didn't seem to be afraid of us hardly at all."

"Maybe it knew we were just married," suggested Mr. Wilson.

She looked at him with indulgent malice. "If it didn't it was the only living creature in that part of New York State that didn't know."

"Sometimes we ran," said Mr. Wilson. "But mostly we walked. You see, we could hear the Falls and so we knew they were there, and they wouldn't go away. There was nothing to worry about. We kind of wanted to make that walk last a long time. It was the only one of the sort we'd ever have. You wouldn't know about that, of course, but some day you will."

"And then we came out of the woods," Mrs. Wilson broke in, "and there they were—the Falls, I mean."

"And there we were." The old man knocked the ashes out of his pipe, and I could see the unburned tobacco in the bowl as he emptied it. His hands shook a little as he started filling it again from a jar on the table at his side. "She was eighteen and I was twenty."

"The two of us stood holding hands and looking at the Falls," said Mrs. Wilson.

The old man lit his pipe with a sulphur match, and the room was filled with the strong fragrance of match and tobacco.

"That was all a long time ago," he said.

"I used to think of it sometimes, when he was in the army." The woman smiled sadly and fondly.

He nodded. "I got into worse woods than that before I was through. And no woman around to hold hands with. Chancellorsville. Little Round Top. That was the kind of woods I got into."

After a long silence I asked the obvious question: "And when you came home after the war you settled down here?"

They both nodded and smiled. "Been here ever since," said Mr. Wilson. "Don't aim to go anywhere else."

That would have been more than forty years. Forty forests through which they had walked together. Just when, in what especial corner of what woods, had they stopped resembling the youngsters who had gazed at Niagara Falls and seen a squirrel on a tree on that spring day of 1856, just when and where had they begun to fade and wither?

I let the question stand unvoiced. I still think about it sometimes.

"Mr. and Mrs. David Wilson," said the *Waterbury Record* in its next issue, "celebrated their golden wedding at their home on Main Street last week. They received many acknowledgments of the day and a host of friends dropped in on them to offer congratulations. Mr. and Mrs. Wilson clearly remember an incident of their wedding journey when they walked through the woods to see Niagara Falls." I did not mention the squirrel. Various other details followed in what I can only call my imitable style.

But I never forgot the Wilsons' walk through the woods. In time it almost seemed to me that, in an earlier incarnation, notebook in hand, I was there—a century and more ago.

CHAPTER SIXTEEN

It's Tough to Grow Old

1

*M*ENTION of the Waterbury Inn set Justin Moody to thinking of days long ago, that he remembered from his boyhood. The Inn, as he said, had had its ups and downs. It had been more of a hotel in 1850, he said, than it was in 1906. When the stages stopped running and the railroad came in, he said, the Inn kind of lost some of its importance.

People used to have to stop somewhere overnight when they were traveling by stage, up from Bellows Falls or White River or over from Wells River, or back again, Mr. Moody told me. On the railroad, of course, they went faster and didn't have to lay over so often—or at all.

It was a great life riding on the stage, Mr. Moody declared, if you were young and could stand it, but people liked to get off at a good hotel, like the Waterbury Inn as it had been in the old days.

After I left Waterbury the Inn turned into an excellent hotel again, but Mr. Moody and I couldn't know that the stagecoaches which Mr. Moody inwardly mourned would be replaced by a new sort of stage with the horses inside; and that the Inn would have another period of glory.

Mr. Moody, on his melancholy days, was not anticipating the future with much pleasure. Mr. Moody didn't believe the present was as good as the past had been, and he suspected the future would be worse.

Not that he seemed to be precisely heartbroken as he leaned back from the front counter and pulled at his gray sidewhiskers. Justin Moody was hardly capable, so far as I could tell, of being heartbroken. He expressed himself with a sigh and a sad smile and compensated for being elderly by reminding the young—myself, for example—of how much they had missed by being born so late.

"There'd be a stage from the south and one from the north," Mr. Moody reminisced, "both of them connecting sooner or later with such places as Boston and Montreal and even New York City. You could go all over this part of the country by stagecoach then, just as you can by the trains now. It just took longer." Mr. Moody drew a long breath and smiled benignantly through the front window at a pretty young woman going by. "It took longer," he repeated, "but I can't see that people have any more time today than they did then. Nor so good a time."

Harry Whitehill had come down the store from his dingy little office and was listening. It seemed to me that neither Mr. Whitehill nor Mr. Moody was seriously pressed for time just then. Mr. Whitehill bustled, but that was not so much because he was in a hurry as because he was a bustler by nature. Harry Whitehill could bustle standing still.

At the moment neither of my employers seemed to realize that they were using up the working time of an employee, meaning me, who was then being paid at the rate of approximately eight and a half cents an hour. Whenever Mr. Moody engaged me in conversation for half an hour, as he frequently did, it cost the partnership about four and a quarter cents. From this I deduce that I must have been a good listener.

"I don't believe they had macadamized the roads in the

village in those days," resumed Mr. Moody. "They were a lot dustier those days when it was dry, and a lot muddier when it was wet, than they are today. And in winter the stages might be a day or so late, though they came through as fast as they could on account of their carrying the mail. They'd throw a few passengers off in the woods if the going got too rough"—here Mr. Moody winked at me to show that he was stretching the truth slightly—"but the United States mail came through. The passengers that did get here would be mighty cold and the minute they got inside the Inn they'd have to have something to drink, because that was what their doctors had prescribed under those exact circumstances." Mr. Moody winked again. "Soft cider," he explained. "They would test it to see if it was soft by sticking a fork in it. Or ginger beer. Old-fashioned, non-alcoholic ginger beer."

Mr. Whitehill laughed politely. "Makes me think—" he began, then thought better of what he may have been going to say and stopped.

"It was best in summer," said Mr. Moody dreamily. "We boys would wait for the stage to come in, either way, over the covered bridge on South Main Street or over the hill here from North Main Street. Then we'd race it to the hotel. I can still remember how good the dust felt between my toes. I guess I was about ten years old then. The stage would sometimes have four horses, and the drivers would lash at us with their whips—not to hurt us but just in fun because we scared the horses. But they always came in whooping, no matter how they'd been walking the horses on the grades."

I tried to imagine a ten-year-old Justin Moody without any sidewhiskers, running whooping along Main Street beside a stage that might have come in from Boston or Montreal. That would have been more than half a century earlier. It would have been before the Civil War.

"Boys don't have as much fun as that today," continued Mr. Moody after a little pause.

"At least not that kind of fun," Harry Whitehill put in. "I like to see a little change, myself. It's better for business. You'd be the first one to complain, Justin, if the Central Vermont stopped running and the stages came back."

It is true that Mr. Whitehill was a progressive kind of man. He had led the drive to build the electric railway to Stowe, so that the summer boarders could get up there more easily.

Justin Moody shook his head. "You can't tell about fun," he admitted. "Maybe being ten years old was part of it. But maybe all this gallivanting around in railroad trains doesn't make anybody any happier. When you hear the oldtimers talk about it you can see that they did well enough without railways. They had ways of enjoying themselves."

"Including," interrupted Mr. Whitehill, "some of the ways folks have today."

Mr. Moody caught Mr. Whitehill's eye and shook his head slightly. "Rob here wouldn't know about that," he said. "Not yet, anyhow."

I did know in a general way what Mr. Moody had in mind. I wasn't quite sure what his attitude toward women used to be when he was younger, but I knew what it seemed to be now. People said of him that he had been around. They also said that he had seen the elephant. He was very polite, and never vulgar.

So I imagined he was thinking not only of when he was about ten years old and the railroad hadn't yet arrived but of when he was my age, that is to say, about eighteen, and the railroad was running new and shiny all the way from Boston and way stations to Burlington and Montreal.

But a customer came in just then and Mr. Moody hurried to wait on her, a young and pretty married woman whose name I don't recall.

2

Justin Moody didn't call himself an old man, not in my hearing. Nor even an elderly man. He would have been more likely to skirt the issue by saying he was no longer young. Still, he did remember things that were nearly sixty years back at that time and are about one hundred and fourteen years back at this writing. Without knowing it, he was a fragment of history.

But I didn't have to look far to find older men than Justin Moody. One of them, Elisha B. Chandler, lived in a house on Main Street that I passed several times a day. The difficulty with Mr. Chandler, who sat wrapped up in afghans and blankets on his front porch in summer and stayed inside out of sight in winter, was that the only impression he made on persons of my generation was that he was very old and much concerned about his health.

I don't recall whatever Mr. Chandler had done for a living when he did do something. He had stopped doing anything for a living about a quarter of a century before his death, but somehow he had a house and a little money and perhaps made some of his relatives think he had more than he actually did have.

At any rate, he began to take to his bed or chair about the year 1880 or thereabouts but was not a candidate for a funeral until 1906 or thereabouts. He remarked to his daughter, so it was said, that he was sorry to be such a burden to her but that he would die as soon as he could; he was not, he said, and I quote this verbatim on good authority, long for this world.

Miss Chandler, the dutiful daughter, was said to have been engaged to marry a man from Boston but had reached a tacit understanding that she would not leave home during her father's lifetime. She was not young when I knew her, but she was a pleasant woman who might have been pretty in the flush of her girlhood. There must also have been a Mrs. Chandler but I suppose her husband had outlived her—she does not figure in my memory.

It was in late 1905 or early 1906, I should say, that one of the Burlington papers sent a reporter to interview Mr. Chandler on his ninetieth birthday. The story he wrote was headed: "Waterbury's Grand Old Man," and he described how chipper Mr. Chandler was, how clear his mind was and how he had almost enlisted in the Mexican War of 1846, but hadn't done so because he didn't approve of it.

Beyond this, the reporter found it hard to dig much out of Mr. Chandler, except that he was the age he was, and had seen a lot of changes, he wasn't sure just what.

The *Waterbury Record* and *Stowe Journal* also had a piece about Mr. Chandler and his birthday, rewritten by me from what was in the Burlington paper. Mr. Whitehill didn't think it was necessary for me to interview him again after the Burlington man had done so; he said it might tire him. Mr. Moody said Mr. Chandler had always been one to get tired easy, even when he was younger.

My Aunt Alice said the person she felt sorriest for was Daisy Chandler, the daughter, and that the way she looked at it the old gentleman stayed alive all that time just to spite her, but my mother and grandmother said she ought not to talk that way.

But all that sticks in my mind is that Mr. Chandler was indeed very old, and that I was glad I wasn't that old, even though being almost eighteen years old was not enough to get my name into the papers. I didn't want fame. I merely wished to go on being my present age, or possibly, some day, old enough to vote, and have more money and not have to get up so early in the morning.

So there sat Elisha B. Chandler on his front porch, when

the days were warm enough, and for me he is immortal in a vague way, like a picture made long ago that has faded. I detect in him a mild, slightly impish sense of triumph in getting to be ninety, after being so certain he was not long for this world.

But that is all.

3

But if Elisha B. Chandler is dim in my memory, another old man, perhaps his equal in years, is still vivid to me. This is William Butler, a relative of the Janes family. Mr. Butler lived somewhere in Massachusetts and came to Waterbury only for brief visits.

William Butler was one of the handsomest old men I ever saw—today he reminds me, as he naturally would not do then, of the late Oliver Wendell Holmes of the Supreme Court of the United States. He had abundant white hair, a sweeping white moustache, and a long, aristocratic face. He was tall, still carried himself well, and wore dark clothes of a somewhat old-fashioned cut.

My Aunt Alice called Mr. Butler "Billie," but not in his hearing, and with a humorous intonation that seemed to say nobody in his right mind could be so familiar.

What I wondered was whether Mr. Butler hadn't been called Billie at some time in his life. His parents and boy and girl friends of long ago certainly hadn't called him Mr. Butler. I wondered if he had ever lived in a town with stages running through on dusty roads, as Justin Moody had, and if he had run barefoot and yelling in the dust beside the horses.

I couldn't ask such questions of William Butler, for though he always greeted me kindly he had an absentminded manner, as though his thoughts were miles and years away. If I had been ten years younger I believe he would have patted me on the head as he went by, but all he did was to incline his own head slightly and smile a little. I wished I could interview him and ask him, what was it like to be living so long ago, and was it any more fun than it was to be alive in the humdrum modern days of 1905 and 1906, with all their dash and scurry.

But William Butler was bent on but one thing when he came to the Davis house from across the street. He came to call on my grandmother, who must have been his junior by quite a number of years but with whom he had some things in common.

They played a little game together. The game was that the year was 1850 and not 1905 or 1906, and that William Butler was courting my grandmother. That was the way it seemed to me. He was courting her in an old-fashioned way, as though he were dancing a minuet with her. She smiled at him, I thought, in a way she had not smiled for a long, long time; and I thought there was in that smile a shadow of what had been in an old daguerreotype she had once brought out for us, showing her as a girl of seventeen.

My grandmother was an educated woman who did not stop reading while she was bringing up her two daughters— my mother and my aunt. She had taught school when she was young, and after the death of her first husband, Josiah Graves, she had gone back to teaching.

She rarely went out of the house in those latter days, except to the porch or to look at her roses. She had recovered from a slight stroke a few years earlier, but she had rheumatism and perhaps a fear that the stroke might recur— though it never did. Indoors she was active enough, and she retained to the last a quick and resilient mind and a keen sense of humor. The result was that she liked to talk to William Butler and that he enjoyed talking with her.

I suspect that Mr. Butler's mind was not as good in 1906 as it had been twenty years earlier. On the other hand, he had kept every scrap of his imposing manners, and I believe I learned from him what an American gentleman of the first half of the nineteenth century had been like.

The thing he did that impressed us most was to bow low and kiss my grandmother's hand. He did this when he arrived and he did it again when he went away.

My grandmother liked it, in a detached, half-smiling way, half-sad, too, as though it brought back to her things and years that not even my mother and aunt could know about.

"What does he find to say?" I heard my Aunt Alice ask her once.

"Enough," replied my grandmother. "Old times. He is a very well-informed man." But that was all she would say about the matter.

When William Butler left he went out by the side door through the kitchen, and not in the more formal way through the front door. He and my grandmother had their little visits in the sitting room rather than in the parlor. The sitting room had a full-length mirror, a horsehair sofa and some comfortable chairs. The parlor, on the west or street side, was heavily carpeted and curtained, with a picture of Lincoln reading the Emancipation Proclamation to his cabinet, every one of whom I believe I could still name and visualize from that one source; a composite of Pilgrim's Progress, and a crayon drawing, done from a photograph, of my step-grandfather, Luther Davis. There was also an orange tree, which sometimes produced one or more small oranges; I had tried one in my earlier childhood and didn't want another.

But I believe William Butler and my grandmother were more comfortable in the sitting rooom. It had to be a big occasion to bring the parlor into full use; the exception was that the parlor had a bay window in which my grandmother often sat, and from which she could look up Main Street and across to the Janes house. The bay window wasn't stuffy, the way the rest of the room was.

Anyhow, William Butler, when he had finished his visit, departed by way of the cheerful dining room and the even more cheerful kitchen to the side door and side porch. My grandmother accompanied him to the kitchen door, or in fine weather came out on the porch. William Butler then bowed deeply and kissed her hand for the second time, and that is the final picture I have of him in my memory: the dark clothes, the coat with tails a little longer than the style then prevailing, the white hair and moustaches, the unforgotten grace with which he bent and straightened up, and turned, and with one last bow walked away.

I was looking at the early nineteenth century, though this did not seem so remarkable in 1905 and 1906 as it does now: now, when even the early twentieth century is historic and vague in the minds of a newer generation. In 1906 I could almost transform William Butler into the youth he had been, a youth who must have been fully grown, walking with a light step and gaiety in his eyes, looking around for someone to love, when my grandmother was still a child, and the nineteenth century was adolescent.

Now, in his remote and dignified way, William Butler went again, for the last time, through the ceremonial motions of a courtship. This was the last dance, and to what inaudible but remembered music?

After one of his visits to Waterbury, William Butler returned as usual to his Massachusetts home—it should have been in or near Boston—and came no more. Indeed, I believe he died before I myself left Waterbury, and I seem to remember my grandmother receiving the news with a sad smile—a smile that was often sad about many things, in a not too unhappy way, but chiefly mourning the passing and tribute of the years.

It was about this time, too, that Elisha B. Chandler died

and had a grand funeral, leaving his daughter free, unless it was too late, to marry her patient suitor. If I am not mistaken the suitor came to the funeral. After all, a long-prospective son-in-law could do no less.

I believe that both William Butler and Elisha B. Chandler were old enough to have been patted on the head by Thomas Jefferson or John Adams the elder, both of whom died in 1826, and both could have conversed in manhood with men who had known George Washington. Of the two, William Butler would have been the more likely to do this, and no such surviving relic could have found anything to complain of in his manners.

I once spoke of William Butler to Justin Moody. Mr. Moody looked at me reflectively. I think now he may have envied me all the years I seemed to have ahead of me. He knew what most of us discover belatedly, that the sorrows of youth are certain to pass, as those of age are not; we can all grow older but who ever grew younger, except in legends and operas?

"It's a tough thing to grow old," said Mr. Moody. He sighed deeply, fiddled with a pencil and gazed out the window at the crowd, such as it was, that was passing on Waterbury's Appian Way.

"But it's tougher not to," he added.

CHAPTER SEVENTEEN

◄••••►

Lilith

1

I HAVE alluded to Lilith, which is a name she never bore and would never recognize, who indirectly killed Jim O'Neill and Lewis Stillman, wrecked the life of John Franklin, the bank cashier, and would have ruined Harry Whitehill if that plump, hustling, hypocritical, stingy, somehow engaging man had not had the stuff of valor in him.

Did I ever see Lilith in Mrs. Marwell's boarding house? I sometimes believe I did. I do not recall her face clearly, but a sort of wild and wicked grace that she had, and how, when she reached out to take a plate or put a plate down, there was a catlike, sinuous quality about her natural gestures. This did not concern me, myself, it was not done for cubs like me, I was not even visible to Lilith as a rule, being so innocent and so absurdly young, but the way she moved and stirred sent chills through me, both hot and cold.

I do not know that this Lilith, with her flexible arms, her fingers that were like weeds in a slow tide in a brook, this Lilith, with her yellow hair and blue-gray-green eyes, this Lilith, with the voice that dissolved men's reluctance—I do not know that she was the one woman who did all the things I have mentioned above.

All I am sure of is that this seemed to me to be so, and that the thought of her troubled me. For the Lilith dream, though beautiful, was not good; though it set the pulses jumping, it was not restful or secure. For an adolescent, a man-cub, it was a troublesome dream, this Lilith dream.

I wanted greatly to be good, to walk purely in the paths of righteousness; that was the way I had been brought up, and that way the way I wanted to go. I wanted to be happy, and how could a person be happy if he were not good? I did not believe altogether in the mild doctrines they taught in the Congregational Church, or in other doctrines taught in other churches, but in virtue I did believe.

And so this dream, this image of Lilith troubled me, for I knew from the beginning she was not virtuous or pure, and that no reformation, no revival meeting, no appeals from the Rev. Kellogg or from the Methodist incumbent or from Father Ryan could change her. The only way you could change Lilith would be to abolish her, she was all beauty and all sin, and that was the terror and wonder of her.

Lilith dwelt in my mind after the tragedies of Jim O'Neill and Lewis Stillman. She dwelt in my mind so much that I almost hoped she would come into the *Record* office some day, maybe to talk over old times (if that were, indeed, the case) with Harry Whitehill. But this didn't seem likely to happen, because every time you heard of Lilith she was being quietly rushed out of town on account of something she had done that was wrong. It wasn't likely to happen, because Harry Whitehill's recollections of Lilith couldn't be too cheerful, and because he had told everything about the affair with her (if she was the one he alluded to) to almost every man who would listen, and the men had told their wives such details as they deemed suitable, she couldn't collect any hush money from him.

But this didn't keep the vision of Lilith from bothering me. More accurately, I should say that no evidence to the contrary kept the thought of Lilith from bothering me, in a not always unpleasant way, when I should have been thinking of something else, or somebody else. I always had a young girl in mind, a sort of Joan of Arc, to whom I paid secret homage, and in whose presence I blushed to the tips of my ears and fell silent. Indeed, this confession is scarcely personal, it is, rather, a minor detail of the portrait of one sort of adolescent in that vintage year, 1906. I am sure things would be different now; I would have a hotrod car and go steady; maybe I would even join the beat generation and live unhappily ever after.

But this was not then possible. I always had an ideal young girl in my mind, and this young girl, though visible, was altogether too pure and beautiful to live in the kind of world this was. The ideal girl, so far as I was concerned, dwelt apart, like a star. This was convenient for me, since I didn't have to think up things to say to her and I didn't have to buy ice cream sodas for her, but I suspect that if all young men had regarded all young girls in this fashion, at that time, the result would have been a progressive depopulation of this continent.

Fortunately, no such catastrophe happened, and the population of Vermont increased slowly but normally—usually, but not always, after the contracting parties had undergone matrimony.

As for myself, I fear that my pure and poetic devotion would have been more likely to bore its objects than to send them into ecstasies. Women were hard to please, in those days, when one approached them with hesitations and inhibitions. They liked the confident sort of young men.

With Lilith, or the dream of her, I had no inhibitions. So long as she was at least half-imaginary and not present in the flesh, I could deal with her as an equal, man to woman, I could talk with her, I could explain my doubts and problems to her, I could draw from her (in the dream) sympathetic and always satisfactorily wicked answers.

I needed, indeed, a little wickedness in my life, and the semi-present Lilith seemed to furnish it. I do not refer entirely to her voluptuous qualities, though she had them. She was warm-bodied but also warm-minded, she was Desdemona, Juliet, Ophelia, she was the sad heroine of *The Scarlet Letter,* she was Lorna Doone, she was a dancer frozen in slow motion on the Grecian Urn (but ready to thaw at a man's breath), she was all the love and desire I did not know a single thing about. She was totally imaginary, and so was the young man who fancied her his ready companion. However, it is pleasant to be imaginary and to imagine, at eighteen; it is harder afterwards.

Sometimes I fancied her walking close with me as I went to the *Record* office in the winter darkness, maybe in a shrieking blizzard that did not love me at all and would kill me if it could, or, again, when spring was coming and the mornings were soft with promise. Sometimes I imagined what it would be like if she went into the composing room with me and asked what the funny pieces of metal in the type cases were, or sat on the counter in the front office and sang to me while I was sweeping out, or if she strode pace by pace with me—for she was always, so I dreamed, a good walker—while I delivered my papers, morning and evening.

I thought I would easily be able, under those circumstances, to give her all my problems, wonderments and puzzlings unashamed, and she would sympathize and find ways out of them. She would stand with me against a world that outside my grandmother's house often seemed hard to deal with.

And sometimes at night she might seem to be close and speaking to me. "Don't be lonesome," she might whisper. "It's me."

I can see that I have not made Lilith a consistent character.

The truth is, she was never consistent, she was wicked, beautiful, and maternal; she had a heart of gold and could have been sent to jail for some of her inclinations, beliefs, and intentions, if there had then been statutes to cover the case; she was whatever I wished her to be at a given moment, and also what I feared she was and ought not to be; she was no fit company for me, even in my night thoughts and daydreams; she was not a suitable acquaintance for any adolescent, but I am sure she knew, and in a way blessed and comforted, countless numbers of them in her endless incarnations.

This was Lilith and she lived, whenever the sheriff or constable would let her, in a pious little town in Vermont in or about the year 1906. I didn't love Lilith. I could never have written rhymes about her. But I did devote a lot of valuable time to thoughts of her.

2

"Look here, Lilith," I would say in those free-and-easy imaginary conversations we had, "I do not want your sympathy. Sympathy is for people who haven't grown up. It is not for men and women of the world. What I want is your friendship and admiration."

I did not use words like these in real life, but this was not precisely real life. Lilith would gaze at me from under half-opened lids (I got this phrase out of a paperback book published by Street and Smith that George Beckett the harness-maker in Williamstown had lent me before I came to Waterbury to live); Lilith would look at me and a mocking light would come into her eyes (that was from another book); Lilith would examine me carefully: "What's there in it for me, kid?" she would demand (still another book); "I'm wasting my time with a kid like you. You're not even dry behind the ears. [This from a fourth volume, possibly.] Go away and grow up."

I would return her gaze, in this dream world, almost fiercely, yet with a certain tenderness; there was never any uncertain tenderness in the books or boilerplate romances I read, or in the story magazines Mr. Whitehill had in his front stands and that I sometimes sneaked out to read overnight.

"You haven't given me a chance to prove myself," I would say, with a far-away look in my eyes and a sadness as of unhappy memories. "When I leave Waterbury I'm going to—." Even in the dream sequences I had a little difficulty in completing this sentence. "I'm going to college, Lilith," I would limply continue. "I'm going to get an education. I'm going to show them a trick or two. I'll come back here rich and well-known."

"And talk long words to me?" Lilith, even in the dream, could yawn at that prospect. My interpretation of this remark, now, is that I didn't want Lilith to be intelligent. If there was going to any intelligence in this imaginary relationship I wished to provide most of it myself. And I wanted Lilith to be rather vulgar. I did not wish her grammar or even her manners to be too good. I would feel more comfortable with her, of that I was certain, if they weren't.

"If you don't understand the words I shall explain them to you," I said. "What I intend to be is a man among men. We will have good times together, but I think you would want me to be a—well, a man among men first."

Lilith fluttered her eyelids at me some more. There never was a girl who could flutter her eyelids the way this non-existent, or only partially existent, Lilith could.

"I like strong men," she mused. "Perhaps you will be a strong man when you grow up."

I interrupted her. "I am no longer a child," I protested indignantly. "I am eighteen. Charles the Ninth of Sweden led a successful invasion of Russia at the age of sixteen. William Pitt—one of the William Pitts—was Prime Minister of England at the age of twenty-one. I'd like a little more respect from you."

"All right." She smiled agreeably. "O. K. You're pretty tall already"—she put her head a little on one side in a pretty way she had—"though you're still kind of skinny." She laughed as an idea struck her. "I think I'll call you Skinny." She continued gazing at me. She wasn't like those girls who pretended to be listening to you if you ever got up the courage to say three words about the weather to them but were really interested in some other person or thing on the other side of the street. "Do you think you could beat somebody up some day—some man who had insulted me or kicked a sick cat or something like that?"

"I certainly could," I assured her, flexing my biceps. "I'd have to get in training first, I guess, but after that I could."

"It isn't so much that I would want you to do it," said Lilith, relenting a little. "I wouldn't want you to get all messed up and bloody. I'd just like to feel that you were able to."

That was just the way I liked it, too.

We had, of course, more serious moments. After the death of Lewis Stillman I never indulged in any adolescent dreams of suicide, but I wondered sometimes if, despite the happy home life I had at Number 27 North Main Street, my existence as a bondservant to Harry Whitehill and Justin Moody was really worth the trouble of getting up in the morning—or at least so very early in the morning.

Lilith could always pull me out of these dismal moods. She did this, however, less by being logical—logic was never her strong point—than by being beautiful and wicked. So long as beauty and wickedness existed in the world I was sure that life would be interesting enough to pursue: the curtain had gone up, the actors and actresses were in their places and, saints or sinners, I waited for them to speak their lines.

I didn't tell anybody about Lilith. I felt that my relatives would have been shocked and my friends startled out of

their wits (as they still may be, but I doubt it) if I would. The general impression was that in my quiet and possibly tedious way—or possibly all the more because I didn't make loud noises—I was an uncommonly good boy.

I knew better, of course. Lilith, in my dreams, knew better. That was our secret.

3

That is to say, it was our secret while our affair, if I may call it that, lasted. Alas, like so much other beauty, so much other not too unwholesome sinfulness, such a great anthology of good and ugly dreams, it could not last.

My intrigue with my imaginary Lilith ended, fortunately, not long before I left home for various experiences and adventures elsewhere recorded. It ended one day as I was tending store while Justin Moody was home for his mid-day dinner and Harry Whitehill was working at something or other in his dark little rear office.

Lilith in the flesh, the girl who, as I believed, had caused the deaths of Jim O'Neill and Lewis Stillman and nearly wrecked the lives of Harry Whitehill and some others (and I hope that now, being both nonexistent and dead, and perhaps enjoying a mercy and understanding she never had, in the flesh, on earth, she will forgive this recurrent mention of her offences) opened the screen door and walked in.

"Hello, Kid," she began, evidently not recognizing me, in spite of all the daydreams and night dreams I had had about her, "Can I subscribe to the *Record* for a year?" She paused and a flicker of amusement came into her eyes. "Unless," she added, "Harry Whitehill wants to put me on the free list." She inspected me with a casualness that hurt. "You new here?" she asked. "I don't think I ever saw you before."

"No," I said. "I'm out back, usually." I pointed with my thumb.

She looked at me again. I was embarrassed, the way I

wasn't in the dreams. "I guess you carry papers, too, don't you?" she asked. I could see she wasn't interested but felt she had to make conversation. This hurt me almost more than her failure to find anything familiar in me. At least, it did until I had a really careful sidewise look at her.

"I can take the subscription," I began again. "If you want me to." I felt the red flush mount into my outstanding ears and descend into my face.

Well, this was Lilith, the lady of my half-good, half-bad dreams. This was Lilith. And what did this real Lilith really look like? She glittered somewhat, with jewelry and with the red-and-white contrast of the clothes she wore. Her eyes, so alluring in my dreams, were dark, shadowed; somewhat— let us face it—bloodshot. Her blonde hair was not well-put-up, it straggled around her pink cheeks and made an island of her right ear. She was plumper, less graceful, less sinuous in her movements, than I had remembered her. Remembered her? Imagined her, reconstructed her, I had better say.

The heavy burden of her perfume filled the store as she stood there. I did not especially like it. The scent and the bright lips, the invitation of her costume and her attitude— these did not belong in my dream, even in the most vulgar and earthy moments of my dream. Suddenly I knew the truth about her. She had to be bought, and I hadn't anything to buy her with; she was an honest woman if the goods she had were the goods a man wanted.

I shifted uneasily. "Mr. Moody isn't here," I resumed. "I can take the subscription if you want me to. Or maybe Mr. Whitehill—?"

She smiled broadly—and wickedly, and in this respect was for an instant the Lilith of my dreaming. "Mr. Whitehill?" she repeated. "Harry Whitehill. I think I might like to speak to Mr. Whitehill about my subscription." She pushed back

an imaginary feather of a fairly plain hat. "I know you could do it all right, but I'm an old friend. I'll just go back and have a pleasant word or two with him. An old friend." She turned toward me as she walked down the store. "Or did he say he didn't want to see any of his old friends?"

"No, he didn't," I answered quickly. I wanted, for an instant, to bring her back and say to her, "If you'd give me a chance I could be a man among men, the way you said. I'd have to get in training first, but I could." But this was the sort of remark I couldn't make to the real Lilith, so different from the imaginary Lilith—and yet so like her, so damnably like her.

I didn't really wish to say those words to her, not really. The scent was too strong, the lips too red.

My heart sank. This, I suddenly knew, had been my great opportunity, a turning point in my life. Here had been my chance to talk, man to woman, to my imagined Lilith, to reconcile her with the true Lilith, and I hadn't done it, hadn't tried to, hadn't wanted to.

The conversation in the back office was too dim to hear, and I didn't really want to hear it. She came back after a while, not smiling. At the door she turned and spoke to me, and a glint of the smile came back.

She waved a delicate hand. Her arm moved sinuously, as though it had several extra joints, and something stirred in me—not, I believe, romantic love. "Good bye, Kid!" she cried. "Good luck to you! Keep on being a good boy, and be sure to say your prayers every night before you go to bed. And don't get mixed up with any bad women! It's too expensive."

She was gone, and I never saw her again, in the flesh— never saw her again till now, when I have remembered her. Poor girl! I could be impersonally polite to her now, I could be attentive, for she might need help getting into and out of chairs, I could offer her my arm when she was crossing a

street, I could talk to her about the old times and how much better they are—and always have been—than the new times. I could ask her, was she ever, even a little, in love with Harry Whitehill, or was he, like several acres of timberland, something she could buy at a low price and sell at a higher price? I would like to know all about her.

But I don't. And in a way I miss her.

4

I heard Harry Whitehill talking to Justin Moody later in the afternoon. I was standing out in front, by the magazine rack, reading in the old *Strand Magazine* some story by the late W. W. Jacobs. My father liked those stories, too, though I didn't know why until years later. I often reread them, to this day.

I don't know why I was standing there, for I should have been at work at something. Maybe I had finished in the printing shop and was all washed-up and ready to go down to the depot for my papers.

Harry either didn't know I could hear, or didn't think I would be interested, or didn't think that I was sophisticated enough to understand. Yet he spoke softly, and it was clear he had already told Justin the beginning of the story.

"She wanted to subscribe for a year," he said. "I wouldn't take her money—naturally. Why should she want to read about Waterbury—or Stowe?"

"Maybe she used to know the editor," Justin suggested.

Harry Whitehill caught his breath, in a sort of reverse-motion whistle. I heard it. "Maybe she did," he said.

"Did she ask for money?" Justin inquired.

Harry lowered his voice still more, but I heard. "Fifty dollars," he replied.

"Did you give it to her? You don't have to, you know. She can't get you on anything, not now. You could sue her, if

you wanted to."

Harry laughed, but not gaily. "Twenty-five," he said. He sighed. "She was a pretty girl, once."

"They all are, once," said Justin Moody.

Harry leaned closer to Justin Moody. "She uses some sort of color in her cheeks," he said. "She didn't have to, once. You should have seen, close up, how red her lips were. And the perfume she uses—." He shrugged his shoulders, almost with a shudder.

"It's hard to understand now, isn't it?" asked Justin.

Harry nodded. "Yes, it is. But I don't want to hurt her. C. C. Graves has moved her on. She needs the train fare."

Justin coughed. If they said more their voices were so low I couldn't make out the words. I had found a story called "Captains All," by Mr. Jacobs, in the *Strand Magazine*.

It was a day or two later that Justin Moody held up his index finger as I came in from my morning newspaper round.

"Listen, Rob," he said. "You're just the kind of boy that stays quiet and respectable because he doesn't know what's going on, and then finds out and starts turning somersaults all over the pasture lot. You're just the kind of boy that gets mixed up with bad women because they're easier to talk to than good women. I saw you with that woman that came in here the other day. But don't you do it, Rob. Don't you do it." He waved his finger again.

This seemed familiar, but I didn't say so. "I certainly won't," I answered meekly. "You don't have to tell me. I do quite a lot of reading."

Justin smiled benignly. "It isn't all in the books," he explained.

But, just as I said, I certainly wouldn't. Lilith hadn't come to me in my dreams since the day she came into the store in reality. I didn't want her in my dreams any more; I wanted somebody who used more soap and less perfume, less painted, lovelier—but, I am afraid, just as wicked.

CHAPTER EIGHTEEN

The Other Side of the Hedge

1

*M*Y GRANDMOTHER'S house in Waterbury, built by her second husband, my step-grandfather Luther Davis, when he became prosperous enough to leave his down-river farm (my birthplace, incidentally), was a comfortable brown wooden structure, with a large empty lot between it and the Lawyer Morse house on the southern side.

The site of the house had originally sloped toward the north, and my grandfather had leveled it off and propped the northern side of it with a retaining wall. On the boundary line he had planted a cedar hedge. To this day, whenever I smell cedar I am reminded of that hedge, and that house, and all that went with visiting or living in my grandmother's house in Waterbury. I also think of a place called Cedro Cottage, which I have described elsewhere, but my grandmother's cedar hedge, which she carefully kept up and caused to be clipped regularly after my step-grandfather's death, stirs more primitive emotions. So much of my childhood as well as my adolescence is distilled from it.

Below the hedge, on ground perhaps six feet lower than the Davis house, and therefore more exposed to flooding when the Winooski or Little River got out of bed in the spring, stood the more modest dwelling in which resided Asa

Baker and his family. I suppose a certain social prestige was derived from living on the upper side of the hedge, simply because it was the last really good site available on that side of Main Street above the Little River bridge.

The Baker house, into which I never entered, may have had two bedrooms, a sitting room, and a big kitchen. In 1906 it did not have a bathroom, but neither did the Davis house. I think it did have running water, which was piped into most houses in the village at the cost of about four dollars a year.

The Bakers were poor, and never pretended not to be, but they were neat. They were not the sort of poor that would wind up in the poorhouse, except under the strain of a wholly accidental series of calamities. The Bakers were probably an old family in Vermont. A man picturesquely known as Remember Baker was one of Ethan Allen's Green Mountain Boys during the quarrels with the Yorkers that preceded the Revolution. It was a name nobody had to apologize for bearing. Nobody could discriminate against Asa on account of his name.

Nobody did, in fact, consciously discriminate against Asa Baker. My grandmother, mother and aunt spoke of him in the highest terms, as did everybody else.

"There's one thing about him," said my grandmother. "If he says he'll come at a certain time he'll come. He's a good, hard worker, and you don't have to watch him to make sure he doesn't take time out for a smoke. There isn't any man around this town, rich or poor, I'd trust more than I do Asa Baker."

This was quite a strong statement, considering the lawyers, the business men, the doctors, the school teachers, and our leading celebrity, Senator William P. Dillingham, but my grandmother meant it. She meant, as she usually did, precisely what she said. She would not call in Asa Baker if she felt

ill, or wanted to draw up a last will and testament, or needed to have a trunk roped up (and when did we ever go traveling in those days without a trunk tied with approximately thirty-two feet of clothesline?) and taken to the railway station. She would call in Asa for the particular thing or things he did well, and would trust him without reservations.

As far as anything my grandmother, mother, and aunt said about Asa Baker and his family was concerned, there was no reason at all why we should not visit back and forth.

2

Of course it is hard to understand the setting of the Baker family in Waterbury social life unless one bears in mind the entire social situation in Waterbury. This situation centered on the churches and included some organizations to which the churches gave rise, such as the Ladies' Aid. There were the usual fraternal orders of the time, and there were one or two literary societies (mentioned elsewhere in these memoirs), whose members met at each others' homes in rotation and tried to acquire culture.

The communicants of the different churches did not usually belong to the same social or literary groups. Waterbury had a lot of good will in its atmosphere, but it also had about as much diversity as to who called on whom as could be found in a much bigger community. At the same time, anybody who tried to divide us into upper, middle and lower classes, in so many words, would have found himself a lower class, all by himself. We didn't quite practice equality but we did believe in it.

There was another peculiarity about Waterbury social life —though it did not seem peculiar at the time. It wasn't often that people invited even their closest friends to drop in at mealtime and get something to eat. Relatives assembled at Thanksgiving time, but that was different. Dinner as a social

weapon hadn't been invented, so far as Waterbury knew. Dinner, at any rate, was a meal that took place in the middle of the day, with the man of the family customarily home from shop, store, or office and hungry enough, as we used to say, to eat a bear. (It wasn't until many years later that I learned that bears, if shot young enough, actually were good to eat.)

Supper was the meal that came in the evening—usually not much later than six. But the word *supper* also suggested to most of us the church supper, a combination of sociability, piety and money-raising which all denominations found useful.

The universal exception to all this lay in the interchanges among relatives, and not only on Thanksgiving Day. My father, a native of Scotland, had no blood connections in Vermont, except his children, but on my mother's side, Waterbury and its environs were dotted with persons to whom we were some sort of kin. Sometimes it took a lot of figuring to make out just what the kinship was. If puzzled we usually settled for uncle, aunt, or cousin.

Since few village houses and no farm houses had telephones, and since no farm wife was ever entirely sure when she could have the horse and buggy to come into town—the horse might be needed for ploughing or some other chore that could not be determined in advance; or, in the cases of really cantankerous farm husbands, was deliberately not determined—the custom of unannounced droppings-in among relatives grew up.

For instance, my grandmother might answer the front-door bell and discover Aunt Lucy standing on the step. Aunt Lucy would state that she had come to spend the day. Then she would move in. My grandmother, mother, and aunt might have other plans for the day, but if Aunt Lucy arrived they would give up or modify those plans and devote themselves to Aunt Lucy. They might complain mildly about it afterwards. They might say, after Aunt Lucy had left amid affectionate farewells, that she could have dropped them a postcard a few days earlier to let them know she was coming.

But you couldn't be rude to people who called on you that way, if they were relatives—and nonrelatives wouldn't call in that way. You would pretend, and my grandmother, mother and aunt did pretend, that there wasn't anything on God's green earth they liked better than a day with Aunt Lucy. They would dig out their best currant jam or greengage plums or blackberry preserves, or all of them, or a slab of mince pie, or the better part of a roast of beef left over from Sunday, or a few slices of ham that was really *ham*, and some cake and cookies and a few other odds and ends, and sit down with Aunt Lucy.

Aunt Lucy was bound by the same conventions that the rest of us were. She had to eat all that was served her at the first helping—all of it, I repeat. Then she had to take a second helping, for if she did not do this her hostesses would assume that she didn't like the cooking. And she had to eat all the second helping, because we were near enough to pioneer conditions to know it was wicked to waste food; and if she could find breath enough she had to praise the food and ask for a recipe or two. That was the code, and Aunt Lucy lived up to it.

Aunt Lucy had a saying, derived, I believe, from one of her own aunts, and so on back, I presume, to the first settlement of Vermont: "I'm afraid I can't eat any more; I've had my sufficiency full." But of course she never said this until she had finished her second helping and had been offered a third.

My grandmother, mother, and aunt, also my brother, my sister, and myself, if present and available, would have been free to go out to Aunt Lucy's house any time we felt like it, and tell her we had come to spend the day. But we hadn't any horse, and though I could have made it on my bicycle I was too modest to go alone and too busy to go anywhere after Harry Whitehill gave me my job; and I don't believe I loved Aunt Lucy the way young men ought to love their great-aunts. I did admire Aunt Lucy, for she was a tough, resolute, and essentially good and upright old character, but I would have hated to spend a whole day in her company.

But of course, the fact that Aunt Lucy could come and spend the day with us, any time she wanted to, didn't explain why Asa Baker's wife couldn't stop by once in a while as she went to and from the postoffice and the stores. Except, possibly, for the theory that since we could see Mrs. Baker's house, and sometimes Mrs. Baker herself, just by going upstairs in my grandmother's house, there wasn't much sense in paying calls back and forth.

But that wasn't the whole story, either.

Waterbury, like countless American villages of that period, was lined with front porches. On Sundays and holidays, in the afternoons in warm weather, nearly every family, or at least its adult members, sat on the front porch and rocked. For variation, if the men of the family were on hand, the wife rocked and the man sat in a straight chair, leaned back and put his feet on the railing. You could count the holes in the bottoms of the shoes of half of Waterbury's grown-up males by strolling along the two or three principal streets on a late July Sunday.

Sometimes, on these occasions, a family would get restless and go walking, and in that case the family sitting on the front porch next door, or on some other accessible front porch, might call to it—assuming that the families were on speaking terms, which was almost but not quite always the case, and of course on about the same social level—and there would be some conversation across the lawn.

The family on the porch might then ask the perambulating family to come up and set for a while—and *set* is the right word. Thus there would be a brief social contact, though as a rule no refreshments of any kind. Certainly there would be no tea, for the kind of tea we mostly drank, when we were old enough and strong enough, was a green tea that would take the hair off a cowhide—indeed, I am not certain that C. C. Warren did not use leftover green tea in his tannery. Black tea figured to a lesser extent, but I don't recall any uncolored Japanese tea or other nonsense of that sort.

Once in a while a porch-sitting family would offer lemonade, especially if it had been having lemonade and couldn't conceal the sticky glasses and other traces. Candy might be passed around, too, if there was any candy, but usually there wasn't. Candy was too valuable to be handed out indiscriminately, even to one's near neighbors.

My grandmother had no front porch big enough to rock on, though she did have a beautiful side porch. The Bakers had a front porch, but it was a plain one. And somehow we never sat, even for an instant, on their porch, nor they on ours.

There were rules about porch-sitting and porch-visiting, just as about every other phase of life. We were a free people but we were also, as was often said, "sot in our ways." In practice, the porch-sitting system was not simple at all. We worked it out—at least, the adults did—but this was accomplished more by instinct than by logic. An observer who knew everything there was to know about Waterbury might have indicated by maps and charts, with possibly a few genealogical tables, who was entitled to sit on whose front porches, but I believe it would have taken ten years of his life.

There was some relaxation of the rules for the young in their courting season. The adolescents might visit each other and sit in each others' hammocks or in rocking chairs on each others' front porches when their elders did not do so. The old-fashioned hammock was an excellent courting mechanism, for it did throw young people together.

Still, we didn't ever sit on the Bakers' porch, nor the Bakers on our porch. It was taken for granted on both sides of the hedge that this would not occur, and it did not.

3

Somehow the system didn't bother me, nor seem wrong to me. This was despite the fact that I was a free-thinking young man. My thoughts may not have been profound but, such as they were, I thought them all by myself. Especially when I was carrying newspapers in the snow or sweeping out the *Record* office or feeding the little job press that said clackety-plunk, clackety-plunk, clackety-plunk hours after hours, and lay in wait for the finger it never succeeded in getting.

I was not convinced, for example, of the existence of a God, and this required me to be ambiguous when the Rev. Mr. Kellogg, in his Sunday School class of rather restless adolescent males, asked me doctrinal questions. I hedged as much as I could, for I didn't want to hurt Mr. Kellogg's feelings. It was clear to me that if there really were no God, Mr. Kellogg would lose his job.

I was also a democrat of the deepest dye. I believed that all men were created equal. I believed that the United States was, and of right ought to be, a free country, that Vermont was freer than the rest of the United States, and that my two Vermont towns, Williamstown and Waterbury, were freer than the rest of Vermont.

One man was as good as another, provided he behaved as well: such was my credo.

Still, it never occured to me that Asa Baker, who behaved

as well as any man in town—and much better than some men who had much more money than he had—ought to be considered as high up in the scale of values as my own family. On the maternal side, that is. My father, an immigrant from Scotland, had to take his chances; people weren't romantic about the Scots in Vermont in those times; my Aunt Alice, I believe, would have liked my father better if he had been foresighted enough to arrange some ancestors who had come over in the Mayflower before he proposed to my mother.

The truth was that in democratic Waterbury in democratic Vermont in the year of our Lord 1906 virtue wasn't enough. We all recognized virtue when we came across it and spoke well of it, and it was an advantage to a man or woman to be considered virtuous. But if virtue alone made a man prominent Asa Baker and his family would have been prominent. Doing useful work wasn't enough, either. If it had been, Asa Baker would have been honored and envied.

But nobody envied Asa Baker. He had moved into a field that few men cared to enter. He was doing necessary work and did not have to fear competition, but there was no future in it. Dr. Janes said he was one of the most useful men in town, and that we could better afford to lose a lawyer or two than to lose Asa Baker. But the lawyers didn't worry.

Asa worked carefully and neatly. He dug a sizable hole in the back yard, broad and deep enough for his purpose. Then he removed the boarding from the back and under side of the privy, which was an indoor affair, reached by passing through the woodshed and next to the barn, and wheeled the contents to the grave he had dug for them. There was no spillage, no waste, no mess, and it may not even have been necessary to close the windows on that side of the house, though my grandmother always did this during this operation.

Asa sprinkled ashes where he had taken the material out. He also sprinkled ashes in the hole he had dug, and then filled it up carefully. In the course of years there might be a finer growth of apple trees, of which my grandmother had several, near by.

When Asa left there was no evidence that he had ever been there, except that everything involved, except possibly Asa himself, was neater and fresher than it had been before. Asa was doing his work, in short, just as conscientiously as Dr. Janes did his, and I suppose these two men could have talked together more understandingly about one or two subjects than any two other men in town. Dr. Janes understood, I am sure, far in advance of today's medical knowledge, that he and Asa Baker were partners in the labor of keeping down typhoid fever and other ailments that could arise out of sanitary carelessness.

But as I said, we never stopped to sit on the Bakers' porch, nor they on ours.

———◆•••◆———

CHAPTER NINETEEN

The Pierian Spring

1

*H*ALF A century and more has gone by since I was a non-innocent bystander in the historic battle between the Philomathian and Hypatia Literary Clubs. Passions have cooled, as in other civil wars. Yet I still feel a deep and illogical loyalty to the Philomathian Club, of which my mother and aunt were members; I still insist the Philomathians were right, though I cannot explain why.

The wars of the Guelphs and Ghibellines, the contests among the wards in Siena, the affrays of the ancient three hundred German states, the battles among the gangs of old New York—none of these move me as profoundly as the civil strife between our two ladies' literary societies in the year 1906. The ladies who took part are inscriptions and memories now, but how alive they were then!

The depths of the emotions this encounter summoned up can be understood only if it is also stipulated that Waterbury, Vermont, was not, in the first decade of the century, a cultural wilderness. Our schools were small but good. Our churches were enlightened, each after its special creed. In the State Insane Asylum we had a retreat for citizens who had too much culture as well as for those who had too little.

We read newspapers, books and magazines. My grandmother, for example, had a nearly complete file of *Harper's*

Magazine going back to the early 1850's—I wish I had it now. When Mark Twain published *Joan of Arc* anonymously in serial form, under the quaint delusion that nobody would guess it was his, we in Waterbury detected the imposture as quickly as people in Boston or New York.

Our women's literary clubs were probably independent parts of a movement that was sweeping the country at the time. They belong now in the same attic with the old-fashioned style of Chautauqua lectures, the inspirational speaker who could still get a fair audience in a Vermont town at ten or fifteen or twenty-five cents a head, and the magic-lantern talk that was just going out as the rudimentary motion-pictures came in.

We were, young and old, really hungry for what we thought was culture. We were not just pretending. We might not always be able to tell culture when we saw it, but we tried. Was it culture when a lecturer and an organist came along on tour, and the lecturer recited Tennyson's *Enoch Arden* while the organist played appropriate music? The Congregational Church had a new organ. Was this a bad way to celebrate the occasion? I remember the combined sounds of the human voice and—perhaps—the vox humana in the opening verses:

> Long lines of cliff breaking have left a chasm;
> And in the chasm foam and yellow sand.

Turning back to the poem, which I never deliberately memorized, I find that my recollection is inexact by precisely two words. The song stayed with me.

Was this culture? It certainly wasn't barbarism. I wish I had heard and could now recall more poetry, and better. Yet *Enoch Arden* has images and music in it, as well as a law named after it.

We did the best we could with what we had. The ladies

led the way, for I don't, indeed, recall any cultural clubs that flourished among the men. Did they consider culture, under that name, effeminate? Maybe.

Another thing about men, of course, was that they were expected to be at their places of business or employment ten hours or so a day, and couldn't conveniently hold meetings at each other's houses to talk of the latest novel or study the situation in Hungary. In the evening they would be too tired to do anything but relax, and Hungary wasn't relaxing—even then.

I know that the Philomathian Club studied Hungary, which may have been a happier subject than it is today, for my aunt or mother brought home the book they used; it had pictures of pretty women in native costume working in the fields, and having a good time. I liked it. But there wasn't anything those ladies wouldn't tackle, including the poems of Robert Browning and the causes of the French Revolution.

2

I don't know what started civil strife among the Philomathians and caused the Hypatias to fire on Waterbury's cultural Fort Sumter. I know only that it happened.

You could never tell what would stir up that sort of trouble. Our village had all sorts of cross-currents, old quarrels, snobberies, things that had begun a generation or two ago, or, at the latest, when all the ladies of both literary clubs were girls in school. My mother, who was extremely tolerant, and my aunt, who was peppery but had a sense of humor, felt these things but did not explain them to me, except by accident.

There may have been a slight friction between the ladies of the Congregational Church and those of the Methodist Church, though these churches often held union meetings,

and young folks would go to or from either church in search of a church sociable—as we called it—at which there would be something good to eat. Or pretty girls. A boy didn't care what church a girl belonged to if only she was pretty enough.

In the clubs' civil strife some surface indications were visible to all, or became known as the gossip spread. Mrs. Rutledge wanted to meet on Tuesday afternoon instead of Wednesday or Thursday afternoon. Mrs. Glennon and a few others desired something more lively to study: they were tired of Hungary and didn't care for the poems of Robert Browning. Mrs. Dorkins had made some slighting remarks about the refreshments served when the Philomathian Club met at the home of Mrs. Limpson. I have not used any real names or any semblance of real names. I wouldn't dare to, even half a century later. But this was the sort of thing that went on.

While it was going on, it was the real news in Waterbury: foreign countries didn't provide news; we had few murders or crimes of any sort; buildings sometimes burned down, but not often; the automobile was not frequent enough to make traffic injuries a common item; we had no one-way streets and no red lights, of any kind; indeed, we were by modern standards a dull town. However, we always had social news, which meant a certain amount of enjoyment, some heartburn and disappointment, and a few squabbles.

Harry Whitehill knew all that was going on. The whole town knew a good deal of what was going on. If Mr. Whitehill had been the city editor of a big newspaper in a big town at that moment, he would have had banner headlines on the battle between the Philomathians and the Hypatias.

But Mr. Whitehill didn't. Mr. Whitehill couldn't. An invisible censor sat at Mr. Whitehill's right elbow. A visible censor produced Mr. Whitehill's supper when he went home from the office. Mr. Whitehill couldn't print what was go-

ing on in the town's cultural circles, because any way he put
it he would be sure to hurt somebody's feelings; you could
not do this in a Vermont town as small as Waterbury and
remain in business.

Any important person's feelings, I should have said, for
the only persons whose feelings did not matter were the
outcasts, the perennial drunkards, the perpetual ne'er-do-
wells, the occasional Lilith who tarried briefly and was then
hurried on her way to some more licentious community. Yes,
and possibly a few Democrats.

So what Mr. Whitehill published did not in so many words
say that the Philomathian Literary Club, like a tired and
world-weary amoeba, had split into two portions. What Mr.
Whitehill published, and this he himself wrote with care, not
trusting his adolescent apprentice with the chore, was in its
way a work of art.

It read somewhat as follows:

"NEW LITERARY SOCIETY. Mrs. Arthur Rutledge, Mrs. James
Glennon and Mrs. Peter Limpson are among the founders of
a women's literary club which will meet regularly to study
current fiction, conservation, and other issues. The new club
was organized at the home of Mrs. Rutledge, who was named
President, with Mrs. Glennon as secretary and Mrs. Limpson
as treasurer."

Such was the news, to the extent that Harry Whitehill could
give it without endangering his own capital investment and
that of his father-in-law, Justin Moody.

Mr. Moody was reading the piece on the day of publica-
tion, as I came back to the office after my mid-day dinner.
"You've got it all there, Harry," he remarked to his associate.
"Except what isn't there."

Mr. Whitehill understood what this meant. "Can you think
of anything else to put in?" he inquired, a little petulantly,
for he had evidently expected praise, just as I did when I

wrote something clever. "We could still change it."

Mr. Moody shook his head. "You know damned well I could think of a lot to put in," he replied, "but if you put it in I'd take my money out of this paper as fast as I could lay hands on it." He meditated a moment or two, then resumed. "Women are peculiar, Harry. I always thought so, even when I was a young man. There's nothing you can do about it. If you tried, they'd just get more peculiar."

They looked at each other without speaking. A fact both may have had in mind was that Mrs. Moody had been, and remained, a loyal Philomathian, whereas her own daughter, Mrs. Whitehill, had been flirting with the Hypatias, even though she hadn't attended their first meeting.

"Sooner or later a married man has to go home," said Mr. Moody in a melancholy tone. "They've got us there, Harry."

3

I could not be an impartial historian of what went on in the continuing battle between the two literary clubs. My sympathies would always be, and still are, with the Philomathians. As a journalist, however young and inexperienced, I tried to hold the scales even. If the Philomathians announced that they had completed Hungary and were going to devote two meetings to the Russian Empire, and after that take up China and Flemish painting in succession, I would, at Mr. Whitehill's request, turn the formal statement into a news item glowing with editorial good will.

On the other hand, if the Hypatias came in with a program calling for a study of our forests and how to save them from extinction, I would give it the best wordage I had at the moment; I meant to be fair; I was in favor of forests, for I meant to take to the woods some day; but inwardly I prayed that something awful would happen to the Hypatias. Not individually, of course, but as an organization. In my scheme

of things the organization was subversive, though that useful word was not then in active circulation.

However, I played it safe, as did Mr. Whitehill and Mr.
Moody, and most of the town's adult males. We all sat
around, young, middle-aged, and elderly, waiting to see
what would happen, and in some cases chuckling at the folly
of womankind.

I didn't do much chuckling, for, in the first place, I was too
young to know all about women, and, in the second place,
I could see that my mother and aunt were disturbed by the
situation.

My grandmother, who did not attend meetings of the
literary clubs, except when they were held at her own house,
remonstrated gently. She said that the members of the Philomathian Literary Club should be glad that the members of
the Hypatia Literary Club were also interested in learning
something. There shouldn't be any scandal, my grandmother
said, about anybody in Waterbury being too well educated.

"Besides," my grandmother concluded, "Mrs. Dorkins
doesn't deny she made fun of Mrs. Limpson's refreshments.
How would we like it if Mrs. Limpson made fun of our refreshments?"

"She wouldn't have any occasion to," replied my Aunt
Alice with some asperity. "That's one thing nobody can ac-
cuse us of."

This was correct, and my grandmother knew it. She had
come of a good heritage and she had brought up her daughters with care. The food at Number 27 North Main Street,
whether for regular meals or for refreshments at the meetings of the Philomathian Literary Club or any other organization likely to meet there, was as good as any in town.
Or in any other town, as I still believe.

But my grandmother had another string to her bow. "Naturally," she went on. "But what I thought the two clubs were

trying to do was to learn something about foreign countries and trees and literature and things like that, and not to see which member could cook best."

My mother hadn't spoken up, but I could see she agreed with my grandmother.

"Mrs. Limpson started it, anyhow," said my Aunt Alice, who was not easily intimidated, even by her nearest and dearest. "If she hadn't been so sensitive about that stale cake she served—and nobody in her right mind can deny it really was stale—it wouldn't have happened."

"I think they're trying to save, the Limpsons, I mean," remarked my mother mildly. "She should have been more patient, of course—"

"She was patient enough with that cake," my Aunt Alice broke in. "She left it in the icebox for a week or ten days before she brought it out for the meeting."

"Mr. Whitehill certainly has a hard time trying not to take sides," I said.

"I should think so," my aunt agreed. "He is not only an editor. He is also married. To a woman."

"A good woman, and good for him," my grandmother commented. "I'd hate to see how Harry Whitehill would have turned out without her."

I wish I could bring back the underlying currents, intimations, memories, that were implicit in such conversations. It was all so very comfortable. The acid in it was like vinegar on a lettuce salad—good in moderation. My grandmother was always, in those latter days, philosophical and kindly. The occasions when she came down into the arena and fought battles were long behind her. Sometimes I, a baffled adolescent, envied her—not for being a woman, God forbid, but for being old enough not to have to worry about many things I did then worry about.

My mother took after my grandmother, as we used to say.

She didn't like to say anything sharp about anybody. My Aunt Alice didn't like to do this, either, but she had a sense of justice, a Calvinistic impulse, a sense of mischief, too, a sprightliness, a sort of wit, that left her discontented with saying the obvious and tolerant things.

I judged that my mother would have forgiven the erring Hypatias and readmitted them to the Philomathian Literary Club, with no mention of stale cake or Hungary or other points of difference, if this could easily have been arranged; my mother, if she could have lived that long, would have been in favor of the League of Nations and of the United Nations, in the belief that if people understood each other they would be good to each other—or, if not good, better.

By some magic of the gene pattern, some gift of inheritance, by thinking these things sadly over, at this late date, I now sympathize with my mother's attitudes and convictions, and my grandmother's. I also understand those of my Aunt Alice, who wanted this to be a more satisfactory world right away, and was impatient with people, especially feminine people (for she liked men well enough) who kept it the kind of world it was. I am myself an iconoclast and a conservative, all at once, and this I painfully realize, not for the first time, as I survey the history of the Philomathian and Hypatia Literary Clubs, in the small town of Waterbury, Vermont, so very long ago.

Do I hear somebody suggest that this bit of history, this moment in time, this concealed and sequestered crisis, didn't matter? I say it did matter. This squabble was democracy; these aspirations for better cake and more culture, an understanding of Browning and the salvation of trees—these were America. It is in this way that empires rise or fall, as the case may be, that republics dissolve or otherwise, that civilizations, turning around three times like drowsy hens, go down into the dust.

But Waterbury, I am glad enough to say, did not go down into the dust. No, indeed. Mr. Whitehill didn't let it.

4

Mr. Whitehill, with cautious assistance from Justin Moody, really ended the intolerable state of affairs under which ladies who should have been bosom friends scarcely spoke to each other when they met in the street.

Mr. Whitehill promoted an Old Home Week celebration. I don't suppose he was thinking entirely about the strife between the Philomathians and the Hypatias. He may not have been thinking at all, for he was not the sort of man that sits around thinking. Maybe he was just responding to what in a larger sphere would have been called historic forces. Maybe something told him that Waterbury was about to have a nervous breakdown, that it was tired of the present and uncertain about the future, and that it needed to have its mind directed to something new. In this case the something new was something old, but that made no difference to anybody.

Mr. Whitehill didn't have to do the work needed to produce the celebration. All he had to do was to publish news articles and editorials about it in the *Record*. If he said it was being discussed he was correct—it was discussed as soon as he printed this statement. It may also be true that the firm that rented the circus tent that was required for Old Home Week stimulated such celebrations for mercenary reasons. Or perhaps the Central Vermont Railroad did a little advertising and put on some extra cars and collected a few extra dollars—not just from Waterbury, of course, but out of the general idea of persuading people to come home; and in those happy or benighted days they could come home only by riding on the railroad.

The celebration began to bud. There was a top committee,

of which Senator William P. Dillingham was the exceedingly
honorary chairman, with Dr. Janes as vice-chairman and doing some of the work in his swift, decisive way whenever his
patients would let him, which wasn't often; a finance committee of businessmen to make some practical arrangements,
chiefly by picking up a little money here and there from citizens they were able, in a genteel way, to blackmail; and a
refreshment committee of ladies from the Catholic, Congregational, and Methodist churches, who were able to forget
for the time being some differences of opinion about the
hereafter in their common interest in what Mr. Whitehill
called Waterbury's Storied Past. Or maybe I invented that
final phrase myself; nothing banal was alien to me in those
elegant days.

One of the committees rented the big, open circus tent, a
transaction which I am sure they found almost too easy.
No elephants or tight-rope performers came with the tent,
but it was fun just the same.

And how those women did work—and it was the women
who worked, mostly—first to prove that the Philomathian
members could cook as well as the Hypatias, second to make
clear that the Protestants could cook as well as the Catholics,
or the other way around. In the general commotion the war
between the two literary clubs, as such, was lost sight of, as
was the difference of opinion between Martin Luther and
the Papacy.

Old Home Week was a sort of circus in the sense that there
was this tent (it even smelled like a circus, and I thought I
detected some tiger hairs on the canvas), that people sat on
benches and were uncomfortable and that some curious
things happened. For me, this was a turning point in history: I saw some oldtimers who had lost their teeth, their
hair, and to some extent their memories, yet had returned
to the scene of their youthful happiness—or so they labeled

it; I saw this not long before I was myself to take flight from Waterbury for a long, long absence.

I gazed at the elderly persons who had come back, or had been carried back, and I felt younger than I had felt for several years. I didn't believe I would ever be as elderly as those elderly persons. I didn't believe the year in which I am setting down these present words would ever arrive.

However, what I started to say was that Old Home Week made people like each other better, or pretend they liked each other better, which is almost as good. The elderly exiles, returning to their ancient home town, seemed to see everything in a rosy light; they thought everybody loved everybody else; they did not dream that Mrs. Limpson's cake was ever anything but fresh, or that Mrs. Dorkins would have noticed it if it hadn't been. They fell on Mrs. Limpson's bosom, and also on the bosom of Mrs. Dorkins. They chortled over the news that Waterbury now had two ladies' literary clubs instead of just one or none; they said this showed the dear old town was booming.

Before the week was over my Aunt Alice, who could forgive people just as fast as she could get annoyed with them, was arm in arm with Mrs. Rutledge, Mrs. Glennon, and Mrs. Limpson, Mrs. Dorkins and Mrs. Limpson were exchanging recipes, and all five of them were recalling, with girlish shrieks of laughter, some things that had gone on in Waterbury when that was the variety of laughter that came naturally to them.

When the tent came down and the elderly visitors returned to their various homes, in such remote places as upstate New York, Boston, Ohio, Indiana, and in at least one instance California, the question must have come up in the minds of the Hypatias as well as the Philomathians whether the civil war should be resumed or not. There was some hesitation, but the truth seemed to be that ladies who had been polite to one another for five or six days were embarrassed at the prospect of being impolite again.

What went on, who acted as ambassador or ambassadress, I can't say. Alice Smith may have been the go-between for the two clubs, she was so frank and funny that everybody liked her, whether or not they agreed with her. She could easily have won my mother over to the peace-at-any-price policy, and my mother would have made it quietly difficult for my Aunt Alice to hold out.

The consequence was that another news item appeared in the *Waterbury Record* and *Stowe Journal* not long after Old Home Week. It read more or less as follows:

"LITERARY CLUBS JOIN. The Philomathian Ladies' Literary Club and the Hypatia Ladies' Literary Club agreed, at a joint meeting held last Friday at the home of Mrs. Arva Smith, to unite in a new literary club, to be called the Pierian Cultural Society, in honor of the famous literary center in ancient Greece. Mrs. Smith will be President of the new club, Mrs. Peter Limpson will be Vice-President, and Mrs. Thaddeus Dorkins will be Treasurer. The first subject to be taken up in the study program will be the early history of Vermont. We hope"—Mr. Whitehill editorialized in the news whenever he felt like it—"the storied past of Waterbury will not be overlooked."

This was the end of that particular outburst of internecine warfare. I do not suppose it ended all the jealousies, suspicions, and ill-natured gossip in the town of Waterbury, forever. It did prove to us all, though, that when a situation required Waterbury people to stick together they did it.

CHAPTER TWENTY

The Midnight Train

1

A FEW minutes after five o'clock on the morning of April 18, 1906, the city of San Francisco was shaken by an earthquake and shortly afterwards half-destroyed by fire.

This calamity would not belong in these recollections if the earthquake had not also shaken Stanford University, thirty miles southeast of San Francisco, toppled over some buildings and killed two men, one of them an undergraduate; if, secondly, my brother William had not been a student at Stanford at that time; and if, thirdly, I had not been planning to join him at the opening of the September term.

The truth is that many of us, young and old, were longing in those days to abandon the lovely environment and bracing climate of our native state. My Aunt Alice had gone to California with her tuberculous husband a few years before I was born. They had had difficult times, and he had come home to die, yet she remembered some things that stirred my imagination. She and Uncle Lucius had lived in the beautifully-named San Bernardino Mountains. Once the burro she was riding had gathered its four feet together and come down hard on a rattlesnake, which my aunt found surprising. She and Uncle Lucius had roughed it, and in spite of the tragedy and apprehension had had some good times.

Sun and warmth, new opportunities, better living in California's uncrowded spaces (as they certainly were then), oranges, peaches, prunes, and plums in the valley, grapes on the foothill slopes and snow on the distant mountains—this was the kind of allure California offered.

But what I wanted was escape. Why did I want to escape? Why did any Vermont boy of that generation want to escape?

At this late date I do not suppose I shall be able to make anybody believe that a young man should yearn with an undying fire to get away from Vermont, though the population figures, in 1906 and later, prove that many young men not only wanted to get away but did.

Today I am glad Vermont is romantic, or seems to be so; but in 1906 I wanted to travel, I wanted to cross the country, I wanted to go to Stanford University, which charged practically no tuition fees and where snow was prohibited, I wanted to go somewhere far away from Waterbury.

I am being careful at this point not to stir up the psychiatrists, who know that wherever you go you carry yourself with you, and that there is no real escape. I don't argue with them. They are good and helpful men.

What was wrong with Vermont? It wasn't necessarily lack of opportunity, for people who wanted to remain at home did so and got along all right. Perhaps I should ask what was wrong then, what is wrong now, what will forever and ever be wrong, with adolescents? If I had not loved Vermont I should not now be remembering it with warm affection and a degree of repentance. If I had loved it a little more I should have remained there.

But I left, or planned to leave, with a sort of whoop. I think I felt hemmed-in. The mountains came too close into the too narrow valleys. There were mountains, also, of old memories, of dead generations, of what one was expected to be—and wasn't. And in one sense the impulse that made my ancestors on my mother's side travel up from Massachusetts, and that had also made my father leave his own native land, made me, as well as my brother, turn toward another land and another promise.

There were depths beyond depths. In California, as I dreamed, I might be a more successful adolescent than I had been in Vermont. I turned toward California, perhaps, as a youngster today may borrow the key of his father's car and scoot madly down the smooth-surfaced highways. In my early day we had no cars to speak of, and no smooth-surfaced highways, but the impulse to scoot was certainly there.

2

On countless nights when I lay half-sleeping in my grandmother's house I heard the midnight train go by. We were so close, in that narrow village, that it was right under my window. I heard the rush and roar, I lifted up to see the lights of the cars, I heard the engineer whistle for a crossing this side of the Winooski River bridge. How musical that whistle, how fantastic that passage of tumult and lights, what romance and joy went by on the midnight train!

As I had done during my childhood days in Williamstown, so now, at eighteen, I still envied the engineer, opening and closing his throttle, easing his engine to the curves, letting her out on the straight, dashing through Vermont in the middle of the night, tied to no locality, bound, maybe, for Montreal. I never thought of a locomotive engineer as sleeping, I pictured him always at the throttle, serene, strong, unconquerable, traveling down the night and into the far-away dawn.

As I thus lay sleeping, on many a night, I dreamed myself aboard the midnight train, all my troubles behind me, all my wealth of family affection and tradition riding along with me—for I did not then know the cost of departures and late arrivals—into an unknown and fabulous world. If there were young and beautiful women in this enchanted world I would approach them confidently, as I had never done in the real universe called Waterbury; they would wait for me with grave but friendly smiles, hand in hand we would venture further and further into wonders and enchantments—but I believe this is sufficient to suggest why I got sleepy.

The midnight train stopped at Essex Junction to leave passengers destined for Burlington, or to take the luckier passengers who were on their way to Canada and the West. Then, as I knew but for many years never experienced, the train flew on into the abysses of the night, faster than the birds of passage I had seen vaguely overhead in spring, toward Montreal; toward Montreal, where people spoke French as though it were a real language and not something made up to be taught in school; and soon past Montreal, or by some other train into which one would be conducted by implacable destiny, the passenger would penetrate the unimaginable distances, the interplanetary ranges, of the West and Far West.

For five years and more I saw the sunset light die out at Bolton Notch, and darkness come, and in due time the midnight train flash by.

There will never be for me another train like that, never a plane bound for the ends of the earth that will carry the same freight of glamour, never a ship, with the white water under her bows, that will be poetry as was, once, the midnight train.

But for a while after April 18, 1906, I feared I would never catch the midnight train, never ride with it into the night toward the inexpressibly alluring world that drew it onward.

I had been duly notified that I would be admitted to Stanford University, that, as the pictures showed, lay brown and red under the foothills above the Santa Clara Valley. But was there any Stanford University any more? For a week no news came through, not even the telegram my brother had sent as soon as he realized that he had been in a big earthquake and was still alive.

San Francisco was burning. One Stanford student, at least, was dead. That was all we knew. No radio, no television, no transcontinental telephone, not even the overloaded telegraph lines, no airplanes, brought us closer to the scene of the disaster. California was further away than any civilized portion of the earth now.

My brother's telegram came at last, one morning as we sat at breakfast in the big, sunny dining-room, with cheerful smells of coffee and griddle-cakes coming from the kitchen. My aunt answered the knock at the kitchen door with almost startling swiftness, tore open the yellow envelope and came in with laughter. "He's all right," she said. And then she broke down and cried.

"I thought he was," said my mother slowly. But she hadn't been sure. None of us had been.

My grandmother reflected for a little. "I used to think," she began, "that God wouldn't allow the very worst things to happen. I knew they did happen, though. I learned that when I was a very young mother, during the Civil War. Being good, and loving their relatives and friends wouldn't keep men from being hurt or killed. It got so I never wanted to see another telegram—it was always grief they told about. This one didn't, and that's a comfort, for once. I'm selfish, I know. I'm glad Will Duffus is alive and well. If I could raise my hand and let that boy at Stanford who died come alive again, and Will Duffus be dead, I wouldn't. I would not." Her eyes were wet. "I'm a wicked old woman," she concluded.

She wasn't then as old as I am now, nor was she at that time or any other time a wicked woman, but in her honor and in loving memory of her I record this speech.

3

Little by little the nightmare lifted, I was wide awake again, it was a real world but not an unendurable one. Not only was my brother all right and in good health, not only was my father all right, who had gone to California some months after my brother did in a sad search for better health. Besides this good news, we also learned that Stanford University, several of its buildings lying in ruins, its triumphal arch abbreviated and humbled, its church unsafe for use, its students scattered and unsure, had announced that it would open the same as usual in the late summer of 1906. That was Stanford for you, that was California for you.

This meant that Stanford University was going to have me, myself, a refugee from the beauty, glory, wonder, and melancholy of Vermont, as an entering student. This meant I could pack up and prepare to go. This meant I could say farewell, a fairly long farewell, to Harry Whitehill, Justin Moody, and the *Waterbury Record* and *Stowe Journal,* to all the customers to whom I had faithfully delivered the *Boston Globe,* the *Boston Herald,* and the *Boston Journal* (but no *Boston Transcript,* God forgive us), according to their tastes; to those adorable adolescent, darkly misunderstanding, superficially scornful girls of my own generation who troubled me so much because I could never talk as I wished to them; to Lilith, the comer and goer, the undying principle of femininity, the wrecker and maker of men's souls and bodies, who had come to me so often in the night and often even in the daytime; to the old houses, and to the river and the hills I loved so much without knowing how much I loved them.

My term of service was about over. I went through the rest of it with a lightened heart and also a sense of foreboding, knowing in advance that the Emancipation Proclamation was about to be signed and issued and made absolute.

Every night, as before, the midnight train blazed through, its wheels throwing sparks as it swung to the curve, its windows glaring where the doomed or happy passengers sat, its whistle blowing down the corridors of darkness, like the shriek of a beneficent banshee.

Some day soon, I mused, as I turned on my pillow and felt the gentle, urgent tug of what I considered to be destiny, I shall be on that train. Some day I shall be where I will not have to please Harry Whitehill or listen to Justin Moody. Some day soon I shall lay down my last stick of type, run my last job through the small press, stand for the last time on the shelf of the thundering flat-bed.

Some day soon. I shrank somewhat, deep inside. I wanted to escape. I was also afraid to escape. I was fitted to the clothing of my work, my town, my relatives, my friends; these were not, and never would be threadbare; would I ever fit any other place or set of people again? (The answer, in case anybody is curious, was no; no for almost everybody in the twentieth century that was just beginning to take hold of us all.)

But every night the midnight train went through, and every night I either waked and heard it, or slept and dreamt it; it could not pass my vigil unheard and unobserved. Beauty and glory and fear rode with it down the dark highways of the night toward an uncertain dawn, and in my bed on the second story of my grandmother's house I was still safe and uncommitted.

My brother wrote that he had rented a room in a house in Palo Alto, a mile away from Stanford University, that he and my father would meet me in San Jose, and that we would not have trouble in finding work enough to keep us going comfortably while we went to college.

The days moved forward. I would have liked to see them go more slowly. Now that the weight was off my shoulders and no longer oppressed my mind I was in no hurry. Let July take its time, let the first weeks of August not concern themselves with speed.

Yet I would have sunk into deep despair if I had been told that I must stay and work my fate out under the shadow of my native hills. I did not want to stay, but it was hard to go.

4

On one of those final days in Waterbury I went uptown on some errand, and returning, saw my grandmother, sitting in her bay window, and waved to her. She did not speak to me then of what she had been thinking. She had sacrificed much for her daughter's children, myself just one of the three. My brother had already gone. My sister alone would remain, a delicate and pretty little girl, four years younger than myself, who had bravely conquered a spell of ill health but still had to eat nourishing food and get plenty of sleep; I know now what a blessed link with youth she was for my grandmother, mother, and aunt after my brother and I had left.

My aunt looked at me sadly as I came in. "Do you know what your grandmother said?" she asked. "She said, that is the last time I shall ever see Robert walking down that street."

It was true. That street was not for me any more, after that summer. It was shut off, more surely than the time, many years later, when I drove back to Waterbury and found North Main Street being tarred and the State Police—my Lord, the State Police, in Waterbury!—turning traffic away on a Maple Street detour.

I could argue with the State Police, who were most polite

and understanding; I could and did; but I could not argue with the years and time, and I couldn't make what wasn't so, and ought to have been so, and hadn't ever been so, become so again.

The State Police let me go through, down the untarred side of Main Street, past the library, on the left, which had been the home of Dr. Henry Janes; past the house, on the right, which had been my grandmother's, and which now offered to passing tourists a lodging for the night. A lodging for the night: that had been my five years in Waterbury, a lodging and a going-on.

But I couldn't foresee all this in 1906. I was a fair-to-middling foreseer, but not that good. I never dreamed, in 1906, that I myself, little Robbie, servant of the *Record's* presses, distributor of journalistic dreams from Boston and Burlington, would ever sit in the driver's seat of a real automobile, and make the thing go, and tell it where to. I never dreamed I would be that important. Or that one could ever do such a thing and not be considered important.

I was going away, in the summer of 1906. That was the reality, and not the dream. I was going a long time and a long way away.

I did not go on the midnight train after all, but go I did, and in the direction the midnight train traveled. For me it was a midnight train, to be sure, a train running into darkness and from darkness into light, a train I had long wanted to take and feared to take. It left Waterbury about sundown on a date I do not more precisely remember, in the third week of August, 1906.

I never knew, I still do not know, how to deal with decisive occasions. I read and reread the words of great men who have dealt with them, but there are no words for the rest of us, the great majority, who are also touched, each one of us, with destiny. Romeo said when told that Juliet was dead, "Is it e'en so?" And I suppose he spoke for everybody, in good or evil fortune.

Frank Carpenter, as on lesser days and shorter journeys, came to take my trunk to the depot. This was, as usual, long before train time. This drummer-boy of the Army of the Potomac, rich, as I conceived, with memories of Antietam and the Grand Review of 1865, was glad enough to take my trunk, and not be asked about the Grand Review or Antietam. If I had been his age in 1861, I conjectured, would I have had the courage to become a drummer-boy? He did not look like a hero.

I could nevertheless have wished, even then, at the last possible opportunity, to ask Frank Carpenter, did they make you march in front of the company beside the color guard, or did they let you do your drumming a little nearer home, and did the enemy fire on the color-sergeant and let the little drummer go unharmed?

But I couldn't ask Frank Carpenter questions like that. Frank Carpenter was a kindly and now elderly man, patient with adolescents, but the time for the asking of questions was past. I didn't know then that anybody would ever ask questions of myself, such as how was it, what was it like, how did you feel to be a boy of eighteen in Vermont in 1906; I didn't suspect that an older me would ever make such inquiries of a boy who no longer existed—and I do hope this is clear to readers, for it is not very clear to me; it just exists and bothers me.

Frank Carpenter might have replied, it was like being alive at whatever age I then was, under whatever circumstances, and that the being alive matters more than the circumstances.

The great miracle called Now was going on when Frank Carpenter first beat his drum for the edification of a portion of Meade's Second Army Corps. It was still going on, though nobody was being invited to step briskly up and get killed, when I boarded the train in Waterbury, in August, 1906.

There was an extra hour or so after Frank Carpenter had taken my trunk and before it was time, even by the traditional standards of our more than punctual family, to walk down to the station. I sat with my grandmother, who would truly never see me again, nor I her; we sat on the side porch and I wanted very much to tell her a number of things.

What I did was to read her some funny stories out of a magazine we happened to have on a near-by table. She laughed a little, but not as much as I thought she might have.

Then there was a silence. I wanted to say, Grandma, you have given me a home and a high-school education, you and my mother and my Aunt Alice—but especially you, because this is your house in which I have found a lodging; you encouraged me to go on studying when I thought I would have to stop; to you I owe a good part of any adequate work I will ever do, and no part whatever of bad work, or weakness or cowardice; these things I wanted to say, and did not; in Vermont we did not, and the Scottish blood did not compel us.

I felt like crying, but laughed instead; and so I said good bye to Mary Ann Davis, my mother's mother, with all her wisdom, all her humor, and all the richness she had made out of living and partly out of pain and sorrow. I was to see my mother again, after a long interval, and my Aunt Alice, but I was never again in this life to see Mary Ann Davis.

We got through the last formalities, at the house and at the depot, with fortitude. I was on the train now, I was alone for a while, just as I had been five years earlier when I left Williamstown for virtually the last time. But today it was different, I was going on a long journey, and, in spite of possible visits and returns, there was no real going back.

It was five years before I saw Waterbury again.

The train came in, extracted me nonchalantly from my

Waterbury life, like an oyster from its shell, and carried me away; I saw Camel's Hump on the left after we had passed Bolton, then it was dark, and I did not know how to go to bed in a Pullman berth.

Next morning early was Canada and a new world, with red-coated Canadian Mounted Police coming aboard for a while, only without horses; and at night the transfer across Chicago, and then the wideness of the continent, the brown-bleached Sacramento Valley, and California, and the new life.

But I know now that the sunset train and the midnight train kept running through Waterbury, with some sad and fatal interruptions, and where I longed to go other young Vermonters also longed, and as I went so did they.

This is what makes room for those who stay home. And where the true romance is, whether in Vermont or somewhere else, I still do not know.